The German-Americans
and World War II

New German-American Studies
Neue Deutsch-Amerikanische Studien

Don Heinrich Tolzmann
General Editor

Vol. 6

PETER LANG
New York • Washington, D.C./Baltimore
Bern • Frankfurt am Main • Berlin • Vienna • Paris

Timothy J. Holian

The German-Americans and World War II

An Ethnic Experience

PETER LANG
New York • Washington, D.C./Baltimore
Bern • Frankfurt am Main • Berlin • Vienna • Paris

D
769.8
.F7
G47
1998

Library of Congress Cataloging-in-Publication Data

Holian, Timothy J.
The German-Americans and World War II:
an ethnic experience / Timothy J. Holian.
p. cm. — (New German-American studies; vol. 6)
Includes bibliographical references and index.
1. World War, 1939–1945—German Americans. 2. United States—
Ethnic relations. I. Title. II. Series.
D769.8.F7G47   940.53'150331073—dc20   95-50143
ISBN 0-8204-3074-9 (hardcover)
ISBN 0-8204-4040-X (paperback)
ISSN 1043-5808

Die Deutsche Bibliothek-CIP-Einheitsaufnahme

Holian, Timothy J.:
The German-Americans and World War II: an ethnic experience / Timothy J.
Holian. –New York; Washington, D.C./Baltimore; Boston; Bern;
Frankfurt am Main; Berlin; Vienna; Paris: Lang.
(New German-American studies; Vol. 6)
ISBN 0-8204-3074-9 (hardcover)
ISBN 0-8204-4040-X (paperback)
NE: GT

The paper in this book meets the guidelines for permanence and durability
of the Committee on Production Guidelines for Book Longevity
of the Council of Library Resources.

© 1996, 1998 Peter Lang Publishing, Inc., New York

Printed in the United States of America.

Table of Contents

Foreword

This work is the result of five years of study concerning the role of the German-American community during the World War II era. An earlier version of this revised and expanded text, under the title *The German-American Community During the World War II Era, With a Focus on Cincinnati, Ohio*, appears as a doctoral dissertation in the Department of Germanic Languages and Literatures, at the University of Cincinnati.

I would be remiss if I did not express my gratitude to those individuals who helped bring this work to fruition. Special thanks go out to my dissertation adviser and book editor, Dr. Don Heinrich Tolzmann, who was tireless in his guidance and direction, and provided much valuable resource information. Dr. Jerry Glenn and Dr. Edward P. Harris offered timely and valuable assistance in the writing of this publication. I am especially grateful to those members of the German-American community, such as Eberhard, Gerhard, and Barbara Fuhr, and Arthur Jacobs, who generously sat for interviews and shared memories of their wartime experiences. Finally, a special word of gratitude is reserved for my wife, Alicia, who provided technical assistance and constant encouragement.

I also would like to thank the Department of Germanic Languages and Literatures at the University of Cincinnati, for academic and financial support during the research and writing of the original manuscript. Similarly, I extend my appreciation to the Taft Committee on Graduate Fellowships, for additional financial support.

Finally, it should be noted that the publication of this volume was made possible by the German-American Studies Program at the University of Cincinnati.

Timothy J. Holian

Preface

This work focuses on the changing status of the German-American community in the years leading up to, during, and immediately after World War II, from a respected and influential ethnic community to one under suspicion of disloyalty and hostility toward its host country. Where possible, the focus of attention has been placed on Cincinnati, Ohio, as an historical center of German-American life and culture in the United States. That said, it should be noted that the German-American experience in Cincinnati during the World War II era was paralleled in many other areas of German-American concentration, including large cities such as New York and Philadelphia, and such midwestern German-American centers as Milwaukee and St. Louis. It may be noted that, while much has been published about the German-American experience in the history of the United States, particularly during and after World War I, relatively little has been written which discusses at length the effect of World War II upon the German element in America.

The present study has been written with that gap in contemporary scholarship in mind. It represents an attempt to share recently uncovered information, as well as to correct a number of historical inaccuracies and misconceptions which have obscured a fuller understanding of the German-American experience. Such misconceptions unwittingly have been furthered at the highest levels of the federal government; in rightly addressing the injustices perpetrated against the Japanese-American community during the war era, the government provided redress for wartime wrongs against this ethnic group, while excluding European-Americans similarly affected by governmental actions during that time. Specifically, in the report *Personal Justice Denied* and subsequent passage of Public Law 100-383 (1988), authorizing compensation for and a formal apology to members of the Japanese-American community and their families, the government acknowledged, and took responsibility for, only the detention, exclusion, and internment of America's ethnic Japanese element. German- and Italian-Americans, among others, were not afforded equal redress under the law; subsequent attempts to alter the prevailing status of Public Law 100-383 to date have proved fruitless. To make matters worse, most contemporary commentators have not based their viewpoints on primary source materials pertaining to the German-American case, the effect being to reinforce inadvertently a number of historical inaccuracies and misperceptions.

Unfortunately, the few previous attempts to document and discuss the German-American World War II experience, especially the issue of internment, have generated considerable controversy. Charges of historical revisionism and ethnic chauvinism have hampered scholars of late attempting to present the facts, which are based on recently declassified government documents; as well as contemporary news reports, and first-hand testimony from members of the German-American community willing to discuss openly and frankly the details of their wartime situation. Many of the aforementioned declassified documents recently have been compiled, as volume four of the documentary history *German-Americans in the World Wars*, making them widely available to interested scholars for the first time.

There are those who would deny historical fact and reality, but existing documentation unquestionably shows that select German legal resident aliens and German-Americans born in the United States, were the victims of a war-engendered anti-German sentiment, including governmental policies such as detention and internment. Thus the purpose of this work is to present documented factual information, in the light of historical, rather than political, correctness. It is the goal of this study to present such information to the reader, in the hope that it will encourage greater attention to the history of the German element in America; generate scholarly discussion of this complex topic; and serve as the basis of expanded study for future scholars in this area.

Chapter I

Introduction

On May 7, 1945, German armed forces brought to an end over five and one half years of war in Europe with their surrender to the Allies. Suffering and sorrow rapidly turned to joy and jubilation in the United States, as millions of war-weary people moved away from war, and towards peace and prosperity in the postwar years. For members of America's German-American community, however, the end of the war was not only the end of a long, draining ordeal, but also the beginning of a period of uncertainty and denial which continues to the present day.

In the half century since the end of World War II, there have been considerable misperceptions and misunderstandings about the situation that German legal resident aliens and German-Americans were forced to endure, beginning as early as the mid-1930s and continuing until three years after the end of the war. In recent years, members of the German-American community have come forward to address such misconceptions, breaking years of silence in speaking of personal experiences during the war, and using governmental documents to show what the government has refused to acknowledge through its own legislation. Many of the misconceptions relate to the Japanese-American community, that significantly greater numbers of Japanese-Americans were victims of wartime bias and discriminatory treatment; also understated was the extent to which German legal resident aliens and German-Americans were subjected to similar difficulties.

Most misunderstood was the arrest and internment of over 10,000 members of America's German community as dangerous enemy aliens and enemy sympathizers, a fact denied by numerous commentators, historians, and scholars who heretofore have been obliged to rely on inaccurate and/or incomplete information in retelling, and virtually rewriting, the history of German America during the World War II era. A case in point is provided by Peter B. Sheridan, incorrectly analyzing on behalf of the Library of Congress the wartime internment of German legal resident aliens and German-Americans, and Japanese-Americans:

> The internment in the United States during World War II of more than 100,000 Japanese-Americans, aliens and native-born citizens alike, has

been the subject of numerous articles and books. Less well known is the fact that a significantly smaller number of German and Italian aliens, and some citizens, were also interned, despite the fact that they comprised a greater population than the Japanese Americans, and were present in larger numbers in equally sensitive and strategic areas of the United States.[1]

Such a viewpoint, that Japanese-Americans were interned *en masse* while only an isolated handful of Germans and German-Americans were subjected to such treatment, reflects a major gap in the historical literature dealing with World War II, specifically the absence of studies dealing with the German-American experience of that war. In 1982, the governmental Commission on Wartime Relocation and Internment of Civilians, in its report *Personal Justice Denied*, concluded that:

> No mass exclusion or detention, in any part of the country, was ordered against American citizens of German or Italian descent. Official actions against enemy aliens of other nationalities were much more individualized and selective than those imposed on the ethnic Japanese.[2]

In commemorating the fiftieth anniversary of the bombing of Pearl Harbor in December 1941, John Chancellor of NBC News and Clarence Page of "The McNeil-Lehrer News Hour," both stated to millions of viewers that no European-Americans had been interned during the war.[3] Numerous postwar publications have also perpetuated the notion that German legal resident aliens and German-Americans were never interned; one narrative even came from a Japanese-American former internee who stated that, "Even today I think why didn't they put the Italians and the Germans in the camps? But the point is the majority of the population is Italians and Germans and you can't do that to the population. Because we are a minority."[4] Another book, entitled *America's Concentration Camps*, made the following, highly debatable assertion:

> ... perhaps the most striking of ironies was the fact that no evacuation was even suggested for the Germans and Italians, aliens or citizens, on the Atlantic Coast where submarines and defense installations were far more numerous, and the dangers of espionage and sabotage apparently greater. Only racism can explain the discrimination.

The book was dedicated to "the past and present members of the Japanese American Citizens League. Through precept and example and their wholehearted devotion to an ideal, they could teach other Americans a great deal about Americanism"; no reference was made to German legal resident alien and German-American internees, whose experience received virtually no mention in the book.[5] Such points of view do not convey the truth of the situation; according to Immigration and Naturalization Service records, 10,905 German legal resident aliens and German-Americans were taken in under the enemy alien program, constituting 34.9 percent of all internees. Contrasted with 11,229 Japanese-American internees, or 35.9 percent of the total,[6] it is clear that inferences and reports that members of the German-American community were not interned, or were only selectively interned, are misleading and highly exaggerated.

The arrest of people considered dangerous enemy aliens, and the manner in which their cases were handled, also has been misrepresented in accounts which hold that only Japanese-Americans were subjected to such treatment. Contrary to popular versions of the story, many German legal resident aliens, and some German-Americans, were not afforded the protections granted Americans under the Constitution, nor even under existing standards for enemy alien detainees. According to Eberhard Fuhr, a former internee who grew up in Cincinnati during the early years of World War II:

> They call my brother in for his hearing, and while he's in there I'm reading the paper. And it says, "Two brothers arrested. They will have a hearing, and then they will be interned." I said to this FBI agent: "It says right here we're going to have the hearing - I haven't even had my hearing yet, but it says 'They will be interned'" ... I was kind of numb. I wasn't allowed to have a lawyer or anything - not that I could have afforded one. But I was definitely told, "You can't have that, you can't have any witnesses" - not even my brother or my pastor from church or anybody from school.[7]

Many others misconceptions surrounding the arrest, evacuation, relocation, and internment of enemy aliens and American citizens during World War II continue to circulate, and in being denied serve to fuel heated debate within and outside of scholarly circles. Common belief holds that German-Americans, as citizens, were never the target of federal roundup efforts. Scholarship in the area, according to Stephen C. Fox, indicates that many were on initial "hit lists," even though action in that direction often fell through: "FBI Director J. Edgar Hoover was also eager to get his hands on U.S. citizens of German and Italian extraction, but he lacked the authority to order their arrests without probable cause."[8] One prevalent theory for why large numbers of Japanese-Americans, but not German legal resident aliens and German-Americans, were arrested and interned, is that racism played a significant factor. In reality, such an assertion does not account for the fact that there was no movement to intern Chinese-Americans, Korean-Americans, and others of oriental heritage; basis for the internment of Japanese-Americans can be found in their wartime status as aliens of enemy nationality, and the fact that they were deemed "dangerous" by the same governmental authorities that targeted, arrested, and interned members of the American German community, for the same reasons. Another widely held misconception was that Japanese-Americans were not given hearings before hearing boards, but rather were sent straight to internment facilities; in fact, Japanese-American detainees were afforded hearings before the same boards, under the same criteria for release, parole, or internment, as were German and Italian legal resident aliens and German- and Italian-Americans. Similarly, many believe that the Civil Liberties Act of 1988, providing Japanese-American former internees with a formal apology and a $20,000 per person compensation payment, applied only to American citizens; in reality, the law applies to Japanese-Americans and Japanese aliens, but excludes all those of European ancestry interned from 1941 to 1948.[9] It is this apparent inequity, more than any other, which has sparked members of the German-American community to take action, to publicize their situation during the war years and allow the full truth to be known, so that future commentators will be able to analyze fully and fairly the injustices done both to Japanese-Americans, and German legal resident aliens and German-Americans.

Terminology of the Present Study

Before entering into a detailed discussion of the German-American community during the World War II era, it is necessary first to define the terminology encountered in the text. Such definitions take on considerable importance in the scope of a topic such as the present, in which controversy exists as to the events in question and how they are described.

Foremost among the concerns to be addressed is which individuals made up the German-American community of the 1930s and 1940s. In the present study, "German legal resident alien" is used to describe those members of the German-American community who were born in Germany, emigrated to the United States, and resided in the United States with permission of the federal government, but were still by World War II without American citizenship. In contrast, the term "German-American" refers to those members of the German-American community who were either born in Germany, emigrated to the United States, and became citizens of the United States at a later date, or who were born in America to German parents or were otherwise of German heritage.

The term "Japanese-American" refers to those who were born in Japan, emigrated to America, and resided in the United States without American citizenship; those who were born in Japan but became American citizens; and those who were born in the United States to Japanese parents or were otherwise of Japanese heritage. While seemingly a contradiction with the practice for members of America's German community, this is in keeping with historical precedent;[10] foremost among sources using "Japanese-American," but not "German-American," as an all-encompassing term is the United States government, which utilized such terminology from the Commission on Wartime Relocation and Internment of Civilians in *Personal Justice Denied*, the official report serving as the basis for the Civil Liberties Act of 1988, and in the legal wording defining those who would receive apologies and compensation from the government as a result of arrest and internment during the war.

The terms "German-American community" and "America's German element" are used in situations which pertain both to German legal resident aliens and German-Americans, as a part of the overall German community present within the United States; the effort is to stress the shared heritage of those who claimed Germany, the German language, or the German culture to be a significant part of their background, when a specific differentiation between the two types of Germans in America is neither practical nor discernible.

Regarding enemy aliens and internment, the definition of an enemy alien, or alien enemy, is taken from federal documentation; according to governmental legal authorities, an alien enemy is considered "the subject of a foreign state at war with the United States," while an alien friend is called "the subject of a foreign state at peace with the United States."[11] The Supreme Court cited a fundamental difference in status between citizenship and alien status, in determining the extent to which people residing in the United States could expect protection and comfort from the federal government; in the case of *Johnson v. Eisentrager*, the court made the following pronouncement:

> ... even by the most magnanimous view, our law does not abolish inherent distinctions recognized throughout the civilized world between citizens and aliens, nor between aliens of friendly and of enemy allegiance, nor between resident enemy aliens who have submitted themselves to our laws and nonresident enemy aliens who at all times have remained with, and adhered to, enemy governments. The years have not destroyed nor diminished the importance of citizenship nor have they sapped the vitality of a citizen's claims upon his government for protection.[12]

Consequently, it also becomes important to examine the federal definition of words such as "native" and "citizen," given their use in determining who was eligible for detention as an enemy alien during the war. By definition, the word "'native' pertains to birth; [a] person remains native of [the] country of his birth, although he moved away and became [a] citizen or subject of another nation or government before coming to the United States." This definition became important in the case of Latin American detainees sent to the United States for internment during the war; specifically, the United States Code Service cited the example of a native of Germany who emigrated to Costa Rica and never lost his original German citizenship, eventually to be apprehended by Costa Rican authorities, turned over to American agents, sent to the United States for internment and later removed to Ellis Island, presumably for the purpose of deportation to Germany after the war.[13] The definition of a "citizen" by the government was left to be clarified in the case of special circumstances; the word

> "citizen" must be construed in light of accepted right of inhabitants of conquered or ceded territory to accept nationality of new sovereign, and if they voluntarily depart from such territory without such election, they do not become citizens or nationals of new sovereign.

Several wartime cases were cited to clarify the application of "citizen" to potential enemy aliens. A Jewish citizen of Austria lost any German citizenship acquired by virtue of the German occupation of Austria, when Germany deprived its Jewish nationals living abroad of citizenship; hence, they could not be considered enemy aliens in the United States. On the other hand, a man born in Bohemia, which later became Czechoslovakia and was eventually ceded to Germany, elected to become a German citizen, and thus was subject to arrest and internment under the Enemy Alien Act.[14]

Regarding detention facilities used by the government to hold arrestees and internees, it is important to differentiate between terms such as "temporary holding facility" and "internment center," and a term such as "concentration camp," in defining the locations where enemy aliens were confined during the war. The term "temporary holding facility" is used to describe a location where German legal resident aliens and German-Americans, suspected of disloyalty or actions against the United States, were detained initially after arrest, pending the outcome of a formal hearing before an alien hearing board on their status. For the purpose of this study, a "detainee" is defined as a German legal resident alien or German-American held in a temporary holding facility, awaiting a formal board hearing on whether he or she would be given release, conditional parole, or internment for the duration of the war. Following the hearing, if a detainee was sentenced to internment, the prisoner was then sent to a designated internment center, under the administration of military authorities or the Immigration and Naturalization Service. In this context, the term "internment center," or "internment camp," is used to describe the physical location where internees were held under military or governmental supervision, until their release or deportation after the war ended. In this study, an "internee" is defined as a resident of a designated internment center, awaiting release or deportation after the conclusion of war.

While many sources, including encyclopedias and dictionaries as well as scholarly works, have used the term "concentration camp" to describe American internment facilities, the present study will avoid this terminology. The *World Book Encyclopedia* continues to use the term "concentration camp" to describe "a place where political enemies, real or assumed, are imprisoned," citing the Japanese-American example during World War II.[15] The *New Encyclopaedia Brittanica*, citing the example of the Japanese-Americans but not the German-American community, describes a concentration camp as being an

> internment centre for political prisoners and members of national or minority groups who are confined for reasons of state security, exploitation, or punishment, usually by executive decree or military order. During war, civilians have been concentrated in camps to prevent them from engaging in guerrilla warfare, from providing aid to enemy forces, or simply as a means of terrorizing the populace into submission.[16]

Webster's Third New International Dictionary defines a concentration camp as "a camp where persons ... are detained or confined and sometimes subjected to physical and mental abuse and indignity."[17] Such definitions touch upon aspects of wartime internment of German legal resident aliens and German-Americans, but also incorporate terminology associated with Nazi prison and death camps, used for the extermination of millions of Jews during World War II; in citing examples of American wartime internment and Nazi death camps under the definition of a concentration camp, itself a stigmatized word, such sources have blurred a clear distinction between the two, and contributed to the uncertainty regarding internment facilities and the internment process itself.

German-American former internees have been quick to point out that American internment centers during World War II were in no way comparable to Nazi concentration camps of the same period. Referring to the Crystal City, Texas, family internment facility, which held Japanese- and German-American internees, a German-American former internee who grew up in Cincinnati, Eberhard Fuhr, expressed the following viewpoint:

> That was humane treatment, no question about it. It was not a concentration camp. We were not abused. We got three square meals a day, and the food was adequate. It was cooked by your own mother. There were no psychological numbers done on us, no Chinese torture, no brainwashing. They didn't send you literature about what the Constitution should mean to you and that kind of stuff. We were kind of left alone.[18]

Thus it becomes clear that internment facilities, far from being camps of torture or excessive punishment, were livable, modest centers designed to accommodate the needs of the government, as well as internees of varying backgrounds and situations.

Purpose of the Present Study

The purpose of this study is to examine and evaluate the changing status of America's German element, including those born in Germany and residing in the United States without American citizenship, as well as German-born American citizens, and Americans born in the United States to German parents or of German heritage, during the World War II era. Where possible, the focus will be placed on Cincinnati, Ohio, as a city with a sizable German-American population, which exhibited tendencies representative of other areas of German-American settlement. In the present study, the position of America's German community with the approach of World War II will be shown, as a respected ethnic group with ties to Germany, whose loyalties were called into question with the rise of Nazism in Germany and the subsequent development and growth of pro-Nazi organizations in the United States, along with American entry into World War II in December 1941 and its effect on the German community. An examination and evaluation of German- and English-language media portrayals of the German element and its ties to Germany during the 1930s and 1940s will illustrate the degree to which newspaper and film sided with and against the German-American community, and to what extent they were influential in shaping public attitudes towards the German-American community with the approach, and after the outbreak, of war with Germany. The role of the federal government relative to the German-American community will also be examined; the criteria and procedures for alien registration, arrest, and internment will receive extensive treatment, illustrated with first-hand commentary by Cincinnati-area internees, among others, on their wartime experiences, and documentation of detention life in temporary facilities and internment centers. Finally, the postwar life of German legal resident aliens and German-Americans interned during the war will be examined, to illustrate the difficulties former internees experienced in adjusting to life after internment at all levels, and in getting legal recognition of their status of having been interned as did the Japanese-Americans. In sum, the goal of the present study is to document and explain the changing status of the German-American community in the United States from the mid-1930s to the mid-1940s, and the results of that change in the postwar era.

In the first chapter, an introduction is given to the topics presented in this thesis, with definitions provided for key terms which appear frequently throughout the remainder of the text. A chapter-by-chapter summary is followed by a brief overview of the treatment of America's German element during World War I, to cite historical precedent of how the German-American community was affected in the course of another global conflict.

In the second chapter, the founding and development of Nazi organizations and activities within the United States is examined, along with an overview of German propaganda which influenced pro-German members of the German-American community, and prompted initial concerns about the possibilities of America's German element constituting a threat to American interests. By examining the rise and fall of pro-Nazi organizations such as *Teutonia*, the Friends of New Germany, and the German-American Bund, rationale can be seen for how an isolated, vocal minority of pro-Nazi German legal resident aliens and German-Americans came to stigmatize a large segment of German-America, and provide critics of Adolf Hitler and the Nazi government in Germany with initial cause for questioning the loyalties of the German-American community. In focusing on Cincinnati as a representative example of German-American communities affected by the outbreak of anti-German sentiment, the role of German-American activities will be examined, along with efforts of pro-American groups, such as the Veterans of Foreign Wars and the American Legion, to censure pro-Nazi groups, real or perceived, and make the general public aware of the potential threat posed by members of the German-American community.

The third chapter will discuss and evaluate the role of German- and English-language media in the changing perception of the German-American community. An examination of the German-language press of the mid-1930s will show its efforts to combat anti-German sentiment, developing with the rise of Hitler and the growth of pro-Nazi groups in America, and assert its presence as a representative voice of German interests within American society. By focusing on the English-language press during the late 1930s and early- to mid-1940s, this study will show how newspapers played a role as a public forum, providing a rallying point for those opposed to pro-Nazi groups and German interests with the approach of World War II, in addition to showing the role a prominent Cincinnati newspaper played as a voice of American patriotism following American entry into the war. In focusing on Hollywood film portrayals of the German element in America, the importance of American film studios in reinforcing a governmental anti-German position will be discussed; a detailed discussion of newsreels and feature films, such as Warner Brothers' *Confessions of a Nazi Spy*, will show the extent to which Hollywood played on fears of Nazi spy and saboteur activity in America to influence public perception of the German element, in turn helping sway public opinion in favor of strict control of the German-American community during the war years.

The fourth chapter will discuss the registration of aliens in the United States beginning in 1940, the arrest of enemy aliens in the wake of American entry into World War II, and restrictions placed on enemy aliens beginning in December 1941. A detailed description is given of the alien registration process in Cincinnati, the local detention facility, the makeup of enemy alien hearing boards, and the effect of property confiscations and travel restrictions on Cincinnati's German-American community.

In chapter five, the internment of German legal resident aliens and German-Americans will be treated. Following a brief overview of the internment of members of the German community during World War I, the legal basis for internment will be discussed in detail, including the criteria used to determine which members of the German-American would be arrested and possibly interned. A survey of internment camps utilized during World War II will show where German legal resident aliens and German-Americans were held, and what conditions were like for those living in one of the camps. After a discussion of the internment of Latin American German aliens in the United States, the story of a Cincinnati German-American family interned at Crystal City, Texas, during the war will show the personal side of arrest, detention, and internment of an enemy alien, and their effect on the lives and careers of internees after the war.

Chapter six of this study addresses the postwar situation of internees, including the difficulties encountered in adjusting to life after internment and subsequent legal differences in the treatment of Japanese-American former internees, and that of German legal resident alien and German-American former internees. The physical difficulty of internment will be treated, including the loss of homes and personal property as a result of internment, in addition to the loss of jobs and careers, and the problem of finding new work after having been interned. The emotional difficulties of internment are discussed in terms of the anger and shame, among other feelings, internees experienced as a result of their situation, and how such feelings played a significant role in the future lives of the former internees. By examining the ways in which Japanese-Americans were given formal apologies and compensation, through nine acts passed by Congress and signed into law, while German legal resident aliens and German-Americans were excluded from such treatment, the study will illuminate the manner in which the federal government has perpetuated the notion that only Japanese-Americans were victims of prejudicial treatment, and arrest and internment, during the war years, through the laws it has passed and the programs it has sponsored which benefit only one group of former internees.

A concluding section will evaluate postwar efforts on behalf of the German-American community to obtain equal treatment for their World War II experiences, and bring together the salient points presented in the course of the study. By evaluating the reasons for the failure of the German-American community to receive satisfaction for their legal claims, and the continued misperceptions regarding German legal resident aliens and German-Americans, the study will address one of the primary concerns of German-American former internees, the possibility that other ethnic groups may suffer the same fate in the future, for the same reasons which, in the case of the German-American community fifty years after the end of the war, have yet to be clarified.

The German-American Community During World War I

In order to understand better the conflict between the German-American community and the American public during World War II, it is necessary to begin by studying the German-American experience during World War I, and its consequences for the German community in America.[19] Due to the outbreak of an anti-German hysteria upon the American entry into World War I, the nation's German community was driven underground in attempts to preserve its heritage, leading to a dissolution of the strong cultural and linguistic bonds which had been forged among those of German stock during the previous two centuries.

Held in high regard by the American public beforehand, German legal resident aliens and German-Americans were first subjected to intense criticism and scorn with the outbreak of World War I in Europe in 1914. Despite a professed position of neutrality on the part of the United States government, the majority of Americans supported British and French interests during the war. The German-American community was vocal in its support of German interests during the early war years, loudly cheering German victories and staging public parades and rallies urging German forces on to victory. Members of the German-American community also contributed heavily to German bond and war relief drives, providing financial as well as moral support for a force that increasing numbers of Americans were coming to see as the enemy. An unspoken polarization of attitudes took place from 1914 into early 1917, leading up to American entry into the war on the side of the Allies.

When the United States entered the conflict in April 1917, there was an immediate outpouring of anti-German sentiment. According to Don Heinrich Tolzmann:

> The U.S. declaration of war on Germany in April 1917 resulted in a tragic display of hysteria directed against everything and anything German. Although carried on by nativist extremists, the majority silently approved, or at least did not speak out against the nativist hysteria.[20]

The anti-German hysteria, in Cincinnati as in other centers of German-American population, took on epidemic proportions, as many manifest displays of German-Americana were subjected to elimination and revision under the climate of war. In Cincinnati alone, German-language school teachers were dismissed; university professors were dismissed or sanctioned under charges of being pro-German; German monuments were vandalized; offices of the German-language press were raided; the German collection of the Cincinnati Public Library was relegated to the sub-basement; and the passage of Prohibition laws, given a final push into law based on anti-German sentiment, eliminated one of the city's most prosperous industries, the brewing industry. Countless names were changed, anglicized to eliminate any reference to the German element; the German National Bank became the Lincoln National Bank, and street names such as Berlin and Bremen were changed to Woodrow Street and Republic Street respectively, among many other changes.[21] Even foods were not above having their names changed; sauerkraut was renamed "liberty cabbage" by many, and frankfurter sausages became "hot dogs." On a personal level, members of the German-American community occasionally were forced by mobs to kiss the ground, swear allegiance to the American flag, sing the national anthem, and perform other acts to "prove" their loyalty to the United States. Infrequently, members of the German-American community were subjected to tar and featherings, with two local German-Americans even the victims of attempted lynchings.[22]

The end of World War I in November 1918 was the end of a harrowing ordeal for the German-American community; according to Tolzmann, "World War I, without question, constituted the darkest hour in German-American history."[23] The damage the war did to the German community in America was permanent; emotional scars left the German-American community searching for a new identity in the postwar era. Linguistic and cultural bonds were broken forever, and cohesiveness among German-American societies and their members were weakened for all time. According to Anne Galicich:

> The National German-American Alliance faltered in April 1918 ... and membership in German cultural and political organizations plummeted. Many German Americans stopped speaking German, even in the privacy of their homes. German aliens rushed to become American citizens, and hundreds of citizens of German descent changed their names.[24]

In the postwar years, the German-American community undertook the long, slow process of reintegration and recovery, ultimately gaining back much of the goodwill lost during the war. A high price was paid for the recovery: German-Americans for the first time became more "American" than "German," submerging their unique position in American culture in a rapid and thorough process of assimilation. In the 1920s and early 1930s, German legal resident aliens and German-Americans again were considered "good Americans" by much of the general public, but the experience of the war would not be forgotten on either side. The World War I experience would continue to affect the German-American community in the years before the outbreak of World War II, strongly influencing the posture America's German element would take with regard to the German nation, particularly after the rise of Hitler; its willingness to assert its German heritage publicly; and the extent to which German legal resident aliens and German-Americans would support American interests before and during World War II.

Chapter II

American Nazi Activities and Their Effect
On the Status of German-Americans

In order to understand the rationale behind American distrust of the German element in the United States, it is first necessary to examine the factors contributing to the changing perception of German aliens and the German American community. More than any other factor during the mid-to late 1930s, the rise of Nazism in Germany and the growth of pro-Nazi German organizations in America played a role in creating distrust of German legal resident aliens and German-Americans. Though the vast number of such members of the German-American community were loyal to American interests, and anti-Nazi in their sentiments, the actions of a small but vocal minority of pro-Nazi German legal resident aliens and German-Americans brought about resentment and distrust towards the German-American community as a whole, reminiscent of the anti-German hysteria of World War I. Many loyal German-Americans were placed in the awkward position of guilt by association; this initial development of an anti-German sentiment would contribute to a later situation, in which German legal resident aliens and German-Americans would have to prove their innocence, despite a lack of evidence of wrongdoing.

For the vast majority of Americans, and indeed German-Americans, Nazism as a philosophy was repugnant by nature. By the 1930s, racial discrimination attracted only a fringe group of fanatics, generally of low education and social levels. Images of a class-based society, led by an ethnically pure, superior race struck at the base of American beliefs and experiences: Most Americans were keenly aware that their forefathers had come to this country on immigrant ships, in search of a better life, in forming the multi-ethnic society known as the United States.

Pro-Nazi German legal resident aliens and German-Americans, hoping for support from other members of the German-American community, failed to realize that times had changed for the German element in America. In the wake of the anti-German hysteria of World War I, the German-American community was reluctant to assert any connection to Germany, political or otherwise; recalling the public image of the Kaiser in World War I, the vast majority of German-Americans were not inclined to promote Adolf Hitler as an ambassador of German politics or culture. A new course of isolationism had taken root with the rapid postwar assimilation of the German element, most notably in the core of German America, the Midwest. Post-World War I immigration restrictions illustrated postwar xenophobic attitudes, ultimately restricting the number of Germans able to come to the United States, and influencing the willingness of the German-American community to give expression to its German character. Three separate laws were passed, in 1921, 1924, and 1929, which provided a limit of 150,000 immigrants per year from countries located outside of the Western Hemisphere. While Germany still received a relatively large quota, determined by an already large German stock within the country, immigration possibilities were still restricted for those Germans wishing to come. In 1930, some 1,600,000 native-born Germans resided in the United States; of those, two-thirds had arrived before World War I. By 1930, there were some seven million Americans of German stock, but of them over seventy-five percent had been born in the United States; the 600,000 post-World War I German immigrants constituted a fraction of the United States' total population of 124 million.[25] What immigration did exist into the 1930s was decisively interrupted when Hitler came to power in 1933, soon prohibited save for exceptional circumstances.

Such changes in the German-American community went unnoticed by the majority of Americans, especially with the rise of pro-Nazi groups in the wake of Hitler's ascension to power in Germany in 1933. Despite the fact that only a few thousand German legal resident aliens and German-Americans, out of the millions in the United States, took an active role in pro-Nazi organizations and their activities, the sight of members of America's German community wearing uniforms and parading on behalf of National Socialism brought back memories of pro-Kaiser activities in the German-American community during the World War I era. This prompted calls from concerned citizens and groups, including veterans' organizations such as the American Legion and the Veterans of Foreign Wars, for monitoring, and stricter control over, German-American organizations, particularly those known or suspected to have connections to the Berlin government. In Cincinnati, as in other centers of German-American population, pro-Nazi organizations such as the Friends of New Germany and the German-American Bund came under close scrutiny from numerous sources, including local Jewish groups and veterans' organizations; and traditional activities such as German Day were monitored with increasing frequency, in an effort to monitor pro-Nazi organizations and identify those members of Cincinnati's German-American community who may have held pro-Nazi sympathies. While leaders in the German-American community attempted to differentiate the vast majority of its members, unsympathetic to Hitler and the goals of National Socialism, from Bundists and other pro-Nazi German legal resident aliens and German-Americans, their efforts met with only limited success. Congressional hearings on un-American activities kept the image of Nazi sympathizers fresh in the public consciousness, and sensationalized reports of Nazi espionage and sabotage groups served to undermine the credible efforts of German-Americans to show that they overwhelmingly supported American interests, and would not side with Hitler in the event of German hostilities with the United States.

Early Nazi Activities in the United States

As early as 1923, proponents of Nazism were in America, seeking to advance their philosophy in German communities in various parts of the country. One of the first spokesmen for Nazism in the United States was Kurt Georg Wilhelm Ludecke, who came to America under the instructions of Adolf Hitler in the early 1920s. His mission was fairly straightforward, namely to recruit members among German nationals for a proposed Nazi party. Ludecke's efforts met with only minimal success. He operated independently of the Nazi party in Germany and without sanction from the German government, and received no financial support from Germany for his efforts.

Before the end of the decade, another figure took the lead in attempts to organize a Nazi movement in the United States. Fritz Gissibl, a prominent Chicago Nazi sympathizer, organized an independent cell of storm troopers; the group, known as *Teutonia*, was incorporated under Illinois state law and was even sanctioned by the Nazi party in Germany.[26] By 1932, it had established local organizations in New York, Detroit, Milwaukee, Boston, Philadelphia, Chicago, Los Angeles, and Cincinnati; membership grew primarily through word-of-mouth advertising and correspondence, though the effects of the Great Depression also contributed substantially to membership increases at the time. By June of the same year, the *Teutonia* group, after joining ranks with others in a rival faction known as "Gau-USA," became known as the Nazi Party, U.S.A., and Ludecke was formally declared official representative of the Nazi party in the United States.[27]

Seven months later, though, when Adolf Hitler became Chancellor of Germany on January 30, 1933, American resistance to the existence of a Nazi party in America brought the group's aims into question among a greater scope of the American populace. In April, Berlin took the formal step of ordering all Nazi cells in the United States dissolved, in an effort to promote a positive public image. The young Nazi government, realizing the need to court a larger audience over time and gain a more positive image abroad, chose to step back and regroup rather than risk more permanent damage to its reputation and movement. Thus the *Teutonia*/Gau-USA group passed into history, although the ideology behind the movement, and its key figures, would soon return to prominence in American Nazi circles.[28]

Consequently, another, less known figure, Heinz Spanknoebel, was given charge of planning and coordinating a new organization which would be the successor to the Nazi Party, U.S.A. Spanknoebel had previously headed the *Teutonia* organization in Detroit, and was now being charged with responsibility for asserting a Nazi presence in America, involving fellow German nationals in strategic locations around the country while building up a favorable reputation for Nazism and the German element among a larger cross-section of the American population.

The Friends of New Germany

The organization which Spanknoebel created became the first notable Nazi venture in the United States. Known formally as the *Bund der Freunde des neuen Deutschlands*, or "Friends of New Germany," the group came into being by the middle of 1933, and was recognized by several of the highest-ranking Nazis in Berlin.[29] Specifically, Rudolf Hess assured Spanknoebel and other members of the organization that the Friends of New Germany would be the official Nazi organization throughout North America.

However, as word of the new Nazi group spread beyond the boundaries of the German community, public outcry again forced the Nazi element to pursue damage control measures; according to Susan Canedy, "America, noting the growing Nazi menace in Germany and mindful of

World War I experiences with German fifth columns, real and imagined, demanded the early policing of the movement."[30]   The Friends was established as a militaristic and openly anti-Semitic organization; its lack of cover for its intentions left it wide open to attack from virtually all segments of mainstream America.   Giving little thought to how most Americans would react to his message, Spanknoebel crossed the country, speaking of the need to "clean up America" from racial amalgamation and corrupting Jewish influences.   Not unpredictably, the group found itself under attack at most of Spanknoebel's stops.[31]

Further negative publicity for the Friends was inevitable, as stories began to circulate of violence at Friends' rallies and meetings.   The most notorious incident involving anti-Friends violence took place in Irvington, New Jersey, near Newark, on May 21, 1934, as a mob of some 1,000 anti-Nazi demonstrators raided a Friends meeting attended by seventy-five uniformed members.   The attack, described as "vicious" by a reporter on the scene, injured more than fifteen persons, with two of them taken to the hospital for head lacerations, while thirty five of the attackers were arrested.   Fighting began literally the moment the uniformed Friends members arrived in their buses, as two cars pulled up alongside the buses, their occupants jumping out and beginning the melee, soon to be joined by hundreds of streetside protesters.   Hoping to find sanctuary inside the hall, Friends members managing to enter found themselves surrounded on all sides by even more protesters, likewise pummeled by the mob as police reinforcements were called in.   As members of the Friends of New Germany became scarcer, the mob began to turn on assembled newspaper reporters and cameramen, smashing cameras, tearing clothing, and blackening eyes in the process.   Upon arrival of reinforcements from the Newark Police Department, an hour's worth of street fighting was finally brought under control, and the inside disturbances quelled, though upon withdrawal of the police forces from the auditorium the mob resumed its attack, launching an avalanche of bricks through second-story windows. Remaining Friends members were left abandoned when their bus drivers, alarmed by the violence as well as several well-placed stench bombs, deserted them by driving to safety, in turn leaving the Newark police in the position of having to find a way to return the seventy-five Nazi sympathizers to their homes in safety.[32]

Though clearly the melee was not instigated by the Friends, they nevertheless found themselves placed at a disadvantage with the law as a result of the confrontation.   On May 23, Newark Director of Public Safety

Michael P. Duffy sent orders to all precinct captains instructing them to prohibit further Friends meetings in their districts. Deputy Police Chief John F. Harris explained that the order was not meant to discriminate against pro-Nazi groups, claiming that the rule would apply to any meeting for which the possibility of trouble might exist.[33]

Numerous other stories helped place American Nazi activities, including those of the Friends, in a negative light. Among other incidents, for example, wide press coverage was given to the actions of Nazi vandals in painting swastikas on Jewish synagogues. To a growing sector of the American public, becoming wary after seeing images of massive columns of Nazis marching in Germany, the Friends represented a hostile force whose presence in the United States needed to be checked.[34]

In turn, the German government was forced to distance itself from the American pro-Nazi groups, and the negative publicity they were generating. German propaganda minister Joseph Goebbels assigned the German Consul General, Otto Kiep, the responsibility of hiring a public relations firm to distribute pro-German information leaflets, brochures, and booklets, though initially Kiep was only allotted $31,000 for this task. As Nazi authorities in Berlin grew more aware of, and alarmed at, the growing public furor in America over the activities of the Friends, they issued instructions to Spanknoebel to halt all inflammatory actions until further notice. The orders went unheeded.

Difficulties ensued for the Friends of New Germany, but by September 1 the group had nevertheless managed to pull together the resources and manpower to begin publishing their own journal, *Das neue Deutschland*. The weekly publication was geared toward German legal resident aliens, as well as other sympathetic speakers of German; each issue also contained a special section, published in English to reach a wider audience, entitled the "German Outlook."[35]

*   *   *

Though some progress was made by the Nazi group with regard to public opinion, governmental interference was not long in coming. With memories of World War I still fresh in the minds of many Americans, with visual images of growing Nazi might in Germany being seen with increasing frequency, and as suspicions mounted about the possibilities of fifth-column activity in America, the American public began to speak with a considerably louder voice, calling for the policing of the Friends and other pro-Nazi organizations. To that end, on March 7, 1934, some 20,000 people came together at Madison Square Garden in New York, to observe a mock trial put on by the American Federation of Labor and the American Jewish Congress, entitled "Civilization vs. Hitler."[36]

After Spanknoebel made known his connections to Nazi Germany, political leaders in Washington quickly developed their own suspicions regarding the Friends of New Germany. Among the rumors circulating in Washington was that Goebbels had personally ordered 300 propagandists to the United States, armed with millions of dollars, in an effort to influence public opinion throughout the country; such rumors, often untrue, themselves contributed to the creation of public hysteria against the German-American community. Consequently, in October 1933, the Chairman of the House Committee on Immigration and Naturalization, Samuel Dickstein, announced a forthcoming probe into the matter, with an arrest warrant to be issued for Spanknoebel. Before he could be served the warrant, Spanknoebel managed to escape the country, with assistance from other Nazi agents in the country.[37]

Dickstein was not to be deterred. His committee, the Dickstein-McCormack Congressional Investigatory Committee, promptly made public its plans to investigate extensively the Friends of New Germany, beginning in April 1934. In January of the same year, Congress had voted, 168-31, to authorize the investigation of Nazi activities in America, overriding the objections of Congressman Terry Carpenter of Nebraska, who claimed that the investigations would only create racial prejudice.[38] Meeting from April to July, the committee held relatively few public hearings; those that were open were conducted in an orderly fashion by McCormack, but the meetings presided over by Dickstein were often characterized by high levels of emotion, and even the taunting and baiting of witnesses. Worth noting is that the Committee invited not only Friends members and sympathizers, but also non-member German-Americans with no connection whatsoever to the group; the inevitable consequence for many of the outsiders was that their own loyalties, and those of the German-American community as a whole, unfairly began to be questioned. Members of the Friends present, however, did themselves, and other German-Americans, little service by accenting key moments in testimony with cries of "Heil Hitler!"[39]

For its part, the general public followed the proceedings with rapt attention, lending support to the committee through its growing obsession with the events which were unfolding. Many Americans turned on their radios and bought newspapers on a daily basis, in order to receive the latest news on the hearings. However, some members of the German-American community were considerably less enthused with the proceedings; in at least one case, the German language press dubbed the hearings the "Jewish Inquisition," and Dickstein America's number one "German hater,"[40] due to the harsh treatment of the German-American witnesses and the inclusion of non-Friends members in the hearings.

Conscious that it was not in a position to fight the U.S. Government, Berlin quickly ordered German legal resident aliens in the United States to curtail all political activities. In October 1934, the head of the Steuben Society, Theodore Hoffman, was received in Berlin by Hitler; Hoffman expressed sharp criticism of the Friends, and pointed out that they were doing far more of a disservice than a service to German interests on both continents.[41] The German government then announced that, henceforth, only German citizens would be allowed to become members of the American Nazi party, and that no Germans could be members of the Friends of New Germany as of October 1935, in an effort to allay American fears. The Friends of New Germany was given specific instruction to take on a more "American" image.

The sudden, unexpected departure of Spanknoebel and the Congressional investigation of the group left the Friends in a state of disarray. Once Kiep was recalled to Germany and the announced measures took effect, Nazi activity in the United States went through a period of reduced activity.[42] For Nazism to survive or even prosper in America, a transitional phase was in order, whereby the "Friends" organization could find new and more effective leadership, in a society renamed but virtually identical in its goals and policies.

The German announcements and actions, though, were largely ceremonial. The American Nazi movement was geared largely towards German legal resident aliens in the United States, not second- or third generation German-Americans. While several other American "hate groups," such as the Ku Klux Klan, voiced their support for the Friends of New Germany and Nazi policy, few members actually involved themselves with the Nazi organization. The vast majority of the members of the Friends of New Germany were German legal resident aliens, for the most part recent immigrants from Germany. For that reason, the new German policy was destined to have only a minimal effect, offering little of use to the American Nazi sympathizers.

Realizing that, the House Committee continued its own investigations of the Friends of New Germany through much of 1934, and in February 1935 it finally came out with its report. For the most part, the report centered on the history of Nazi organizations in the United States, detailing their growth and development. While claiming that most German-Americans were loyal and honest people, but that there was sufficient evidence that Nazi activity within the United States had been on the rise in recent years, the committee took the opportunity to pat itself on the back for its work, stating that the adverse publicity the Nazi groups had received as a result of the hearings had served to halt their growth.[43]

Such boasting, which sounded good in the media, was less than accurate in reality. From October 1934 to March 1935, membership in the Friends had doubled, and group activity was noticeably on the rise. Such activity was conducted in remarkably high-profile fashion, including expressing support for Bruno Hauptmann, the German-born carpenter accused of kidnapping and murdering Charles Lindbergh's baby; sponsoring a dance to celebrate Hitler's birthday; and conducting a mass rally in New York City.[44]

Though Congressional action was something the Friends had little ability to manipulate, the group, to a certain degree, played upon German loyalties in traditional settlement areas, in an effort to strengthen its power base. By comparing itself with German National Socialism and reiterating the "Germanness" of the group, they were able to draw sympathy from many Germans; indeed, the Friends had a stated mission of making all German-Americans aware of their Germanness, in an effort to instill in German immigrants a sense of duty or obligation to the movement. Such a goal was achieved with relative ease in some areas, in which the German population tended to group together in well-defined communities, in clubs and societies which drew upon traditional German elements. The Friends liberally altered the basic components of National Socialism to suit the American audience they were trying to reach, adding anti-black overtones to their position against communism and the Jewish element.[45]

Still, any successes the Friends may have had within the German community were more than negated by the reaction of the general American public. Seldom out of view due to their uniformed parading and rhetoric, the group found little acceptance or sympathy from even the most vocal First Amendment supporters in America. Increasing reports of persecution of Jews in Germany, and even attacks on Christian churches there, as well as a growing pattern of violence within Nazi circles, left most of the remaining open-minded observers with little cause or desire to support the Friends.

Fritz Kuhn

In order better to understand the best known of America's pro-Nazi groups, the German-American Bund, it is worthwhile to examine the background of the man who, more than anyone else associated with it, not only brought the group national notoriety, but also established Nazism as a significant presence in the United States. Fritz Kuhn was the first elected president of the German-American Bund, and in short order he transformed the fledgling organization into an extension of his own personal philosophies, ultimately called the "American Führer" in his resemblance to Adolf Hitler.

Fritz Kuhn was born in Munich in May 1896. Spending his formative years in Germany, he grew up in a middle-class family under the influence of Kaiser Wilhelm. Kuhn acquitted himself well in World War I, earning the Iron Cross as a lieutenant in the infantry. After the war, though, deep disillusionment set in for Kuhn, as the Versailles Treaty imposed harsh restrictions on his country. He took refuge from economic and social problems in the *Freikorps*, and studied chemical engineering at the University of Munich. He received the equivalent of a Master's degree in 1922; the following year he married Elsa Walthers and left Germany, at the height of its postwar economic crisis, for Mexico. There he spent five years, working for an oil company in Tampico, as a chemist, a cosmetics manufacturer for three years in Mexico City, and for another year as a teacher at the College of Mexico City. He finally gained permission to enter the United States, his long-time goal, in 1928, and soon settled in Detroit, hoping to land a job in the automobile industry.

Kuhn spent the next eight years in Detroit, working first as a chemist in the Henry Ford Hospital and later with the Ford Motor Company. Early in his Detroit stay, Kuhn joined a local German American fraternity, longing for a connection to his birthland; eventually, Kuhn became a member of the Friends of New Germany. Through an aggressive and enthusiastic style, Kuhn quickly rose within the organization, becoming the leader of the Detroit regional group of the Friends. Although Kuhn sought and attained United States citizenship in 1934, there was little doubt that his heart remained with Germany, and with the Nazi regime which had recently come to power in Germany. He remained highly active in the Friends of New Germany, and when the group met in Buffalo on March 28-29, 1936, as a prelude to reorganization as the German-American Bund, Kuhn was elected president of the organization. At this point, he made his pro-Nazi interests a full time profession: He soon quit his chemistry job at Ford to devote full time and activity to the Bund.[46]

Kuhn was a large and hulking figure, standing five feet eleven inches tall and weighing just over 200 pounds. His face was steely, with graying brown hair combed straight back. In character he was forceful and decisive, aggressive in most affairs while exercising foresight and intelligence in articulating his points.[47] Former Bund members associated with him often portrayed him as highly professional and dedicated in conducting Bund business; though he struck many as somewhat distant and cold, he seemed to inspire high levels of admiration and trust among other members of the organization. Many of his fellow Bundists were quick to point out that Kuhn was fiercely devoted to the United States and its strength as a nation, believing more in Nazism as a political philosophy that could be applied to the United States than in Germany as a superior nation state;[48] Kuhn was destined nevertheless to make a less positive impression on the American public, striking many through his public statements and writings as the embodiment of all that was evil in National Socialism.

After Kuhn was elected president of the Bund, he disposed of the title of president, preferring instead to be referred to as the *Bundesführer*. In this function, he eagerly and energetically took his case for Nazism to assembled audiences, speaking at numerous Bund rallies and conventions. According to Kuhn, Germany and its Nazi government were a bright, shining light, one which could lead America boldly into the future. He made great use of his tendencies toward sensationalism, speaking in loud, aggressive tones in a heavy German accent, with German flags, swastikas, and Nazi embellishments as backdrops for his lectures. Though he lacked the forcefulness and magnetism that Hitler possessed and utilized so effectively, he nevertheless was widely regarded within the Bund as its most effective messenger and an ideal spokesman for the group's aims. Kuhn did not lack support: Fellow Bundists eagerly pledged loyalty to and support for Kuhn, eagerly proclaiming him to be the "American Führer" and the dominant leader of the pro-Nazi movement in the United States.[49]

The German-American Bund

After the demise of the Friends of New Germany, some felt that the threat of Nazism in the United States had begun to decline. In reality, such was not the case; in 1936, the Friends reorganized and retitled itself. The new organization, founded in Buffalo in March 1936, formally took the name of the *Deutschamerikanischer Volksbund*, or German-American People's League; before long, it came to be known by the shorter name of the "German-American Bund," or simply as "the Bund," under the leadership of president Fritz Kuhn. By emphasizing and taking advantage of basic insecurities exhibited in the German communities of America following World War I, which in turn were further compounded by the effects of the Great Depression, the Bund became the most influential and, not coincidentally, threatening Nazi organization to appear in the United States, better organized and funded than any of its predecessors. From the lower classes to the highest levels of politicians, the Bund attracted unprecedented attention and publicity throughout the country, and impacted upon foreign policy decisions on two continents.

Consistent with previously announced regulations, the German-American Bund proclaimed that only United States citizens could become members of the organization. Specifically, according to the organization's constitution, each applicant had to be both an American citizen and an Aryan, and two references had to be furnished by each applicant, one residing in Germany, the other in the United States. There were two distinct types of members: Regular members held full voting and participation rights within the Bund, while members of the "sympathizer sections," while paying the same amount of membership dues, did not receive voting privileges. For all members, there was a $1.00 initiation fee, plus dues payments of 75 cents per month; by the end of the decade, the Bund generated some $900,000 of income per year.[50] By this time, though, in an effort to generate additional funds, Bund dues were raised to $1.00 per month, with sixty percent of the total going to the national organization and forty percent given over to the local group.[51]

Beyond membership dues, the Bund was able to receive operational funding for its various activities from numerous sources, such as the

German-American Business League, partly in exchange for which the Bund published business directories recommending where its members should shop. By the end of the decade, annual Bund income was estimated in the millions of dollars, at least a part of which supposedly was forwarded on occasion to the Nazi regime in Berlin.[52]

The Bund was composed of three separate divisions: East, Midwest, and West, with headquarters in New York, Chicago, and Los Angeles respectively; each division was divided into districts, corresponding to the states in a particular region. Further, in the 47 districts/states (all states save for Louisiana were represented), there were 100 smaller units, the local organizational groups.[53] At the annual national convention, representatives of the local units elected the national president of the organization. In turn, the president selected all other officers of the national organization. Local unit heads, on the other hand, were selected by the department leaders, subject to the approval of the president, Fritz Kuhn.[54]

The Bund centered its operations not only in highly populated areas, but also in places which historically were centers of German immigrant population. East coast cities were an important center of Bund activity, given past immigration patterns and the abundance of employment opportunities there. In that area, according to division leader August Klapprott, there were twenty local units in October 1940, including ten in New York state and city, with some 5,000 members total; four local units were counted in New Jersey at that time, involving some 500 members.[55] Traditional inland German centers, such as Cincinnati, Milwaukee, and St. Louis, were actively exploited by the Bund, if less so than in the national center of New York and New Jersey.[56]

Through effective promotion, Bund membership rose higher than for any previous pro-Nazi group in America. Martin Dies claimed that Bund membership had risen to around 100,000 by 1940, though other sources felt that figure to be high: Justice Department and FBI sources held that Bund membership was only in the 6,500 range, a figure which the Ambassador to Germany, Hans Heinrich Dieckhoff, had filed with the German Foreign Office. Other sources cited much higher figures: Congressman Samuel Dickstein, who it is remembered headed an earlier probe of Nazi activity in America, stated that Bund membership ranged as high as 450,000, while Fritz Kuhn boasted that the Bund was home to 230,000 Nazi sympathizers.[57] Local Bund membership estimates varied as widely as did national ones; while available evidence indicated that membership in the Philadelphia branch of the Bund stood at around 100 in September 1939, a local government official estimated actual Bund membership to be more than ten times that amount.[58] It is unlikely that an exact count of Bund members will ever be determined; shortly before the Special Committee on Un-American Activities convened hearings on the Bund, Fritz Kuhn ordered district and unit Bund leaders to destroy all existing records. By all indications, his orders were carried out. Officially, each of the members was nameless; the national offices of the Bund kept no records of names of members of the organization.

The Bund, as its membership requirements showed, looked for more than just German support for its aims. The group also gained a following among other extremist groups, particularly those which espoused racial supremacy. Among others, Ku Klux Klan brotherhoods, the Black Legion, the Gold Shirts, the Pan-Aryan Alliance, the Social Justice Society, the Knights of the White Camellia, the Silver Shirt Legion of America, and a host of "Christian" organizations (including the Christian Front, the Christian Mobilizers, and the Christian Crusaders) fell in with the Bund, lending vocal support and an occasional presence at organizational meetings. Kuhn admitted in later testimony that leaders of several of the groups had spoken at Bund meetings, with Bund members in turn frequently appearing as speakers at meetings of the listed organizations. Similarly, Bund camps frequently made themselves available as meeting places for various other radical groups, solidifying contacts and increasing revenues at the same time. For example, on August 18, 1940, the Ku Klux Klan held a meeting at the Bund's Camp Nordland, in Andover Township, New Jersey, at which the Klan paid no rental for the Bund facilities, but agreed to patronize the camp restaurant and pay the Bund's standard twenty five cent parking fee. Additionally, August Klapprott, Eastern Division leader of the Bund and director of Camp Nordland, delivered an address of welcome to the assembled Klansmen.[59]

Further, the Bund assisted the sympathetic groups by publishing some of their materials in its official publication, the *Deutscher Weckruf und Beobachter*; in most of the features, the Bund explicitly approved of the activities of the other extremist groups. As an additional gesture of solidarity, the Bund distributed or sold at its camps, meetings, and other gatherings much of the literature produced by their companions. The Bundists themselves already had a standard reading list, including Hitler's *Mein Kampf*, the books of German propagandist Julius Streicher, booklets by Pelley such as *Liberation*, and the Reverend Charles E. Coughlin's publication *Social Justice*.[60]

Not limiting its activities to adults, the Bund established a Nazi youth program within its ranks, opening summer camps for children to be drilled in Nazi ideology and German military tactics. To prepare youth group leaders for their responsibilities, numerous candidates from across America were secretly sent to Germany for special training, under the auspices of a Nazi propaganda agency in Germany, the League of Germans Living Abroad.[61] Stating that they practiced sports, Bund authorities in America outfitted children with sticks and wooden guns in teaching the youths how to march and conduct combat exercises.[62] Uniforms were standard equipment; members of the youth groups wore outfits similar in many ways to those of the Hitler Youth, and the Nazi salute was designated as the standard gesture of greeting. In terms of education, nothing of American ideals and institutions was instructed within the camps, and youth attendees were encouraged to be extremely critical of the United States and its government.[63]

Beyond word-of-mouth promotion and occasional propaganda pieces, the Bund utilized one major instrument to spread its doctrine throughout the United States. The *Deutscher Weckruf und Beobachter*, or the "German Wake-Up Call and Observer," was published in New York City and circulated by the various group units around the country. Founded in 1936, the journal published pro-Nazi editorial views and articles, and attempted to provide "equal time" for its views to be heard. Many of the features were deliberately inflammatory, attempting to whip the membership into a frenzy in supporting the Bund and its stated goals. In a December 10, 1936 article, detailed descriptions were given of Kuhn's trip to the Berlin Olympic games, lauding Hitler and quoting Hitler, who met with Kuhn personally, as saying, "Go back and continue your fight," corroborating a quote on the front page of the August 13, 1936 issue. Another issue echoed a core belief of the organization, stating that, "We may have lying in the closet different citizenship papers and yet we are all German men and links of a big German community of hundreds of millions." Similarly, an October 1936 issue of the *Weckruf* imparted a related editorial view:

> If you prefer the term "American-Germans" to the term the "German-Americans" you do so ... for the reason that we are first of all Germans in race and blood and language. We belong to the great humanity of

German people. By obtaining your citizenship you have not lost your German character. You remain what you were, Germans in America. American-Germans because we do not become Americans by taking out our second papers. [64]

Another issue openly pledged "Our eternal loyalty to Germany and our eternal loyalty to Der Fuehrer."[65]   More than any other previous Nazi organization in America, the German-American Bund and the *Weckruf* openly proclaimed their ties to the Fatherland, seemingly fearless of the potential repercussions among a greater anti-Nazi population in the United States.

Ultimately, the impact the *Weckruf* made outside of the Bund, and on the Bund's treasury, was considerably less than they had hoped for. Despite numerous attention-getting tactics, circulation for the paper never grew past 5,000 copies, and most of those were given away free.

*   *   *

The Bund augmented its boisterous publication with even more boisterous rallies, meetings, and public events. Bund officials reckoned that negative publicity was inevitable no matter what course they took; by maintaining a high profile, they believed the group would at least gain a greater membership base than previous organizations had attained, and consequently a greater power base to build on. So confident was Fritz Kuhn that the organization's influence was spreading, he devoutly proclaimed that German-Americans would in short order form a voting bloc based on principles of race, one which would draw on the vast number of American citizens of German heritage to reject the national concept of America as a "melting pot" nation.

Bund activities took place in numerous locations, under a wide variety of pretexts. In August 1936, a Bund delegation headed by Kuhn attended the Berlin Olympic games. Carrying $3,000 in cash, the Bundists donated the money to Hitler for his winter relief fund, and later marched in parades under the swastika. Traveling on to Hanover, Kuhn delivered a speech in which he proclaimed, "We feel bound with Germany and are fortunate to belong to such an organization. To be in Berlin and see the Fuehrer eye to eye was for us an experience. We will bear everything and will continue to fight further for the cause."[66] Also in 1936, an estimated 20,000 Bund members came to Madison Square Garden in New York, to hear the Chairman of the American Olympic Committee, Avery Brundage, speak on the Olympics. Among other featured speakers was German Ambassador Hans Luther. This rally, while significant, was smaller than the one held in the same place on February 20, 1939, ostensibly to celebrate Washington's birthday. While some 22,000 people attended the rally, estimates held that a good percentage of those present were simply curiosity seekers, wondering just what the spectacle happened to be; many also may have been attracted by the promise of free beer inside.[67]

In 1937, approximately forty pro-Nazi Americans of German descent traveled to Stuttgart, to attend the Fifth Congress of Germans Abroad. Wearing Bund uniforms, the attendees regularly saluted their comrades with the shout, "Heil Hitler!," and gave speeches frequently punctuated with cries of "Sieg Heil!" During the trip, they, on behalf of the Bund, reiterated more than occasionally their intention of fighting against Communism, the C.I.O., Jewish influences, and boycotts against Germany in the United States.[68]

*   *   *

Given the Bund's high profile, it was simply a matter of time before their activities attracted nationwide harsh criticism, sporadic reprisals, and governmental attention. The effect of Bund activities was magnified by widespread coverage in the media, particularly in German-American centers such as Cincinnati. On February 26, 1938, the Superior Court of Indiana enjoined the Bund from holding meetings in the state, claiming that "Nazi activities are dangerous to the well-being of the commonwealth."[69] On March 24, a full-scale riot broke out after an anti-Nazi crowd stormed a Bund meeting in Philadelphia. Over twenty people were injured in the clash, mostly in fistfights that continued until the riot squad arrived; one man, Sam Bernstein, was cut on the face when someone struck him with a blackjack. Philadelphia police inspector William Soull had been told that the rally had been intended as a celebration of Hitler's seizure of Austria. William Kunze, Philadelphia Bund leader and featured speaker, denied this was true, however, claiming that it was simply a monthly meeting with no fixed program or agenda. Taking no further chances, policemen were posted inside the hall to prevent resumption of the meeting. Violence was not limited to the meeting hall; after police broke up the free-for-all, various members of the Citizens' Anti-Nazi Committee paraded down the street, carrying signs reading "Down With Hitler and His United States Followers." After picketers later disbanded, sporadic fistfights broke out along the street as well.[70] On September 5, 1939, Bund Camp Deutsch-

Horst, on the Meramac River near St. Louis, was destroyed by fire. The blaze, estimated to have done $4,000 damage, was considered suspicious by fire authorities, with a fifty-gallon oil drum found among the ashes.[71] In Sellersville, Pennsylvania, state motor police put a guard around the quarters of the local Bund meeting place after a rally attended by Fritz Kuhn. Local Bund officials claimed that, in the aftermath of the meeting, they had been threatened with a "citizens' assault."[72]

As unpleasant as the attacks and negative publicity may have been, governmental interference into the Bund's affairs had a much more pronounced effect on its existence. Following the Bundist excursion to Stuttgart, and its resultant publicity, the Federal Bureau of Investigation was prompted to undertake an in-depth study of the Bund and its activities, eventually issuing a thousand page report with its findings. Then, after Fritz Kuhn returned from Germany in May 1938, having claimed to have been welcomed by Hitler with open arms, the government began a new and even more substantial investigation into the Bund. The Congressional investigation, chaired by Martin Dies, was conducted by the House Un-American Activities Committee.

In a preliminary report on Nazi-Fascist groups in the United States, issued one day before the outbreak of World War II in Europe, Dies' committee found that the primary aims of such organizations were twofold: 1) To provoke a radical change in the American form of government; and 2) to collect or coerce dues and/or other monetary contributions "from such misguided citizens as will support them."[73] In addition, the committee concluded that such groups were in fact engaged in a form of racketeering, as well as subversive activity in an effort to attain their goals. In issuing its report, the committee appealed to the sensitivities of American citizens, decrying the roles of and measures taken by those who would otherwise threaten the established order:

> In these times, when democracy is harassed from many sides, pee-wee Hitlers, aspiring Fuehrers and would-be Caesars have arisen in our midst urging our people through an unprecedented volume of propagandistic literature to resort to force and violence against large sections of our population. We call special attention to the deplorable prostitutions of such words as "patriotism" and "Christian" to the selfish ends of these fascist racketeers. Critical days call for clear thinking and strong faith in our democratic institutions.[74]

Shortly thereafter, Dies' subcommittee took up another issue of national importance, namely the employment of Bundists in military establishments and plants vital or related to national defense. As early as September 7, the Federal Bureau of Investigation made public its findings that at least seven U.S. Army and National Guard officers had participated in Bund rallies, along with the fact that Nazi agents in America had laid plans for establishing Bund camps within twenty miles of every federal military establishment in the greater Philadelphia area.[75]

By October 1940, Representative Joseph Starnes of Alabama had provided information in the Dies subcommittee that "hundreds" of Bundists were employed in plants vital to national defense. Among the findings presented were that, in one plant alone, some 300 Bundists, Communists and aliens were employed, with fifty in another and some 600 others located in another industrial area; the subcommittee also brought to light acts of sabotage in several other plants. As part of his rationale behind the evaluation, Starnes stated that the subcommittee had "judicially determined" that the Bund was "the agent of a foreign government" and that it was "not American in its concepts and practices. There is no place for it in this country."[76]

Damage to the Bund was not done exclusively by members of the subcommittee; current and former Bundists contributed vital information which helped turn the hearings, and public opinion, decisively against the Bund. In one instance, a former member testified that the group had planned to march on Wall Street, to kidnap "some big bankers" and "hang them up from the nearest post or tree."[77] The witness, Richard Werner, stated that Bundists were trained for a time "when blood will flow in the streets of the United States"; that ninety percent of the New York members were trained in martial arts every Wednesday evening during the wintertime; and that summer rifle training at a New Jersey Bund camp was "almost compulsory."[78] Publicly and privately, the image developed rapidly that the Bund was a bloodthirsty, revolutionary organization that would go to any length to spread Nazism in the United States and impose its will upon the majority that opposed what it stood for.

Confronted directly by the United States government, and in the face of mounting protest against its existence by the American public, the downfall of the Bund was hastened. Under the auspices of celebrating George Washington's birthday, the Bund held a rally on February 20, 1939 at Madison Square Garden. New York Mayor Fiorello H. La Guardia gave the group a permit for the meeting, citing freedom of speech laws, under the condition that there would be no violence advocated, and that the affair proceeded in an orderly fashion. Security was extraordinarily tight for the event, with some 1,000 police officers, including 150 plainclothesmen, expected to be on duty. In response to the rally, anti-Nazi groups threatened to disrupt the event; the first of several bomb threats was made at the Gardens two days before the event, though no such device was found in a thorough sweep of the building.[79] The next day, following increased signs of trouble arising from anti-Nazi picketers, an extra 330 policemen were assigned to the event, and sidewalk picketing outside the Gardens was forbidden; Bundists were also forbidden from holding any part of their function in the streets, including the use of loudspeakers to broadcast the proceedings indoors to those outside.[80] The rally itself proved to be relatively uneventful; only one minor incident was reported indoors, and the New York police officers on hand, raised during the day to a total of 1,700, made only thirteen arrests, all on minor charges. An estimated 22,000 Bundists attended the rally, while police speculated that about 10,000 people were on hand outside, to protest or watch. By the estimates of all involved, it was the largest police turnout ever for such an event.[81]

The massive anti-Bund protest in New York was typical of a growing wave of anti-Nazi agitation in America as the decade came to a close; much of the anti-Bund protest came from fellow members of the German-American community. In San Diego, another "George Washington celebration party" by the Bund on February 25 met with jeering, heckling, and egg and tomato hurling.[82] On February 24, a St. Louis beer garden owner moved back to Frankfurt am Main, Germany, after his flattering remarks about Nazis prompted a demonstration in front of his cafe, and a significant loss of business over time. The beer garden, considered one of the most popular eating places in St. Louis among German-Americans, was given the "cold shoulder" by members of the German-American community in an expression of outrage over the comments. Efforts by local Bund leaders to find meeting halls were also rebuked. The German House, traditional meeting place of St. Louis German-American groups, suddenly announced that it was "booked solid indefinitely" when the Bund approached it; other meeting halls in St. Louis also turned away the Bund, after its leaders revealed their identities to hall owners.[83]

Heavy police patrol and strict enforcement of laws also served to hinder Bund efforts to meet and promote its agenda. On March 12, 1939, a Brooklyn meeting of the youth division of the German-American Bund was outnumbered by patrolmen from the local police, placed on special duty in anticipation of anti-Bund violence. 342 members of the youth division were reported present at the meeting, to undergo calisthenics, marches, drills, and dances in storm trooper and Hitler Youth uniforms; 250 patrolmen watched over the proceedings, with another 350 officers placed on standby duty at nearby precincts, in the event of an altercation between Bundists and protesters.[84] During Fourth of July celebrations, Bund leaders at Camp Nordland ignored a New Jersey law that prohibited the wearing of uniforms similar to those used in a foreign nation, and disregarded regulations against giving the Nazi salute;[85] two days later, the Bund camp lost its liquor permit for use of the Nazi uniforms. In his ruling on the matter, State Alcoholic Beverage Control Commissioner D. Frederick Burnett cited the prominent use of the swastika on the uniforms, as a distinct reference to the German nation, despite Bund objections that the symbol had its origins in Indian culture.[86]

Due in large part to the intense public pressure, attendance at Bund functions dropped noticeably during 1939. Typical of other locations, Fourth of July celebrations at Bund Camp Siegfried, on Long Island, were attended only by about 2,000 people, compared with an estimated 10,000 the year before. The previously mentioned Camp Nordland celebration drew approximately 1,000 members, a significant decline from past attendance. Declining membership and attendance prompted a financial crisis in the organization; the Bund attempted to cut costs where it could, legally or otherwise, in an effort to stave off economic ruin. It did not take long for law enforcement officials, carefully monitoring the Bund at every turn, to uncover financial irregularities within the organization. In March 1939, an inquiry was launched to determine if the Bund had paid New York City taxes on the sale of propaganda materials. In May, Kuhn was charged with the theft of $14,548 of Bund funds. With little money at their disposal, the Bundists were powerless to provide their leader with much defense; Kuhn was convicted of grand larceny in November 1939, and sentenced to two-and-one-half to five years in prison.[87] With the arrest of Kuhn, the Bund lost not only its most effective leader, but its direction; growing smaller daily in the wake of Kuhn's arrest, the organization lost any effectiveness it had possessed beforehand. On December 8, 1941, in the wake of the Pearl Harbor bombing, what remained of the executive committee of the Bund voted to disband the group.[88]

*   *   *

Despite the fact that the German-American Bund was the most successful pro-Nazi group in the United States, there are several reasons why the organization, like previous pro-Nazi factions in America, was unable to succeed in rallying the German-American community. Leland V. Bell has equated the Bund's failure with a lack of understanding of American politics and culture:

> Basic to the Bund's failure to capture a mass following was this attempt to relate a foreign ideology to the American scene. This mindless effort produced ludicrous interpretations of American life and showed that the Bund lived in an eerie world of fantasy and fabrication.[89]

Bell also cites the Bund's deliberately confrontational style, and unconcealed resemblance to the German Nazi party, as a reason for failure; by antagonizing anti-Nazis and alienating others who might have been objective listeners, the Bund sharply reduced its chances for success:

> The propagation of National Socialist racism infuriated American anti-Nazis. Contributing also to their anger were the Bund's other Nazi characteristics which Kuhn made no attempt to disguise. As in the NSDAP, the *fuehrerprinzip*, or leadership principle, underlay the basic organization of the Bund and gave Bundesfuehrer Kuhn the final authority over every sphere of the movement's affairs.[90]

Susan Canedy discusses the failure of the Bund in terms of both governmental and public disapproval; while the Bund did itself a disservice in many ways, the people and their government ultimately determined the fate of the group, rather than the Bund exercising control over the people:

> For the most part, the Dies Committee merely voiced opinions and passed judgments that were shared, and indeed expected, by the American public. It was looking for spies, acts of sabotage, popular front organizations, and individuals connected with foreign governments. It found all those things, but, sadly, not necessarily because they were there.[91]

This point is of interest in discussing the Bund's right to exist, and how it affected German legal resident aliens and German-Americans not involved in the movement. The Bund represented only a fraction of the

German-American community, as a tiny but vocal minority capable of generating sensational press coverage. As Canedy makes clear, the Bund broke no laws by its existence, nor did it advocate action against the United States government; by standing up for what it believed in, something unpopular with the vast majority of Americans, it came to be regarded as a threat to American interests:

> The German American Bund was tried and convicted on the basis of the perception it engendered. Its existence broke no laws, nor did it advocate revolutionary principles or the forcible overthrow of the government. What it did advocate was its chosen doctrine - that of National Socialism. Under the First Amendment, its activities were legal and protected by the Constitution. The reaction to the German American Bund ... indicates popular support for the government and for ideal American values.[92]

In comparing moderate members of the German-American Bund with their vocal counterparts, Canedy also expressed the plight of the German-American community; a large majority of German legal resident aliens and German-Americans were lumped in with Bundists in a blanket condemnation of pro-German, not just pro-Nazi, interests in America, in the absence of evidence of wrongdoing or subversive behavior: "The group as a whole was punished for crimes committed by the few due to the solidarity which the group portrayed. [The German-American community] was called upon to pay for the sins of its alleged master."[93]

Cincinnati and the Pro-Nazi German Element

Pro-Nazi organizations such as the Friends of New Germany and the Bund preferred to locate in cities with high German-American populations; in the mid- to late 1930s, these groups attempted to wield influence in Cincinnati, as a traditional center of German population. Leaders of such movements played heavily on the sympathies of German-Americans and German nationals in the city, appealing to their loyalties to the Fatherland and on nostalgia for the old country. In principle, such a strategy was sound; as late as 1935, some six out of every ten Cincinnati residents were of German extraction, with many of them still participating in one or more of the over forty German societies located in the area. Though weakened as a result of World War I, the local German community was still an identifiable segment of the city's culture and population, continuing to exert influence in virtually every aspect of Cincinnati life.

Despite the efforts of the Friends and the Bund, though, the vast majority of German-Americans in the city rejected Nazism and its proponents. Additionally, there is little evidence to show that German nationals in Cincinnati were swayed by the pro-Nazi movement of the 1930s. While many German nationals professed a devotion to Germany as their land of birth, only a small minority felt that such a devotion extended to politics as well. To that end, Eberhard Fuhr cites the example of his father, Carl, as a German national residing in Cincinnati during the 1930s:

> My father was very pro-German. He really was a true German patriot, no question about that. And I was brought up in that way. To love your country. 'This is your fatherland, you were born there, this is really your roots.' All those kinds of things.

Though Carl Fuhr took a passionate interest in politics, according to Eberhard, his first preference was for the American political system; in 1938, Carl had even worked for the Republican candidate for Governor of Ohio. With regard to German politics, Carl desired a constitutional monarchy based on the model of Great Britain; in his view, says Eberhard, Hitler "was a transient kind of thing," a leader who would help stabilize the country before inviting the exiled Kaiser Wilhelm to return.[94]

Nevertheless, there were a relative few people among the German element who saw Nazism as a solution to America's social and economic problems of the Depression era, people who were willing to advocate openly National Socialism and the guiding principles of Adolf Hitler. Doubtless many in the general public were shocked at the appearance of Nazi sympathizers, at public rallies as well as private meetings, which in several cases lead to a fervent effort to head off the Nazi presence in Cincinnati. As early as 1934, campaigns were waged to expose the pro-Nazi element in the city, and by 1935 the Cincinnati German community was put on the defensive, following what was called a pro-Nazi rally. By 1938, veterans' organizations and others were outspoken in their condemnation of the Bund, portraying Bundists as un-American hate groups bent on undermining the American lifestyle.

*　　　*　　　*

The first concerted effort to combat the Nazi presence in Cincinnati came from the city's Jewish community, which was already well informed about the extent of Nazi persecution of the Jewish element in Germany. Working to prevent the possibility of any such occurrence on these shores, Cincinnati's Jewish element responded promptly and vociferously to fight what they saw as a threat to their existence. Though numbering only around 18,000 in a city of 450,000 residents,[95] the Jewish community was already well established and highly respected in Cincinnati, recognized as the birthplace of reform Judaism. Behind several outspoken leaders, two prominent newspapers in *The American Israelite* and *Every Friday*, and countless community members ready and willing to take on the Nazi element, the local Jewish community stood at the forefront of the Cincinnati anti-Nazi movement; partially to that end, the Jewish Community Relations Council was founded by the mid-1930s.[96]

In January and February 1934, *The American Israelite* fired the first shot in the battle against local Nazi sympathizers, publishing a series of reports exposing Cincinnati Nazis. On January 18, the paper reported that a Friends' meeting had been held at the Friars' Hall, at 2436 Clifton Avenue. Addressing those present was Albert Knoedler, the leader of the Cincinnati branch of the Friends, while the featured speaker was Fritz Gissibl, who had come in from Chicago to talk in place of an absent Walter Kappe. The fact that two of the most prominent Nazis in America, Gissibl and Kappe, were associated with the local meeting went neither unnoticed nor unmentioned by the *Israelite*, specifically referring to Gissibl as the "Nazi Kingfish in America."[97] Despite the paper's heavy-handed tone against the Nazi element, editors of the *Israelite* made a point of mentioning that the majority of Cincinnati German-Americans neither had nor wanted anything to do with the Nazi organization, referring to the "complete absence of the respectable and prominent German-American element from the meeting."[98]

The *Israelite* continued its series of reports on February 1, publishing an article concerning Alfred Knoedler's refusal to apply for American citizenship. Knoedler, who had been in the United States since 1928, had been eligible to apply for citizenship for ten months, but had steadfastly refused to pursue the matter. In response, the *Israelite* noted the fact that few members of the Friends were American citizens, further challenging the group to "name one member of the well-known German-American community who belongs to their group."[99]

The Jewish Community Relations Council was also successful in its efforts to expose Cincinnati's Nazi German element, albeit in a different manner than that employed by *The American Israelite* and *Every Friday*. During the mid-1930s, members of the JCRC managed to infiltrate several secret meetings of the Friends, and subsequently filed detailed reports on their activities.

One such report was dated January 25 and discussed a secret meeting held at 76 McMicken Avenue. To gain access to the meeting, those attending had to enter the large building and ascend a flight of stairs, until reaching a sign reading *Teutonia Sing Chor*. Of the three rooms present on that floor, one could hold up to 200 people, the second approximately 100, and the third room some fifty persons. While the first, largest, room was decorated with numerous "ever so dirty" American flags, the second, middle-sized room, was decorated with a swastika-emblazoned German flag, a blue, white and red German flag, and a large picture of Adolf Hitler. Some sixty people were present at the meeting; the roll call indicated a total membership of seventy. Speaking to the assembled group, Alfred Knoedler made the dubious claim that the group enjoyed the support of various German veterans' organizations, otherwise praising the Cincinnati chapter of the Friends as being "much more cautious and thorough-going than other chapters in larger cities."[100]

Another such meeting took place on March 2, 1935, at the Masonic Lodge on Clifton Avenue. The featured speaker was Walter Kappe, by that time a New York resident who returned to Cincinnati on a semi-regular basis to speak to the Friends. During the meeting, also reported on by *The American Israelite*, Kappe made "vicious, unretracted anti-Semitic outbursts," with the approval of members present.[101]

Logically, expressions of pro-German, and especially pro-Nazi, sentiment went underground in the wake of American entry into World War II in December 1941. Nevertheless, several incidents were exposed by the local Jewish community. On August 9, 1942, a Jewish Community Relations Committee member attended the Cincinnati German Day celebration, noting that "because of the inclement weather, and because of the prevalent fear to identify oneself with the German organization," only around 1,000 people attended the festivities. While there, though, one woman named Paulina Miller spoke on her "National Socialistic ideas" and openly espoused her "sympathy for the New Germany," also volunteering the information that her fiancee was an aviator in the German air force, according to the observer. Similarly, several days later the Banater Societies of Cincinnati held their annual picnic, at Steuben Social Park in North College Hill. The event, referred to in the August 15, 1942 *Cincinnati Enquirer*, was also attended by a JCRC witness, who claimed that pro-Nazi speeches and activities took place, despite the fact that public sentiment ran contrary to such an exhibition.

*   *   *

On August 18, 1935, representatives of the Friends of New Germany, soon to become the Bund, attended the annual German Day celebration at Coney Island. In participating in the day's rally, various members paraded behind the Nazi swastika, wore swastika arm bands, sang one verse of the "Horst Wessel Lied," and repeatedly gave the "Heil Hitler" salute as a greeting. Not surprisingly, objection was soon forthcoming from the local Jewish community. Several days later, the *American Israelite* published an editorial blasting the German-American Citizens' League and, particularly, Glenn Adams, a Republican candidate for reelection to city council and officer of the day at the celebration. Meeting on August 28 at the Central Turners Hall, the German-American Citizens' League adopted a resolution making light of the incident, claiming that "nothing occurred that could rightly be construed as an insult to anybody ... we look upon the controversy as much ado about nothing and, therefore, consider the matter closed." Further, the resolution defended the presence of the swastika flag, calling it the official flag of Germany; regarding the "Horst Wessel Lied," authorities noted that the one verse chosen was selected to demonstrate its inoffensiveness to any race or nationality. The resolution was unanimously adopted by more than 100 delegates, representing 41 of 42 organizations affiliated with the League. One measure was taken to appease the Jewish group: The Friends of New Germany was officially censured for their part in the affair, and consideration was given to asking the Friends to resign their membership in the League.[102]

For several years thereafter, German Day celebrations in Cincinnati continued without incident, as normal proceedings reigned without hint of controversy. In 1937, far from focusing on the Bund, Cincinnati German-Americans enjoyed a celebration at the Cincinnati Zoo, featuring a food show, apple pie baking contests, music by such luminaries as Billy Bryant's showboat troupe ("Ten Nights in a Bar Room"), health classes, a card party, and baby beauty contests for children aged six months to two years. The biggest, and least controversial, attraction was the food show, daily at the Zoo from August 29 through September 6, from 10 a.m. to midnight, with 175 booths to satisfy the heartiest of German appetites.[103]

Some six months later, though, such lightheartedness gave way to dissention and controversy, as the German-American Bund and its activities in Cincinnati came in for scathing attacks from the Hamilton County Council of the Veterans of Foreign Wars. On March 1, 1938, local commander Lindley P. Moore sharply denounced the Bund's work as "a deliberate, audacious effort to foist European hatreds upon peaceful America." Responding to the statement of the German government that no German citizen in the United States would be allowed to belong to the Bund, Moore only snapped, "No American, either." He made clear that true German-Americans, and all others in the country, were better off without the Bund and its strong-armed tactics:

America can get along very well without the Bund, without the Bund's military camps, without the Bund's use of the German national flag upon American soil, without the Bund's overemphasis upon a fanatic, alien nationalism, without the Bund's heiling of a foreign dictator. Several years ago, an outstanding veterans' organization adopted unanimously a resolution denouncing a group known as the "Friends of New Germany." The Bund is the equally undesirable successor of the undesirable "Friends of the New Germany." We are against the Bund under whatever substitute name that may be used to disguise its real character.[104]

Lindley went on to express his view that a "dual allegiance," that is, a German in America also professing loyalty to Germany and its goals, was not possible; one had to choose one side or the other, and serve it devotedly:

No man can serve two countries. In these trying times, every man has his mind pretty well made up as to which country he prefers. If that country be not America, we believe the man's place is not in America. It is time that Americans pierced through mere words and lip service. It is time that we come to distinguish between those who simply protest they are good Americans and those who really are good Americans. [The Bundists] live by emotion, not reason; by fanaticism, not common sense; by hyphenated, twisted loyalties; by divided allegiance, not by traditional Americanism. This land has no need for two flags, no need for European hatreds, no need for terroristic organizations. We need more of the desire to live together in peace, more insistence upon freedom, more respect for all men, regardless of race or religion.[105]

Such a view, an extension of the nativist thoughts fully developed during World War I, was commonly held by many at the time, partly out of patriotic convictions, otherwise in part inspired by a deep-rooted distrust of the German element remaining from the last war, and a sense of distrust of the motives of Hitler and National Socialism.

Still, Moore hastened to point out his view that Bund members represented a minority of troublemakers in an otherwise respectable German-American community:

> Finally, we wish to pay a tribute to that great body of Americans of German descent, true Americans, who have no sympathy, no time, and no money to support any effort to inject European discord into the United States. They are far in the majority among Americans of German descent. Our quarrel is never with them.[106]

This view is important, for in it one can see that the anti-German hysteria of the World War I era, and its suspicion of all things German, was unlikely to recur in the same manner; what hysteria did exist would be expressed in part through the internment of German legal resident aliens and German-Americans deemed dangerous to national security and the public welfare.

At least one prominent Cincinnati Bundist tried to put out by fire by downplaying Hitler's influence and the scope of Bund activities in the city. On March 1, Albert Zimmer, president of the Cincinnati chapter of the Bund, was quoted as saying that "Hitler should mind his own business and quit dictating to America," though he claimed later that evening not to have used those exact words and had no further comment to make on Hitler. He added that there in fact were no German citizens in the Cincinnati chapter of the Bund, excepting the few in its associated Prospective Citizens' League. Zimmer also denied that the Bund had any connection whatsoever with the Nazi party or the German government.[107]

*   *   *

The VFW condemnation of the Bund, and Zimmer's own comments, were but the tip of the iceberg, for throughout the month of March 1938, both organizations occupied prominent positions in Cincinnati's news headlines. On March 5, Albert Zimmer formally resigned his presidency of the Cincinnati chapter of the German-American Bund. He refused to comment publicly on his resignation, saying to a reporter only, "Yes, I have resigned, but I don't wish any publicity on the matter."[108] Zimmer's probable motive for resigning can be deduced from what little he did say. Given the extremely adverse public reaction to the Bund, Zimmer and other Bundists were wary of the spotlight of media attention. By nature a secret organization, the Bund discouraged reports on its activities; recent revelations of Zimmer's role as president undoubtedly undermined his ability to lead the Cincinnati chapter effectively. The publicity the newspaper reports generated thus can be seen as a natural cause for Zimmer's desire to step down, partly for the benefit of the Bund and partly for the good of his own reputation.

On the evening of March 5, Zimmer had informed officials of the Hamilton County council of the Veterans of Foreign Wars that he would resign. Further, he offered to appear at a meeting of the council at the Disabled American Veterans' Hall, on Melrose Avenue, on March 8, in an effort to "reaffirm [his] Americanism."[109] That Tuesday night, the Veterans struck a further blow at the Bund in its meeting, condemning the activities and teachings of the Bund in a resolution; Zimmer did not appear as planned at the meeting. Zimmer's whereabouts for the evening were a mystery; inquiries at his Harrison Avenue home yielded only a response that he was out, and would not have had anything to say even if he were at home.[110]

In its resolution, the Veterans, representing thirteen V.F.W. posts in the county, pledged to expose all "isms," including the Bund, in American society, and urged all governmental bodies in Hamilton County to prevent "any Bund, Fascist, and/or Communist camps from being established within this county." The last part of the resolution was occasioned by reports that plans existed for establishing a Bund camp inside Hamilton County in the near future. The unanimous vote on the resolution was taken at a private, executive session, but was made public immediately.[111] Specifically, the resolution against the Bund contained the following grievances:

> 1) The Veterans opposed and condemned Fascism, Hitlerism, and Communism "as forces that attempt to destroy democracy and the American Constitutional system of government";

2) the Veterans found that alien organizations existed within the United States, "originating, fostered, and promoted by alien nations that preach loyalty and allegiance to foreign governments, their dictators and foreign flags";

3) Adolf Hitler had unequivocally stated the notion that "Once a German, always a German";

4) the Bund, previously the Friends of New Germany, had utilized false names to conceal its real identity and "expressed its allegiance to Hitler and his policies";

5) the Bund was "an instrument and an agent of Adolf Hitler, advocating divided allegiance, hyphenated citizenship, loyalty to a foreign power and to its flag and emblem," as well as an institution which "slanders democracy, is opposed to free speech, free press, rights of labor unions, and rights of religious freedom";

6) the Bund "represents the wild and savage forces of hate, fanaticism, and violence as opposed to liberty, justice and reason";

7) wherever the Bund had organized and held meetings, "disorder and strife" took place; and 8) the Bund had attempted to create military camps "to instruct youth in the German military drill and German war tactics."[112]

Given those grievances, the Hamilton County council of the Veterans then listed their specific resolutions relative to the Bund:

1) The council reiterated their opposition to the activities listed;

2) the council was of the firm belief, based on evidence and opinion, that "the propaganda activities and teachings, both public and secret of the Bund, militate against and are detrimental to the national defense of the United States";

3) the council intended to "engage in a county-wide educational policy of exposing all un-American 'isms,' including the Bund, and point out the advocates and the agitators" within such groups;

4) the council would ratify the anti-Bund declaration made by Commander Moore on March 1;

5) "all municipal, township, and village authorities and all other governmental agencies within Hamilton County, and the County Commissioners thereof" would be petitioned to prevent any Bund camps from being established in the Greater Cincinnati area; and

6) copies of the Veterans' resolution were to be sent to all municipal and county authorities within Hamilton County, to state and national authorities within the V.F.W., to the Governor of Ohio, members of Congress from Hamilton County, all veterans' and patriotic organizations, and to the press for publication.[113]

On March 16, Hamilton County Commissioners acknowledged receipt of the Veterans' resolution.[114] Other attention was forthcoming, though, as on March 24, Ohio Attorney General Herbert S. Duffy made public a letter he wrote to Fritz Kuhn in New York. Having already received several tips in addition to the Veterans' document, Duffy was attempting to determine whether Nazi organizations in the state of Ohio were involved in any illegal activities, with the intention of prosecuting the Bund "to the full extent of the law" if such was found to be the case. Such a position by Duffy is indicative of the prevalent attitude of the time, namely the fear of some type of illegal activities from a group which neither had broken the law nor advocated doing so; reminiscent of the fear of German spies and saboteurs during World War I, it was fostered by hostile press and radio coverage of the Bund, newsreel footage emanating from Europe, and negative Hollywood portrayals of the German element in America.

Duffy indicated that illegal activities of the Bund included violations of the criminal syndication law, in which attempts to overthrow the government by using or inciting violence, a felony, were punishable by lengthy jail terms or worse. To that time, though, no one had been sent to the Ohio Penitentiary for such a violation in the almost twenty years the law had been in existence. In his letter to Kuhn, Duffy specifically referred to three Bund camps said to be located in Ohio: 1) German Center, in Cleveland; 2) Youth Camp #5, in Cincinnati; and 3) Camp Richthofen, in Dayton. Additionally, Duffy asked Kuhn to provide the following information on the Bund camps:

1) The names of all local chairmen and other officials of the three camps in Ohio;

2) the scope of the Bund camp activities;

3) the purpose for which the camps were organized;

4) the address of the camp meeting sites; and

5) any other information on the three camps.[115]

The Veterans' Americanization Committee had already looked into various reports that camps would be established at specific points. However, as of the date of their resolution, they had found that none of the reports held any basis of truth. Citing Bund policy to maintain a camp near each large metropolitan area, the Veterans insisted that each report would be taken seriously and fully investigated.[116]

On March 25, it became clear that conflicting versions of the Bund camp story, a reflection of a certain degree of discord, were being expressed by Cincinnati and national Bund leaders. That day, a Bund associate spoke out on the issue; he refused to use his name out of fear of adverse publicity, a concern expressed previously by Albert Zimmer. According to the unnamed associate, there was not a single Bund camp in Hamilton County, nor even a single one in existence throughout the Midwest. Beyond denying the existence of a local Bund camp, reputedly located in Norwood, the speaker publicly denounced a New York Bund officer's assertion of the existence of a Dayton camp as "ridiculous," saying "the Bund has had only five members in Dayton. How could they support a camp?"[117]

Such a view directly contradicted the remarks of James Wheeler Hill, secretary of the Bund in New York. Hill, in responding to Duffy's written inquiry announced two days earlier, claimed that the Bund had not three, but rather five, camps in Ohio. He fleshed out his comments by citing that two new camps had been founded one month earlier, namely Youth Camp No. 47 in Dayton and Youth Camp No. 14 "near Norwood." The two youth camps were described by Hill as recreation centers for young men. Further, Hill claimed that the Bund's membership number had grown to 180,000 in America, and that a recent investigation by the Department of Justice had given the group a clean bill of health.[118]

Police authorities in Cincinnati, though, sided with the unnamed local Bund follower's view. According to George Heitzler, Chief Deputy Sheriff, law enforcement officials in Cincinnati knew of no open Bund camp in the area, stating, "Unless the word 'camp' is being used to mean 'lodge' or 'chapter' for a group that might meet in some hall, I don't believe they have any camp here."[119]

* * *

The Veterans of Foreign Wars was not the only patriotic organization in Cincinnati to take exception to the German-American Bund.   Like the Veterans, the American Legion passed resolutions condemning the Bund, made the Bund a primary topic at meetings and conventions, and spoke out sharply against their beliefs and actions. On March 25, 1938, the Hamilton County Council of the American Legion, meeting at 322 Broadway, approved a resolution submitted by Mariemont Post No. 146, lashing out at groups which undertook "subversive activities." The document contained three main resolutions:

> 1) To endorse and approve "the continuation of the investigation of all subversive activities and also the individuals in any way associated with them";
>
> 2) to use the receipt of established fact from reliable sources such that "the full spotlight of publicity be given those persons" involved with the Bund; and
>
> 3) that "no stone be left unturned and all steps be taken" to remove Bund members from public offices and teaching positions.[120]

In July 1938, the Cincinnati branch of the American Legion again took a stance against the Bund, in a resolution of protest against the group's activities during its twentieth annual departmental convention in Cincinnati.   These activities, the Legion gathering pronounced, were "designed to corrupt our youth and citizens, to undermine our government, to militate against our defense and our constitutional guarantees." Throughout the July 23-26 convention, the resolution, submitted by the Eli Wittstein Post, formed the basis of discussion. Post members maintained that the resolution was necessary in order to make aware and educate the American public on the inherent dangers of organizations such as the Bund, specifically:

> because the German-American Bund and its affiliated organizations, under pseudo-patriotic names to conceal their real identity, represents savage forces, violence, class and religious hatred, divided allegiance, and hyphenated citizenship as opposed to our love of liberty, justice, and democracy.[121]

The resolution made plain the Legion's view that Bund activities stood in contrast to American ideals and attitudes, proclaiming the Bund and its methods of operation to be enemies of all things patriotic Americans held dear:

> [The Bund was] an alien organization created, fostered, and promoted by an alien nation which preaches loyalty and allegiance to a foreign government to its dictator and its emblem. It teaches thousands of the youth of our country in their camps and classes to hate everything American, to pledge allegiance to and salute the "Swastika of Nazism," and to fight for it when called upon.[122]

In addition to the resolution, the local Legion gathering made plans to ask the 1938 National Convention of the American Legion to undertake a similar action, on the grounds that the Legion, which was organized "to preserve the American system of government ... fosters a one hundred per cent Americanism."[123] Additionally, local commander Sam Kraus sent a copy of the resolution to the Ohio Department headquarters of the Legion at Columbus, asking them to take concurrent action against the Bund.

*   *   *

While the Bund's influence as an organization waned after 1939, following the arrest of Fritz Kuhn, the Bund returned to the public eye on occasion, as further information, or at least rumors, on its status and activities became available.

On April 3, 1941, Middletown resident Martin Coffey addressed a meeting of the Galbraith Post, American Legion National Committee on Americanization, of which he was a member, at the Hotel Gibson. Coffey, whose speech was announced with the promise that he would "name names" in exposing un-American activities, spoke at length on the threat of Communist infiltrators and German-American Bund activities. Coffey asserted that there were 82 Bund branches in the United States, with one of them located in Cincinnati, and that many "loyal and patriotic Americans" were being "duped" into lending their names and making monetary donations to "fellow traveler organizations."[124]   Specifically, Coffey claimed that, as of January 1, 82 active units of the Bund had been located, including Ohio centers in Cincinnati, Cleveland, Dayton, and Toledo. Further, Coffey speculated that the location of the Bund units was far from coincidental, claiming that they were deliberately placed in areas of strategic importance for the United States' defense industries; by implication he indicated that the Bund may have been responsible for local acts of sabotage:

> Perhaps it is significant that 47 of these bunds are located in strategic spots within three miles of plants engaged in the business of national defense. The second largest bund in the country is located less than two miles from the Hercules Powder Company where a disastrous explosion occurred a few months ago. Twenty-five members of that bund were employees of the Hercules Powder Company and the day after this explosion nine of them failed to appear for work and they haven't been back since.[125]

Additionally, Coffey claimed that several incidents, in the Cincinnati area and elsewhere in Ohio, were out of the ordinary and implied that the Bund may have been a factor:

> Right here in your own back yard, the King Powder Company, at Kings Mills, has had three explosions and a fire within the last five months, more of that sort of thing than they experienced during the last 15 years. Only recently, and it hasn't been published yet, the authorities found 500 sticks of dynamite in the vicinity of the wharves in Toledo and every stick of the stuff was foreign-made.[126]

In concluding his discussion of the Bund and other possible subversive elements, Coffey suggested several measures to combat the activities of such groups. Among those measures were the following:

> 1) Intensive educational work among school children, including such things as patriotic essay contests and scholarship prizes;
>
> 2) sponsorship by the American Legion of some 6,000 junior baseball teams throughout the country;

3) insistence on the deportation of people found to have served subversive groups or enemy governments;

4) abolition, at least on a temporary basis, of the international postal agreement which permitted the circulation of millions of pieces of foreign propaganda, free of postal charges, within the United States;

5) the refusal by authorities of the use of public buildings for meetings held by subversive organizations; and

6) an increase of at least 1,000 in the number of FBI employees available for investigating subversive groups and activities.[127]

Thus it can be seen that, while members of the Friends of New Germany and the German-American Bund attempted to establish a presence in Cincinnati during the 1930s and early 1940s, the efforts met with stiff resistance from the local Jewish community, veterans groups, and anti-Nazi members of the public.

Conclusions

The question remaining to be answered is to what extent Nazi propaganda in Cincinnati, and elsewhere in the United States, was effective or posed a danger, and to what extent it simply stirred up emotion which could be directed against members of the German-American community, both those who were members of the Bund and those who were not. Few people in the United States, of German background or not, were swayed by Nazi propaganda efforts to support the cause. There can nevertheless be little doubt that the Nazi propaganda, combined with negative media coverage of the Nazi element and biased entertainment portrayals of the Nazi element as an aggressive, hostile group, did manage to convey a more subtle, unfavorable impression, thus helping to foster an increasingly negative change of perception of the German element in America, from the mid- to late 1930s into the 1940s. To this end, one can describe the *Zeitgeist* of the mid- to late 1930s, indeed the general atmosphere regarding the German-American community, as having taken on an excessive excitability and anxiety, symptomatic of a growing anti-German hysteria found even in the most German-influenced parts of the midwestern United States.

Such excessive excitability and anxiety had been precipitated partially by the Bund and its predecessors, and their deliberately unsubtle means of conveying their message. However, more than that was needed to create the overt fear of the Bund and other pro-Nazi groups, relatively small organizations which in reality were far more of a nuisance than a threat. The previously mentioned negative media coverage and biased entertainment portrayals, along with the provocative style the Bund and other Nazi groups utilized, helped create an excessive fear of such groups, as evidenced by the Congressional hearings of the 1930s, and galvanized public sentiment against not only pro-Nazi groups, but also other members of the German-American community.

The widely held fear of the German-American Bund, for example, can be seen as unwarranted, given the insignificant membership levels in the organization, as well as the fact that the German-American community made clear the fact that the Bund represented no one but the Bund itself. For its part, the German-American community wished only to be judged on its own merits, rather than on Bundist terms.

While it is much easier in hindsight to recognize the relative insignificance of the Bund and other pro-Nazi groups as a threat to American stability, and to assess the effect of their activities on the status of German legal resident aliens and German-Americans, there are other areas in which it is more difficult to ascertain to what degree the German-American community of the 1930s and early 1940s was impacted by the changing perception of the German element within American society. One issue worthy of examination is whether the American public had been able to make a clear distinction between the Bund and the German-American community in general, given the fact that the German-American community had made significant attempts at drawing a distinction between itself and the Bund.

The answer is a qualified no. To be sure, some people were able to make the distinction; generally speaking, the majority of people were not able to, nor in fact chose to, distinguish between the two very different groups of German-Americans. Such a point is underscored by the Congressional hearings, which not only called Bundists as witnesses, but also German-Americans who clearly were neither Bundists nor sympathizers. By including the latter group of German-Americans, the distinction was blurred for most people beyond recognition. The distinction was further rendered invisible by the tone of the hearings, which would be repeated with more notoriety during the McCarthy Communist hearings, in which witnesses were subjected to baiting tactics and harassment. Beyond the hearings, the general public found its ability to distinguish between Bundists and otherwise unquestionable German-Americans blurred by American-made films, which fed the growing hysterical fear of Nazis spies across the nation. Not only did the Hollywood portrayals of the German element represent a falsification of the situation of most German legal resident aliens and German-Americans in the United States, but also one which could, and likely did, place in question the loyalties of German-Americans on a broader scale than had even the Congressional Hearings.

Additionally, one must take note of the point that if in fact another anti-German hysteria were to take place leading up to and during World War II, it would necessarily have to differ from that expressed during the World War I era. It often has been said that there in fact was no anti-German hysteria during World War II, a statement which, upon close examination of the situation, can be disputed. The statement can only be seen as true in the sense that there was no World War I-style outbreak of anti-German sentiment; indeed, the replication of such a reaction would not have been possible to begin with; most of the World War I acts against the German-American community, such as the renaming of streets, banning of German instruction, and destruction of German monuments, had not been remedied in the intervening period. In other words, a new anti-German hysteria would have to be re-directed and focused elsewhere from before, most notably in terms of the more widespread use of internment of German legal resident aliens and German-Americans, the model of which was established during World War I, though used to a lesser extent.

In conclusion, then, we can see that the German-American Bund, in addition to other pro-Nazi groups of the 1930s and early 1940s, contributed significantly to the negative *Zeitgeist* evident during the period, as well as the changing perception of America's German community as a whole. Their posture and activities, while not expressly illegal, nevertheless helped to create an hysterical fear of Nazis in the United States, which in turn placed other uninvolved German-Americans in the position of also being cast into suspicion. While not solely responsible for the anti-Nazi hysteria developing in the United States during that critical period of time, these organizations did little, if anything, to quell the fear of German spies and activists on American shores, reminiscent of the period of the First World War. Also, by failing to work with the German-American community in an effort to distinguish between pro-Nazi German-Americans and disinterested, or hostile, German legal resident aliens and German-Americans, these groups further blurred the distinction between them, helping to create a situation which clearly could endanger the position of all German-Americans within American society.

Chapter III

Media Perception and Coverage of the German-American Community

In order to determine the extent to which the German element in America fell victim to changing perspectives during the World War II era, it is necessary to examine media coverage of the German community during that time, particularly with regard to the perceived threat of the Nazi element and fifth column activities. To be sure, the general public in America formed opinions based on its own perception of self-interest and what may have constituted a threat to its well-being; for many Americans, the German element remained a respected and admired community, based on long standing reputation and contributions to the nation's development. However, given the vast audiences commanded by newsprint and radio media around the country, as well as the growing film industry in Hollywood, it is inevitable that these powerful forces would play a large role, often subconsciously, in shaping the American public's perception of German legal resident aliens and German-Americans, and the degree to which the latter would come to be considered an undesirable or even threatening element in times of war, or when national security interests were at stake. Even many anti-Nazi German-Americans came to feel stigmatized by adverse coverage of occasional Nazi activities in the United States, conducted by a vocal but tiny minority, and by implied questioning of German-American loyalties.

It can be seen as inevitable that the activities of American Nazi sympathizers during the 1930s, would influence the way that the German-American community was reported on by the mainstream press, and consequently the impression such coverage would make upon the American public at large. English-language newspapers of the 1930s, in search of stories known to generate reader interest, frequently seized upon reports pertaining to the Friends of New Germany and the German-American Bund; the result was a preponderance of anti-German, and by extension anti-German-American, news coverage. Such reports lacked a contrasting range of focus that represented the interests, and loyalties, of the vast majority of German-Americans during that time.

In turn, it also is important to analyze the position of the nation's German-language press of the time, in an effort to determine to what extent it strove to emphasize German-American loyalty to the United States and deflate potential sources of controversy or counter negative portrayals of the German element. Despite protestations to the contrary from outside the German-American community, it is clear that during the 1930s and 1940s, German-language newspapers, in Cincinnati and elsewhere, reflected foremost a strong pro-American viewpoint, subjugating the interests of America's German community to those of the United States as a whole. This stands in marked contrast to the pro-Kaiser proclamations of America's German-language press before American entry into World War I, a move which would lead directly to the anti-German hysteria of the late 1910s and early 1920s. Clearly, the German-American community had learned a valuable lesson from its earlier, harrowing experience.

Its best efforts notwithstanding, the German-American press quickly discovered that it could not compete with a new and popular English-language forum, capable of subtly and overtly influencing public opinion: Hollywood film portrayals of Germany and the German-Americans. Films portraying members of the German-American community as potential spies and saboteurs gained in number, and popularity, after the outbreak of World War II in Europe; by the time America entered the war in December 1941, it was clear that Germany was a nation hostile to American interests, a situation which guaranteed the acceptance and popularity of the spy/saboteur motif in portrayals of the German-American element. Such portrayals, while occasionally accurate, often bordered on the ludicrous in efforts to blend a terrorist threat with wartime entertainment. The result was the reinforcement of Bund-generated anti-German feelings, which would culminate in an anti-German wartime hysteria best noted for the wartime detention and internment of select members of the German-American community, as dangerous enemy aliens and Americans of questionable loyalties.

The Perspective of German-Language Newspapers

With the outbreak of war in Europe in 1939, many of America's German-language newspapers saw the need to declare emphatically their loyalty to the United States and its interests in a time of German war. Clearly remembering the World War I era, when German-language papers boldly sided with German interests in a period of American neutrality, ultimately to see the United States enter the war on the side of Great

Britain, America's German journalists had no desire to relive the experience of that time. The German-language press took an interest in events in Germany, yet chose not to become involved in a movement which might again result in a situation as disastrous as that which they had encountered during World War I. Most German-language papers wasted little time in distancing themselves from German interests in times of armed conflict, wishing not to be perceived as biased at a time of heightened sensitivities. Further, given the pervasive sentiment of recent years against the Friends of New Germany and the German-American Bund, many editors went to great lengths to deny any sympathy with American Nazi elements, as well as any contacts with members of the Nazi regime in Berlin.[128]

While the German-language press in America managed to survive the anti-German hysteria of World War I, it emerged in a considerably weakened state, and with a change in orientation. Far from rebuilding itself to levels of prewar influence and regaining ground lost to the hysteria, postwar German-language newspapers declined in number and circulation, as well as quality, due to an accelerated process of reader assimilation and a subsequent lack of cohesion in traditional centers of German-American population. Consequently, the number of German-language newspapers in the United States fell from a peak of more than 800 before 1917 to 201 in 1932, and only 181 by 1939.[129]

Other tendencies illustrated the weakened state of German-language newspapers in America. Once published in every state in the country, by 1940 only twenty-six states continued to produce papers for the German audience.[130] Many of the newspapers previously published on a daily basis, became weekly or even monthly issues as readership declined following World War I. With the naturalization rate of Germans in America running higher than that of any other immigrant group by the 1930s, combined with a virtual stoppage of immigration during the late 1910s and much of the 1920s, the assimilation process was more visible in that community than anywhere else; estimates that twenty-five percent of America's German element continued to read German-language papers were considered "much too high."[131] Also, while the German-language press still represented the highest individual total of the 1,047 immigrant newspapers in America by 1939, it unquestionably had lost ground to other, newer immigrant groups.[132]

Additionally, remaining German-language newspapers reflected a growing apolitical trend from the 1920s onward. As Carl Wittke observed:

> The German press no longer was active politically and tried to avoid controversial issues. The disastrous experience of the war years had convinced many publishers that it was wise to have no editorial policies. By 1940, papers like the Cincinnati *Freie Presse*, the *Wächter und Anzeiger* of Cleveland, and the *Tägliche Tribüne* of Omaha contained almost no editorial comment.[133]

During the 1930s and early 1940s, existing German-language newspaper editorial policies on political issues were defensive in nature; Nazism had little impact on America's German-language press. For the most part, the German-language press came out solidly and vocally against Nazi Germany and its policies, expressing opposition to developments in Germany. Remembering the experiences of the past, most of America's German-language newspapers attempted to avoid the issue of Nazi Germany, maintaining instead an American isolationist policy, if not condemning the Nazis outright, while otherwise reiterating their position of unquestioned loyalty to the United States and its interests.[134]

Consequently, during the 1930s, America's German-language press found itself on the defensive, attempting to prevent a recurrence of anti-German sentiment while reassuring others of its loyalty to American interests. More than ever before, the German press strove to keep a low profile in times of crisis, at the same time presenting itself as a civic-minded, if less influential, voice of conscience for America's German element. Such a posture was seen in Cincinnati as much as in other traditional German-American centers, and the *Cincinnatier Freie Presse* serves as an example of an American German-language newspaper which strove to emphasize its loyalty to the United States, yet also found itself under attack for perceived pro-Nazi biases.

In November 1938, an announcement was made in Berlin that Frederick W. Elven, president of the *Freie Presse*, was to be awarded the Order of Merit of the German Eagle, Second Class, concurrent with his retirement from the paper. Seventy-three years old at the time, Elven was known for having built up the *Freie Presse* more than a quarter century earlier, as well as for having supervised the absorption of another Cincinnati German-language paper, the *Tägliches Cincinnatier Volksblatt*, or simply *Volksblatt*, in 1919. It should be noted that he was known to have traveled "extensively" to Germany following Hitler's rise to power.[135] Members of the German-American community maintained that Elven, a native of the Schwarzwald area, was unfairly stigmatized for his German travels; he came to the United States in 1890 and worked as an apprentice reporter in Detroit, before moving to Cincinnati in 1900 and joining the *Freie Presse* staff.[136] In reality, Elven usually traveled to Germany in an effort to gather news and features for the *Freie Presse*, as well as to study conditions in the land of his birth.

Responding to criticism of his travels, and to past descriptions of him as being a staunch supporter of the Third Reich, Elven at first claimed that he would only accept the award if it were based upon his service to the German people in the capacity of editor of the *Freie Presse*, such as his Sunday feature "Umschau," a highly popular and widely circulated digest of news from various German newspapers he subscribed to. In fact, Elven previously had gone on record as approving of many of the early Third Reich accomplishments, but was "unalterably opposed" to its ideals of racial and class superiority.[137]

Ultimately, Elven opted to dissociate himself from the Nazi regime by turning down the award, explaining his refusal by saying that he was no longer interested in any country except the United States. Emphasizing that his personal policy was "the United States, first, last and always," Elven stressed that he wanted to help defend local and overseas Germans from the Nazi stigma, by demonstrating that not all Germans were Nazis and should not all be blamed for Hitler's acts.[138]

On September 18, 1939, the *Freie Presse* announced its platform for German-Americans, during the course of the war in Europe and into the future. The paper published eleven points, in English, falling into three distinct categories asserting the local German community's devotion to Cincinnati and the United States. The three points which made up category one illustrated the paper's devotion to the American way, calling for the following:

1) "Absolute and unswerving loyalty" to American ideals and principles;

2) a continued and consistent effort to teach, by frequent admonition or repetition, such a spirit and instill it in "the mind and heart of every citizen of German extraction"; and

3) "strict obedience" to all American laws and customs.

Category two presented six points devoted to the local German community and how it might assist in the promotion and development of the city of Cincinnati. Looking beyond the German community, the paper called for Cincinnati's German-Americans to promote the welfare of the city as a whole, for the benefit of all of its citizens. Specifically, the paper called on its readers to assist the city in the following manner:

1) Cooperate with others in an effort to uplift "the social, cultural and business life of Greater Cincinnati";

2) cooperate in an effort to promote and further develop a "proper and adequate" sewage disposal system in the city;

3) help in the development of a rapid transit system;

4) participate in the "perpetuation of good government," without regard to personalities and racial or ethnic factors;

5) aid in the extension of park, boulevard and playground plans throughout the city; and

6) advance Cincinnati's prestige as a center of music and art.

Category three represented two further points, in this case devoted to advancing spiritual values associated with the traditional American ethic. The *Freie Presse* called on readers to set a positive moral example by the following:

1) Helping to develop and foster spiritual virtues, in part through "closer co-operation with scriptural laws and edicts"; and

2) assisting in the promotion of "a spirit of brotherly love," as well as "adherence to the Golden Rule."[139]

While such initiatives were meant to dispel any concerns the American public may have had about the loyalties of the German-American community, other events managed to undermine those efforts. For example, in November 1940 Albert Guise, then editor of the *Freie Presse*, was forced to disclaim all responsibility for letters the Dies committee said were written by a man named Ludwig Schmitt, who reportedly had posed as "editor" of the paper. The letters were written to the German Consulate in Cleveland, suggesting that the consul use his influence to procure the Trans-Ocean News Service at no cost. According to Guise, Schmitt was merely a translator for the *Freie Presse*, and had no authority to make such a request.[140]

*   *   *

Despite strong efforts by the *Freie Presse* and its editorial staff to stress its devotion to American interests, as well as dispel reports that it functioned as an outlet for pro-Nazi propaganda, several instances during the 1930s called into question the role of the newspaper as a mouthpiece for Cincinnati's German community. One of the biggest drawbacks for the *Freie Presse* during the 1930s and early 1940s was the fact that it had employed Walter Kappe, one of America's foremost Nazi sympathizers and later a suspected saboteur on behalf of the German government. Kappe had moved to Cincinnati from Chicago in 1931, and upon being hired by the *Freie Presse* as a telegraph editor and translator proceeded to use his position in furthering a propaganda campaign against the local Jewish community. Though Kappe was fired by the paper in 1934, subsequent reports on his anti-American activities significantly tarnished the reputation of the *Freie Presse*. More importantly, as the paper claimed, an "incomplete description of the Kappe affair" had cast undeserved suspicion upon the Cincinnati German-American community, assuring others that all local German leaders fought vigorously against Kappe and his pro-Nazi activities.[141]

In an effort to minimize the damage, the paper published an article in August 1942 downplaying Kappe's earlier role there. The paper took exception to implications by the FBI that Kappe was one of the highest figures in the Nazi espionage movement while in Cincinnati; according to the article, the presumption made by the FBI was that "the *Freie Presse* and the population of German extraction in Cincinnati had had something to do with Kappe and his un-American activities." Defending itself, the paper insisted that Kappe's position at the paper had been "subordinate," in that much of his authorial work came in writing about club parties, theater performances, and literary topics; the reason for his dismissal after nearly three years of employment, they asserted, was his pronounced anti-Jewish posture and espousing of National Socialist ideology. On an economic level, the paper claimed that Kappe's "biased and muddling articles" had done financial damage, in that valuable advertising dollars had been lost due to his controversial positions. Finally, the *Freie Presse* stated that the management of the paper had changed from that time, and implored readers to believe that "the paper cannot be any more patriotic than it is."[142]

Cincinnati's Jewish community also came out strongly in opposition to the *Freie Presse*, in maintaining that the paper served as a pro-Nazi publication during the mid-1930s. To support such allegations, the Jewish Community Relations Council put together a series of reports describing the perceived pro-Nazi tendencies of the paper. Among other assertions, the reports maintained that the *Freie Presse* directly aided the Nazi cause by publishing "colored reports in favor of Nazi propaganda,"[143] while at the same time attempting to link Nazism as a movement with German culture, in an effort to dispel notions of Nazi aggression and keep the Cincinnati German-American community misinformed, or at least uninformed, about growing, worldwide condemnation of the Nazi regime.[144]

Local Jewish newspapers likewise were outspoken in their condemnation of what they felt was a pro-Nazi bias in the *Freie Presse* during the mid-1930s. Two Cincinnati Jewish papers, *The American Israelite* and *Every Friday*, were particularly vigorous in their efforts to bring to light any anti-Semitic references made by the *Freie Presse*. For example, citing "a climax in a well prepared scheme to force local merchants to spend their money at the *Freie Presse*," *Every Friday* published a front-page article on February 9, 1934, in which it shed light on the blacklisting of large Cincinnati retail outlets who refused to advertise in the *Freie Presse*. Indeed, on February 4 an advertisement had appeared on page two of the *Freie Presse*, less than subtly indicting some of Cincinnati's largest stores for succumbing to pressures from the Jewish community:

Co-Citizens!   Take Notice!

The following firms, apparently under the pressure of certain Jewish atrocity propagandists, have refused to advertise in the *Freie Presse*:

Shillito's
Rollman

Fair Store

German Women and Men buy of the firms who advertise in
the *Freie Presse*.[145]

In another example of investigation of the *Freie Presse*, *Every Friday*
published an article in July 1934, looking into the finances of the German-
language newspaper. According to *Every Friday*, very few "reliable" local
businesses advertised in the *Freie Presse* and that its building, located at
905 Vine Street, was mortgaged "up to the limit," specifically in the sum
of $68,250. *Every Friday* maintained that the "visible income" of the *Freie
Presse*, from advertisements and total circulation, failed to cover weekly
bills by hundreds of dollars; the implicit assumption was that Berlin, or
short of that the Nazi element in the United States, somehow covered the
deficit.[146] In sum, Cincinnati's Jewish newspapers of the mid-1930s
openly denounced the *Freie Presse* as a pro-Nazi organ, one which pursued
a "line of Nazi propaganda as to foreign policy and achievements of the
Nazi Party"; in formulating their opinion, they confidently asserted that "in
following the *Freie Presse* from day to day one must come to the
conclusion that the paper is fully controlled by Nazi propaganda
officials."[147]

As a result of declining readership in the German-American
community, combined with the watchdog efforts of Jewish and other anti-
Nazi groups, German-language newspapers assumed a more centrist role
during the mid- to late 1930s and early 1940s than had previously been the
case. Far from taking on a pronounced pro-German stance in times of
controversy, German-language newspapers went to great lengths to
dissociate themselves from elements of Nazism, real or perceived, and
drew upon their experiences in World War I to assert their patriotism and
community spirit at virtually every turn. The efforts of newspapers such
as the *Cincinnatier Freie Presse* to distance themselves from people and
activities associated with Nazism were successful in deflecting a certain
amount of negative publicity; however, lacking a clear rallying point for
the German-American community in troubled times, German-language
newspapers continued to experience a decline in readership, as well as a
reduced frequency of publication. Due at least in part to the stain of
Nazism in America, as well as to suspicions that the German-language
press could, or would, function as pro-Nazi propaganda organizations
within the United States, German-language newspapers lost readers and
valued advertising dollars in the years leading up to World War II,

hastening the decline of such publications in the United States, and their lack of availability to the nation's largest ethnic group.

The Perspective of English-Language Newspapers

While German-language newspapers served to express views held within the German community, and attempted to defend it from unjustified anti-German attacks, their ability to influence public opinion was only a fraction of that of America's English-language newspapers. The key to the position of superiority held by the English-language press can be found in two areas. First, English-language newspapers had a much higher circulation than those in German, even in traditional German-American settlements; and second, most English-language newspapers benefited from daily circulation, and the resulting immediacy of news and viewpoints presented. In contrast, by the late 1930s and early 1940s, only a handful of German-language dailies continued to exist; the relatively few German-language publications remaining often published on a weekly basis, at best. Thus, it was inevitable that English-language newspapers would come to have greater success in influencing public perception of the German question.

Before American entry into World War II in December 1941, the English-language press, in Cincinnati as elsewhere, had played a significant role in informing the public of developments involving the German community. As early as August 1940, it had even been instrumental in assisting German aliens in complying with federal regulations, serving as a primary source of information as to how native Germans were to comply with the alien registration program. In Cincinnati, the *Enquirer*, *Post*, and *Times-Star* each had devoted space to providing registration instructions, with the *Cincinnati Post* even providing step-by-step illustrations to clarify the process. Further, each of the papers reported not only details of how registration progressed, but periodically updated information, such as the number of registrants and changes in procedure, in addition to publishing reminders of registration places and deadline dates.

However, other "civic-minded" efforts to report on German-American matters in Cincinnati, fell less into the category of assisting Germans in complying with the letter of the law. On the contrary, several journalistic efforts, furthered by the local Jewish community among others, attacked Cincinnati Germans for their efforts to continue meeting and functioning under umbrella organizations, as well as for contributing to German war relief and prisoner of war collections. Even with the outbreak of war in Europe, and the ongoing movement to register German nationals as aliens, many local German organizations continued to meet regularly and openly, albeit with a lower profile, during 1940 and 1941. Despite, or perhaps because of, their openness and sympathetic approach to a homeland at war, these groups were regarded with suspicion by many non-Germans. One group, the Jewish Community Relations Committee, even sent supporters to meetings of various local German societies, in an effort to monitor the themes and tone of group discussions. The spies, posing as local Germans to gain access to meetings, strove to uncover pro-Nazi, or at least anti-Semitic, activities and bring them to light through the mainstream media.

One of the activities uncovered in the meetings, and subsequently reported to the English-language press, was the effort of Cincinnati's German-American community to contribute to those Germans affected by the outbreak of war in Europe, as well as to German prisoners of war in Canada, and other Germans in need or far from home. One such effort brought to light was a November 1940 letter, from Dr. Franz Koempel of the American Committee for the German Relief Fund, soliciting contributions for poor Germans. The letter subsequently fell into the hands of a local Jewish leader, Benjamin Epstein, whose public response was to claim that the sponsors of the organization were "prominent in the more dignified pro-Nazi circles." No substantive documentation was provided to bear out what circles those were, nor to show any connection to the local German community. Epstein also asserted that the government had uncovered evidence that money collected, after care packages had been sent to Canada, was diverted to Berlin, for Nazi propaganda programs, though again no proof of the assertions was provided.[148]

In one case, the *Cincinnati Post* served as a watchdog for German-American efforts to aid German prisoners of war. In an April 12, 1942 appeal, the *Freie Presse* published a letter by a gentleman named Forsten, who had requested that Cincinnati German-Americans doing their spring cleaning consider donating any surplus items they might find to "our war prisoners," namely German prisoners of war in Canada. He also claimed that the United States Government had given him permission to collect items to send away.[149] In response, the *Post* claimed that Forsten in fact did not have permission to gather such material, as well as that local

German organizations had subsequently been warned away from the campaign.[150]

Efforts to report pro-German fund-raising activities did not discriminate between pro- and anti-Nazi groups. For example, the United Banater Association, not unknown to take a pro-Nazi stance on governmental and other affairs, was castigated by the local Jewish community for its efforts at a July 21, 1941 meeting, to raise funds for German war prisoners in Canada.[151] Also reported was a meeting on July 22, of the Bavarian Mutual Support Organization, in which they collected and donated twenty five dollars to German war relief.[152] Up to that point, there had been no indication, nor any expressed suspicion, of any Nazi sympathy within the group. Similarly, in November 1941, the Women's Civic Union raised ten dollars for German prisoners of war, while at the same time the Bavarian Club made plans for a dance at Cincinnati's Alms Hotel, with half of the proceeds designated to go to German war prisoners. In each case, groups not known to have pro-Nazi allegiances were stigmatized for helping those who, officially at least, were not considered to be "enemies" at the time.

*   *   *

Following American entry into World War II in December 1941, English-language newspapers took a more active role in reporting on the status of German nationals, especially those considered to be "enemy aliens." With Germany now officially an enemy of the United States, the uneasy silence many Americans held regarding German legal resident aliens and German-Americans quickly became a loud voice of anger and aggression, cloaked in the guise of patriotism. Coverage of the German element by the *Cincinnati Post*, through editorials and letters to the editor, provides a representative example of the mindset of Cincinnati residents toward potential spies and saboteurs, both locally and nationally, and is typical of viewpoints expressed in other major American cities.

"Cincinnatus," in his *Cincinnati Post* column of February 27, 1942, voiced the feeling held by numerous people at the time regarding German aliens, especially those being detained under suspicion of pro-German loyalties. Like many others, "Cincinnatus" held the view that those who sided with German interests, and those proclaiming their German heritage, were guilty of ingratitude, turning their backs on the nation which had welcomed them and their families, and had given them equal rights. He surmised that "they were just futile Nazis anyway, whom no Americans would follow," referring specifically to those detained as enemy aliens as "pipsqueaks playing at being big shots in their master's plan to take over the world."[153] As Americans hastened to make known their feelings on German aliens and the German-American community, English-language newspapers became a primary forum for exchanging viewpoints, and by extension helping to shape public opinion. In Cincinnati as in other German-American centers, observers contributed their perspectives to the newspapers on an almost daily basis, in forums such as editorials and letters to the editor, with the implicit goal of converting others to their particular points of view.

Predictably, a number of comments called for stricter control of aliens in America, in some cases inclusive even of those not deemed as "enemy" aliens by the government, as well as those who might feel sympathy for their plight. As one writer put it, "any intelligent individual can see (that) any man closely allied with the Nazi regime would continue his nefarious work regardless of how often he swears not to do so." Freeing internees, the writer claimed, would create "a menace to the principles and safety of our democracy."[154] On a related topic, several writers addressed the continued availability of perceived pro-Nazi propaganda, and the need to strengthen laws against such material. One person lamented that downtown Cincinnati merchants continued to stock, and sell, "literature which stresses race hatred, disunity, and lack of confidence in the men of authority in our government," citing the example of "effective defeatism" in *Social Justice*, by Father Charles E. Coughlin, a man whose work had been espoused by the German-American Bund. Another writer, using the initials "F.L.C.," advocated tightening restrictions against those who might spread Axis propaganda. Echoing a growing sentiment against the German-American community, he maintained that, "Clearly even traditional concepts of civil rights must be adjusted to the facts of modern warfare."[155]

One person writing to the *Post*, Vernon Sennett of Norwood, cited the segregation of Axis aliens in Brazil as a potential American policy, criticizing the United States for not taking firmer measures to ensure national security. In the view of Sennett, contemporary American alien policy was akin to saying, "'In case of fire, don't call the fire department, it will eventually burn itself out,'" while calling for anyone holding any type of allegiance to an enemy nation to be "quarantined for the duration."[156] A more extreme posture was taken by a Covington housewife, in calling for an automatic death penalty for convicted spies and saboteurs, claiming that "you cannot tame a mad dog by patting it on the head."[157] Another writer took exception to a request by twelve Cincinnati doctors to release another physician, possibly Dr. Wilhelm Huebener, being held as an enemy alien. The writer, likewise a doctor, opined that many local doctors, including perhaps himself, had been friendly with the detainee. However, as the writer put it, "with patriotic American citizens friendship for alien enemies ended when we declared war." The writer, as did other contributors in subsequent letters, also asserted that anyone who had lived in the United States for a long time, yet had not become a citizen, naturally placed himself under suspicion.[158] The disturbing train of thought developing over time was not only that the government could not possibly intern someone unjustly, but even more so that those who supported releasing interned aliens, for whatever reason, left themselves, and their motives, open to suspicion.

The subject of spies in America, real or perceived, sympathetic to German interests, provoked not only the most commentary locally, but also the most emphatic. Following the arrest of eight men on espionage charges in 1942, Cincinnati area residents, as elsewhere, quickly made known their feelings. One writer expressed the feelings many Cincinnatians held, imploring "this bunch to be shot right away, so as to have no more expense. [I]f there are any more like them in this country, they will think twice before they start anything."[159] When the following day another writer, Mark Millikin, urged a more restrained response, claiming that people had become "a little hysterical" about the threat of espionage and sabotage, a barrage of letters followed which took him, and those holding such a view, to task. Millikin opined that it was far from a heroic response to place someone in front of a wall and shoot him, with the only acceptable option beyond jail for spies and saboteurs being to take them through the country and show them "our comparative prosperity, peace and freedom ... on every occasion," before deporting them.[160]

Response to Millikin's comments was swift and sure. One writer, using the initials "R.H.," rebutted Milliken's views, saying that "it may not be heroic to shoot spies but it's better than to let them in our defense plants and blow up hundreds of plants and workers."[161] Another writer addressed the issue of fairness, claiming that "it certainly would be an insult to our men at the front" were judges to go easy on the eight accused, echoing the widely held view that America could not win the war "by showing mercy to ruthless barbarians."[162] Another prevalent theme of the time was the need to make an example of those who would work against the United States. As one writer said, "I do not thirst for the blood of spies, but spies should be made to die quickly for the sake of example."[163] A more angry reaction was expressed by Charles F. Henessey, in writing that it made his "American blood boil" when fellow countrymen were dying for freedom, while those such as Millikin "have the audacity to say we should go slow" in dealing with accused spies and saboteurs. As he put it, anyone found to have done harm to the United States should be "tied by their ankles and pulled through every street in these United States until dead."[164] Clearly, the intense feelings of wartime had polarized feelings against those considered dangerous to American interests; those who advocated a cautious approach, and by extension those who might show themselves to have something in common with the enemy, whether actually guilty of a charge or not, left themselves open to the possibility of discrimination, if not persecution.

Other comments of a patriotic nature can be classified less as taking on an overt anti-German tone, than as showing support for government policies against the German element, including enemy alien arrests, hearings, and internment. On December 17, 1941, "B.G.," writing to the *Post*, lauded the FBI's handling of enemy aliens, opining that it was a "praiseworthy government that withholds the names of men it had arrested," should subsequent developments show that detainees were "proved innocent of wrongdoing."[165] Similarly, a *Post* editorial of December 13 praised the government for its decision to establish enemy alien hearing boards, stating that "boards of review should serve a useful purpose in providing a 'jury' type of consideration," claiming that alien internment "will not be done now, as it was not done during the first World War."[166]

For his part, "Cincinnatus" commended the government's actions against enemy aliens, while attempting to reassure others that all those targeted by federal authorities would be treated with as fairly as possible. On December 19, the editorial writer commended the government for "setting an excellent example of coolheadedness for the citizenry of this country," further praising Attorney General Francis Biddle for urging citizens not to engage in "amateur spying" or mistreating aliens.[167] Further attempting to quell any outbreak of anti-German hysteria reminiscent of the World War I era, "Cincinnatus" reassured aliens and members of the German-American community that "the spy and saboteur will be given quick punishment, but the average alien ... may rest assured

70

that he will not be interned nor otherwise molested by the government."[168] Regarding possible spies and saboteurs, "Cincinnatus" praised governmental authorities for vigorous prosecution of those detained, stating that "there is no other rational way of dealing with these spies than shooting or hanging them. The lives of ... spies do not seem as important as the lives of hundreds of American workmen who might be slaughtered."[169]

While such forums often urged restraint on the part of patriotic Americans in dealing with those of German heritage, they did not go far enough to prevent many from exposing, and attempting to drive underground, the German element in America. Clearly, if the German element was to prevent a wholesale outbreak of anti-German feeling, for patriotic reasons or otherwise, it would have to take the initiative to distance itself from those with whom its members did not sympathize. Thus, on various occasions, members of the German-American community availed themselves of the opportunity to use the local English-language press to their own advantage, attempting to make others aware of the persecution they endured on occasion, as well as to reinforce the distinction between those simply of German heritage and those who actively supported or sympathized with the Nazi cause.

Not the least of such writers' goals was to equate the belligerence of overly zealous American "patriots" with that of the Nazis themselves. In a December 1941 letter to the *Post*, a German-born worker lamented that, based on how he was treated by his coworkers, if he weren't sure he was among U.S. citizens, he would suspect that he was surrounded by Nazis. According to the writer, his coworkers regularly called him a Nazi, and regarded him with distrust and animosity due to his heritage. In reply, he told readers of the *Post* that "I am an American who loves America even more than those who have always had it. It makes me sad to see Americans taking up some of the manners of the Nazis."[170] Another writer, a German refugee, reported his experience while riding on a Cincinnati bus. Speaking in German with another refugee, they were quickly berated by a fellow passenger ordering them to "Cut out that Dutch! If you can't talk American, you should go back where you came from." The writer was less concerned with the insult than the fact that "[the passenger's] manners were the same as of the Nazis," from whom they had escaped.[171]

Accusations not only of overt, but also covert, anti-German sentiments and actions were also made by local Germans willing to discuss their experiences. One German refugee, writing to "Cincinnatus," spoke for a large number of recent German immigrants. He expressed anguish at the fact that he felt like a criminal in America, simply because he had a German accent. Pointing out that he despised Hitler and the Nazis for having placed him in a concentration camp and confiscating his possessions, he said that he "suffered disagreeable incidents only because the German accent remains on my tongue."[172] Another "Cincinnatus" column took up the case of a local refugee from Hitler's Germany who found himself distrusted due to his accent and background. The immigrant wrote that "people grow cold at the sound of my voice. I can hear them thinking 'This man is a Nazi,' though I am one who above all other men must love America," as his refuge from Hitler and Nazi Germany. Further, he discussed his experience in trying to get a defense job, only to feel "condemned" when he said that he had come from Germany. As he explained it, "There isn't one who would work with more zeal than I to make the things that are needed to defeat Hitler." He also noted that his own father had died in a Nazi concentration camp.[173]

In fairness, though, some writers made the point that the German element was being treated better than had been expected, at least compared with the World War I experience. One person communicated his experience at the Cincinnati Public Library, where he asked for a German book in March 1942. He stated that the librarians were most helpful, evidently not considering him to be a "saboteur, fifth columnist or other form of traitor," all the while expending extra effort to help him find the desired book. He contrasted his experience to that of Cincinnati Germans in World War I, when German-language books were removed to the basement, and when "nobody dared ask for one without putting himself in peril of suspicion and inquisition."[174] Another German exile writing to the *Post* discussed her role as a volunteer, in an effort to show her appreciation for the freedom America, and not Hitler, had given her. Discussing her work with the American Red Cross and the Civilian Defense, she saw her work as "a holy mission for the highest ideals and principles," as well as "a light in the night of hatred, which obscures now the whole world," equating such service to reaffirming a belief "in the ultimate victory of Democracy over the forces of evil."[175]

Hollywood Film Portrayals of Germans
and the German Element in America

There can be little doubt that Hollywood film portrayals played a significant role in the changing perception of America's German element during the World War II era. Far from reinforcing traditional images of German immigrants as thrifty, proud, hard-working and honest people looking to assimilate and contribute to American society, movie depictions of America's German stock frequently leaned towards the controversial, preferring depictions of Nazi spies and Bundists in films full of foreign intrigue. Such images of America's German element as being unpatriotic or working on behalf of Adolf Hitler needlessly fanned flames of prejudice against the German community, without providing a contrasting viewpoint representative of the majority of German-Americans of the day.

Precedent for World War II-era portrayals of America's German element had been set some twenty five years earlier, as film companies actively engaged in the production of propaganda films during World War I. Such a posture was based on a well-known ability of motion pictures to convince the audience of a particular point of view, based on visual images "taking place" right before the viewer's eyes. The importance of film to World War I, as well as future, propaganda efforts has been recognized by Richard Wood and David Culbert:

> When films first appeared in 1895, enthusiasts immediately recognized the medium's potential for persuasion. World War I marked the first worldwide use of film to do four things: record actual fighting, help train combatants, make civilians on the home front aware of the need for sacrifice and patriotic commitment, and, finally, sway neutral opinion. The very idea of propaganda, as a part of state policy is one of the results of World War I.[176]

With regard to swaying neutral opinion, several types of movies portrayed the German element in a negative light, reinforcing existing stereotypes and fanning the flames of ethnic hatred in the mid- to latter part of the 1910s.

One of the most popular film vehicles during World War I was the spy drama. These films, much like newspaper columns and articles of the day, played a large part in turning American citizens against the German element, implicating countless Germans loyal to the American cause by repeatedly portraying German agents and spies as operating on American shores. While some films dealt with German spies in Europe, many others characterized the presence of German spies on the home front, even before war with Germany was declared in April 1917. As early as 1915, the film *Over Secret Wires* depicted German spies operating in the United States, making contact with German submarines about American shipping activity off the coast of Oregon; in *Paying the Price* (1916), foreign agents were shown operating in Washington, attempting to steal a secret formula for a high explosive.[177]

With the American declaration of war on Germany, numerous other spy films were made, exploiting the existing state of war and taking advantage of prevailing anti-German sentiment. Particularly in 1918, spy films with domestic settings were released with frequency. Some utilized the theme of seduction (*Her Debt of Honor*; *Suspicion*), in which the wives of a senator and research scientist respectively, have an affair with a German spy, who attempts to gain access to vital information from them. Many other films showed Nazi spies and saboteurs working to destroy vital areas of American interest, such as the shipbuilding industry (*The Road to France*) and sugar plantations in Hawaii (*The Marriage Ring*), while stealing plans for a new American rifle (*The Kaiser's Shadow*) and papers from a munitions plant (*Claws of the Hun*).[178] Although many of the films were realistically made and to an extent plausible, several others bordered on the ludicrous in their portrayals. For example, in *Mr. Logan, U.S.A.* (1918), cowboy hero Tom Mix uncovers, and subsequently foils, a plot by German spies to take control of a tungsten mine.[179]

While such movies provided valued entertainment in times of international crisis, the end effect of many of the spy films was to help turn public sentiment against America's German element, in an effort to rally patriotic sentiments amongst American citizens. Far from providing a balanced portrayal of the role German-Americans played in the United States, such portrayals reinforced prevailing stereotypes of Germans in America as "dirty Huns" and called into question the loyalties of countless Germans and German-Americans in the United States; as Larry Langman and Ed Borg point out, "According to American films, the home front was no guarantee of safety from enemy machinations."[180] In fanning the flames of anti-German sentiment, Hollywood set a visual image to widespread magazine and newspaper commentary condemning America's German stock, directly influencing the anti-German hysteria of the time.

*　　　　*　　　　*

One notable effort in filmmaking geared towards informing, and influencing the viewpoints of, the public on German-American matters was the American newsreel. As early as the 1910s, and especially during the 1930s and 1940s, newsreels served to pass along timely information on current events affecting people's lives. During World War I, newsreels played only a minor role, inadequately covering ongoing events in Europe more due to obstacles created by civilian and military organizations, than by any lack of effort by the newsreel industry.[181] Further, the credibility of wartime newsreel footage was damaged by revelations that at least some of the coverage was faked, as evidenced by a September 1914 comment by John D. Tippett, the London representative of the Universal Film Manufacturing Company, claiming that "anything [the viewer sees] in America of any consequence is fake. ... Cameramen are absolutely forbidden to go anywhere near the points of interest."[182] A November 1915 report in the *Literary Digest* took reports of fakery a step further, publishing an illustrated description of how war-film faking was conducted in England. However, such problems did not deter President Wilson from establishing the Committee on Public Information, on April 14, 1917, eight days after the United States had declared war on Germany. The committee was given the responsibility of "providing news, information, and indoctrination materials" to American civilians.[183] Named after its zealous chairman, George Creel, the so-called Creel Committee came to be dubbed "America's first propaganda ministry."[184]

By the 1930s, movie studios had agreed on a common policy for handling controversial subject matter, namely that such material should be avoided. To this end, the Fox Corporation announced in 1931 that its theaters and newsreels would not be allowed to show scenes of a "controversial nature ... on which reaction might be divided." Regarding Nazi Germany specifically, at least one, unnamed, film company stated that no news from Germany whatsoever was to be used, unless in the case of a revolution against the regime itself.[185]

In 1938, the movie industry's self-imposed ban on controversy was put to the test by Time, Inc. and its decision to show its *March of Time* newsreel "Inside Nazi Germany - 1938." Introduced in the spring of 1935, *The March of Time* was considered a radically different type of newsreel, with a revolutionary style for its day, uniquely mixing cinematic exposition and unconventional journalism. An Academy Award winner in 1937 "for having revolutionized one of the most important branches in the industry," it featured open editorialization which both infuriated enemies and alienated friends in the course of a fifteen- or twenty-minute report.[186] "Inside Nazi Germany" attempted to shed light on living conditions in Germany under Hitler and the Nazi government, discussing working conditions, military strength and activities, and persecution of Communists and Jews, among other topics. Included in the report was a segment on German propaganda efforts in the United States. Claiming that "propaganda extends far beyond Fascist frontiers," "Inside Nazi Germany" gave prominent attention to Fritz Kuhn, repeatedly referred to as "Führer Kuhn," and the New York branch of the German-American Bund. Among the newsreel's assertions were that Kuhn had claimed "to have enrolled 200,000 U.S. Germans under the Swastika," as well as that Kuhn had established 25 summer camps and drill grounds, including in Cincinnati and Cleveland among three Ohio locations, "where those German-Americans who believe in Nazi teachings can imitate Hitler's mighty military machine."[187] Clearly, in citing the example of the Bund, the newsreel was attempting to arouse public passion against the Nazi element in the United States and, by extension, to question the sympathies not only of Germans living in America, but also those of German stock. To further the emphasis, the newsreel cited the example of a grass-roots movement in Southbury, Connecticut, aimed at preventing the Bund from establishing a camp in town. At a town meeting on the matter, one elderly speaker attempted to distinguish the town's view of its traditional German element, in comparison with those with avowed Nazi sympathies, claiming "We have no quarrel with what we term 'the older order of German people.' But we do object, and we do protest, against the insidious, treacherous activities of Nazi agents masquerading as American citizens."[188] While such speeches met with much applause, they offered no practical solutions as to how one distinguished between "insidious Nazi agents" and those German-Americans who might wish to utilize the camp, for less political means, as a gathering place for fellowship.[189] Hence such meetings, and the coverage given them by prominent forums like *The March of Time*, could not help but have an adverse effect on the German-American community, leading others to unduly question their loyalties and associate Germans in the United States, and the German-Americans, with a regime they were not in touch with.

*　　　　*　　　　*

During the late 1930s and early 1940s, Hollywood film producers saw themselves as leading figures in an effort to prepare Americans for the coming war. For the better part of the 1930s, movies tended to have a domestic orientation, given the fact that moviegoer concerns centered around economic problems born of the Depression and resultant economic deprivation. By the latter part of the decade, though, as progress was seen in the domestic crisis, such a focus was superseded by a foreign orientation based largely on the rise of European fascism.[190] Initial Hollywood forays into political filmmaking during the mid- to late 1930s were cautious and restrained; a prevailing isolationist sentiment in America made decisive expression both financially and politically risky.

With the outbreak of war in Europe, though, a realization of the threat of Hitler's power was soon felt, and Hollywood quickly moved to align itself openly with the expressed position of the Roosevelt administration, and a growing public sentiment that Hitler and the Nazis were enemies of American interests. Consequently, by the end of the 1930s political cooperation between Washington and Hollywood became reality. Pre-December 1941 movies began to exhibit overt propaganda content, with the unstated but nevertheless pervasive goal of shaping public sentiment against Nazism and its proponents.

Several early forays into anti-Nazi filmmaking took on the pretensions of Hitler and his endeavors in Europe. One of the most notable examples came in 1940, when Charlie Chaplin was featured in *The Great Dictator*. The film spoofed Hitler and his mannerisms, in the process reminding viewers of his domineering intentions; the film ended with an impassioned anti-Fascist speech by Chaplin himself. Yet other portrayals were more cautious before American involvement in the war. Many of America's pre-war political films were less inclined towards dealing with individuals; rather than specific people, Hollywood portrayals leaned towards a commentary on those who would try to impose their will on the American people. James Combs comments on this tendency in *American Political Movies*:

> ... [the studios'] pre-war messages usually tended to view the overly ambitious seeker of power as alien and pathological, someone whose will to power propels him or her so against the American grain that he or she becomes doomed by demonic excess. ... We expect the machine politico to take a minor fall ... and the would-be dictator, too, take a drastic fall, one in which he really suffers for his excessive reach for power.[191]

Such depictions, though, inevitably drew comparisons with contemporary figures; in America, in the late 1930s, the most obvious figure fulfilling such images was the leader of the German-American Bund, Fritz Kuhn.

Several major films of the day exhibited parallels between the main character and figures such as Kuhn, including Orson Welles' masterpiece *Citizen Kane* (1941). In that film, Kane "flirts with a kind of American populist fascism but is defeated by scandal,"[192] a scenario not unlike Kuhn's pro-Nazi posturing and leadership until his arrest for embezzling Bund funds in 1939. Further, Kane takes the stance that people will think "what I tell them to think" as a result of his machinations; ultimately he abandons his early "principles" for a new preference, namely power associations, among which he even poses with Hitler. According to James Combs, in a viewpoint representative of Fritz Kuhn:

> Kane is reduced to being a mere "citizen" because he finally was willing to do the wrong thing. ... power was sought as an adornment of the ego, and became a destructive intoxicant that made its seeker predictably ignoble.[193]

By the late 1930s, subtle anti-Nazi propaganda began to give way to a more explicit treatment of Nazism as a threat to American interests. Such a posture came about partly because of political realities; increased Washington concerns with Nazi threats and the imminent outbreak of war in Europe, combined with a strengthened commitment by movie makers to cooperate with governmental interests, brought about the new perspective. No less important, though, was the role of public sentiment; Hollywood film producers eagerly noted a pronounced anti-Nazi and, specifically, anti-Bund sentiment throughout the country.

Given the public's fascination with a small number of pro-Nazis demonstrating in the United States, it was only a matter of time before Hollywood tapped into that interest, creating movies depicting Bundists and other Nazi sympathizers as spies and saboteurs determined to infiltrate American security interests. While such story lines made for interesting movies and handsome profits, they were almost exclusively fictional, defaming a larger number of people by citing the example of a relative few.

Portrayals of German-Americans and German nationals as spies for Hitler's Germany did not go unnoticed in the German community. Nor did they go unchallenged in at least one case, though ultimately the effort proved to be futile. On May 12, 1939, Fritz Kuhn, individually and on behalf of the German-American Bund, filed a suit in the amount of $5,000,000 against Warner Brothers Pictures for libel and damages, for their portrayal of America's Nazi element in the movie *Confessions of a*

Nazi Spy. Also sued in the motion were Milton Krims and John Wexley, authors of the scenario, and Leon G. Turrou, the government employee who investigated the German spy ring a year earlier.

Confessions represented Hollywood's first overt propaganda salvo against Hitler's Third Reich,[194] and the first film to challenge directly the Bund's role in American politics:

> ... while the other studio heads feared that anti-Nazi films would alienate mainstream America in 1939, the brothers Warner stuck to their convictions. They overcame or overlooked the Hays Office objections, official objections of the German government to the U.S. State Department, death threats during the film's production, and bomb threats at the premiere, to produce the first American film that proclaims the Nazis to be an international menace.[195]

In the film, an FBI agent named Renard, played by Edward G. Robinson, investigates Nazi underground activities in America, in which spies organize a network of agents and collaborators in American defense plants, military branches, and other strategic areas. German-Americans who oppose the Nazi agents are either beaten up by Nazi supporters or kidnapped and sent to German concentration camps. Renard systematically uncovers key spies in the Nazi network until finding Schneider, the weak link in the organization. Schneider is a reluctant spy, urged to espionage by a wife in search of "the good life." He impersonates a medical officer and calls hospitals for military personnel figures, in an effort to learn troop strength in the New York area, and provides reports for the relatively paltry sum of fifty dollars apiece. During interrogation, Schneider fingers another figure, Dr. Kassel, who is head of a Nazi Bund; Kassel agrees to turn informant for the American government, but is kidnapped by German agents before surrendering to the FBI and is smuggled out of the country on an ocean liner, ultimately to be turned over to the Gestapo. By that time, though, Renard has uncovered enough information to round up all of the key Nazis before they could do any further harm.

More than any other film to date, *Confessions of a Nazi Spy* was an attempt to illustrate the potential harm of Nazism in the United States, as furthered by Nazi agents and sympathetic German nationals in America. No less important was its unspoken goal of convincing loyal Americans of the Nazi threat to the nation's internal security. H.M. Glancy sums up the Bund portrayal in *Confessions* in the following manner:

> ... the German-American Bund is seen to be the center of a Nazi spy ring, gathering intelligence on the American military and attempting to spread class resentment. The Nazis are predictably stereotyped as sneering, goose-stepping fanatics out to rid America of its Constitution and Bill of Rights. ... the hysterical tone of the non-fiction sequences tends to overstate the Nazi threat to America itself. Thus even the heartfelt political input is somewhat misguided.[196]

Similarly, Larry Langman and Ed Borg take exception to several aspects of the film's characterization:

> The one-dimensional spies lack plausibility at times; the strong-arm men in their employ are stereotypes; and the preachy voice-overs during lengthy newsreel shots of Nazi troops on the march and invading other countries are unnecessary and redundant. ... While the film lauds the American democratic ideals over the German Fascist state, it remains a product of its time. Only two types dominate the American landscape of this film: white Anglo-Saxon Protestants - the good guys, and the Nazis - the bad guys.[197]

By including portrayals of German-American children singing Nazi songs and goose-stepping at a Bund camp in Wisconsin, Warner Brothers played on parental fears of child exploitation and the notion of German-American indoctrination of unsuspecting and, worse, unquestioning youth. Also, newsreel footage of Bund rallies, showing intruders being beaten up, helped portray members of the German-American community as being violent and aggressive.

Several important figures in *Confessions* took exception to the manner in which the movie was made. Illustrating disagreement within the ranks, Milton Krims resigned from the project during filming, citing differences with director Anatole Litvak. Krims had preferred that the movie be made as much as possible in a documentary fashion, with only key background events fictionalized. Litvak, though, chose to dramatize events in a manner similar to Warner Brothers' more traditional format of gangster films.[198]

Doubtless to the pleasure of Warner Brothers, though, public reaction to the film generally was swift and sure, falling into line with the moviemaker's premise. According to Jay Robert Nash and Stanley Ralph Ross:

> *Confessions of a Nazi Spy* frightened audiences with the real threat of Nazi tyranny which was the courageous aim of Warner Bros. This film established the studio as the leading film company of socially oriented productions. ... in the U.S. audiences cheered for Robinson and hissed the Nazi goons. Distributors had been warned that Nazi sympathizers might start riots in the first-run theaters showing the film so squads of detectives patrolled the theaters to arrest would-be agitators. Litvak's direction is unabashedly biased ... his hatred for the Nazis seethes throughout the film and audiences supported that prejudice. At one point a Nazi spy protests to [Renard] about the mass arrests of his fellow agents. When he is told: "After all, New York harbor is still within the jurisdiction of the United States," viewers applauded and cheered.[199]

Predictably, the Bund expressed its unreserved distaste for *Confessions*, editorializing that "The producer of this nightmarish concoction has drawn for his material on the choicest collection of flubdub that a diseased mind could possibly pick out of the public ashcan."[200] According to Kuhn, the film portrayed, through speech and use of insignia, uniforms, and Bund camps, the German-American Bund as an organization whose president and membership abused the rights of American citizenship and suggested that the Bund was connected with a worldwide system of espionage launched by the German government in Berlin. Further, Kuhn asserted that several other portrayals of the Bund in the movie were incorrect and/or inappropriate, including:

> 1) The Bund being characterized as working to undermine the Constitution and the Bill of Rights, under the guise of "Americanism";
>
> 2) that the organization's name had been changed from the Friends of New Germany to the German-American Bund by order of the German government, and that both organizations had been maintained by the German government; and
>
> 3) that, according to Kuhn, "the president of the said German-American Bund [was portrayed as] a member of the German espionage system, a spy and/or connected with the spy ring, a conspirator, informer, hypocrite, liar and ruthless character."

In contrast, Kuhn insisted that he and his organization were nothing but patriotic and loyal to the United States, and that they were consistent in their endeavor to "respect and honor the flag."[201]

For its part, the German government intervened to a certain extent, banning the film in Germany and otherwise dissociating itself from the negative images seen in the film. Eighteen other countries also banned the film, out of fear of offending Hitler. For example, on June 20, following a protest by the German Minister to Cuba, the Cuban Department of the Interior prohibited further showings of the movie, despite the consistently large crowds coming to see it.[202]

Kuhn's arguments, however, failed to impress the courts where it mattered most, in the United States. On June 20 Federal Judge Vincent L. Leibell dismissed his application for an injunction to prevent further showings of *Confessions of a Nazi Spy*, pointing out that it was not customary to grant an injunction in an alleged libel case.[203]

For its part, Warner Brothers was not about to back down before the Bundists. In late June, the film company made clear its intention to advance the starting dates of "two more important films of a controversial and political nature," one being *Underground*, a chronicle of secret anti-Nazi activities in Germany, the other, *The Man Who Walked With God*, the story of the Rev. Martin Niemoeller, deposed head of the German Lutheran Church.[204] While there is little doubt that Warner Brothers produced the movies for their entertainment value, film scholars also have speculated that the company had an interest in making *Confessions* and other anti-Nazi films; the head of their German sales division, a Jew, was beaten to death in Berlin in 1936, and the Warners themselves were Jewish.[205]

On September 5, Warner Brothers formally replied to Kuhn's suit, alleging that the Bund, as represented by Kuhn, was "conceived and originated by the Nazi government" in Berlin and functioned under its direction. Conceding that the film was made up of incidents taken from the records of two espionage cases, Warner Brothers stated that it was fully satisfied of the truthfulness of the incidents portrayed.

Additionally, the company took advantage of the opportunity to attack the Bund in the media, with the counsel for Warner Brothers, R.W. Perkins, going on record with the following:

> The Bund and its members are active militant propagandists of Nazi
> ideology, and endorse and actively support and would plant and
> propagate in the United States the undemocratic principles of Adolf
> Hitler, and are, therefore, disloyal to the United States and abuse the
> rights and privileges of their American citizenship.

Perkins further charged that the Bund was intended to destroy the
Constitution and the Bill of Rights of the United States, under the "will and
dominion of Nazi Germany."[206]

Ultimately, faced with the reality of a minuscule treasury, dwindling
revenues, and the likelihood of a protracted, expensive court battle, the
Bund realized that it was in no position to take on Warner Brothers for the
long haul. On October 2, 1940, the Bund as an organization discontinued
its court action, although Kuhn, by now in jail, had not yet given his
blessings to the move. Representing the Bund, Vahan H. Kalenderian
claimed that he wanted nothing further to do with the suit.[207] For his part,
Judge John C. Knox gave Kuhn until November 15 to "do something
definite" about the suit, before the case would be dropped from the trial
calendar. Realizing the futility of continued action, Kuhn formally
dropped the suit on November 22, bringing the matter to a close.[208]

$$*\qquad*\qquad*$$

Despite the Bund's inability to take action against Warner Brothers,
the filmmaker was not yet given a completely free hand in fashioning films
portraying the German element in a negative light. From September 9-26,
1941, the United States Senate held hearings on the role of propaganda in
American motion pictures, in response to widespread concerns that some
Hollywood studios, such as Warner Brothers, were trying to lead the
United States into war with Germany. Among secondary concerns of the
Senate were that a Jewish element in Hollywood was responsible for the
push towards war, in retribution for Nazi atrocities, and that the
Hollywood film community of the time provided commissions for family
members, rather than giving them by merit.[209]

While a number of Hollywood directors and studio executives were
called to testify during the hearings, it was the testimony of Harry Warner
which received the most attention. From the outset, Warner denied that
his films were "propaganda," claiming that Warner Brothers only was
depicting the world as it existed, based on facts gathered from reputable
sources. According to Warner, in a prepared opening statement:

> *Confessions of a Nazi Spy* is a factual portrayal of a Nazi spy ring that actually operated in New York City. If that is propaganda, we plead guilty. ... In truth, the only sin of which Warner Brothers is guilty is that of accurately recording on the screen the world as it is or as it has been.[210]

Warner made special mention of how his company came to have first-hand information about the German-American Bund. Referring to *Chicago Daily News* correspondent John C. Metcalfe, he pointed out that Metcalfe, in the course of his own work, joined the Bund in an effort to gather primary information, which Warner Brothers in turn utilized in movie making. Warner cited the use of numerous contemporary newspaper and magazine sources, including the *American Magazine* article "An American Fuehrer Organizes an Army," and reaction in local communities where the Bund operated, in creating *Confessions of a Nazi Spy*, maintaining in the process that he "cannot conceive how any patriotic citizen could object to a picture accurately recording a danger already existing in our country."[211]

Further, Warner denied the notion that he was foisting upon the American public films that they did not wish to see, citing the number of people having seen movies like *Confessions of a Nazi Spy* and the profitability of such films. According to Warner, a wide variety of civic, patriotic, and labor organizations endorsed *Confessions*, and voluminous correspondence from viewers commended the filmmaker on the movie; to this end, Warner brought with him to the hearing 550 letters, telegrams, and postcards, from 110 cities, offering congratulations and support. Warner also pointed out the support received from the German-American League for Culture, reading from a newspaper release which stated that the League "wholeheartedly supports this excellent educational picture which in the highest sense of the word is fostering true Americanism by exposing the un-American spy activities of the Hitler agents in this country.[212]

Such points, well made as they were, were not the focus of debate among Senate members, though, as questioning proceeded along different lines. Specifically, Senate interrogation was designed to provide perspective on the extent to which films such as *Confessions of a Nazi Spy* shaped public attitudes, and at whose expense, at the discretion of a given filmmaker. In his opening statement, Warner had already sounded a dangerous train of thought towards those who would oppose his portrayals of the Nazi German element, regardless of their reasons why. According to Warner:

> I would not deny that after seeing nazi-ism portrayed on the screen, the American people will have a new appreciation of the liberties and freedoms that they enjoy under their Government. But would our critics deny that this is in the public interest? Could they possibly have a friendly feeling for the Nazi regime, which destroys the rights of the individual and conducts its foreign relations on the basis of might makes right?[213]

Sen. Charles Tobey, of New Hampshire, expressed the Senate view in questioning Warner, pointing out the following:

> If monopoly exists and if that monopoly bends its powerful efforts to propagandize the American people into hysteria, so that excitement rather than calm judgment should guide them in the matter of getting into the war, it is important ... that the matter be looked into.[214]

Clearly, the Senate was concerned with the fact that Hollywood film portrayals, unrestrained in their scope and focus, could exert undue influence on the American public and its perceptions, not only of Nazi Germany but also of Nazis, real or perceived, in America, and by extension the German-American community as a whole. While the Senate ultimately would refrain from imposing restrictions on the motion picture industry, it made clear its position on mass media portrayals of the German element: Attempts to influence the opinion of mainstream America, and implicate America's largest ethnic group as being un-American or unsympathetic to the American cause, would not go unnoticed or unmentioned as long as the nation remained politically neutral.

*   *   *

The Bund's pre-war lack of success in combating Warner Brothers, and subsequent governmental unwillingness to intervene, made clear that Hollywood portrayals of German-Americans would go unchecked as long as hostilities towards Germany persisted. In the years to come, with no restraint on filmmakers' creative minds, other portrayals of the Nazi element in the United States were exhibited, seemingly less credible than even *Confessions of a Nazi Spy* had been. In particular, spy comedies became a staple of Hollywood film production during World War II.[215] Most notable among such movies is *All Through the Night* (1942), a well-received but improbable spoof of spy dramas. In the film, the American underworld was brought in to fight Nazi spies, reckoning that a Nazi takeover of the United States would be harmful to their own racketeering interests.[216] With an all-star cast including Humphrey Bogart, William Demarest, Jackie Gleason, and Phil Silvers, public interest in and acceptance of the film was virtually guaranteed. Among hero Bogart's feats are discovering a secret room with short wave radios, a Nazi flag, and a portrait of Hitler; uncovering an important meeting of Nazi sympathizers, at which plans would be finalized to blow up half of New York harbor; and thwarting a plan to blow up a U.S. warship anchored nearby.[217]

Thematically, anti-Nazi filmmaking in Hollywood remained virtually the same after the United States entered the conflict, as it had been before December 1941. One wartime Western, *Wild Horse Rustlers* (1943), showed Nazis dressed in western-style clothing, showing up in the West in an effort to rustle Army-bound horses, only to be foiled in the end by cowboy heroics.[218] The film, part of the "Lone Rider" series, featured twin brothers, one a patriotic ranch foreman and the other a Nazi agent with an exaggerated cowboy accent. Somewhat predictably, the patriotic brother initially is blamed for the evil deeds of his brother, but manages to sort out the trouble in the end and claim the role of hero.[219] Similarly, in a prewar vein, *Nazi Agent* (1941) takes up the theme of twin brothers of opposite sentiment; Conrad Veidt plays both of the brothers, one a loyal German-American and the other a Nazi spy.[220] Even the Bowery Boys, renamed the East Side Kids in such low-budget films as *Bowery Blitzkrieg* and *Flying Wild* (both 1941), clash with foreign agents, including Nazi spies who would steal the blueprints for a special American fighter plane.[221] Also, the movie version of *Watch on the Rhine* (1942) pursues the German-American question "as a matter of ideological commitment of a vaguely left-wing but also nationalistic identification;" a Nazi sympathizer learns of an anti-fascist's plans to return to Germany with funds for the resistance movement, at which time he threatens to inform the German embassy, only to stir Americans out of their self-imposed political lethargy.[222]

Another point not lost upon the German-American community was the portrayal, in a positive light, of the Soviets in Hollywood films. Given the fact that movies of the 1920s and 1930s generally portrayed Bolsheviks as tyrants and brutes, or at best "comic bunglers or bureaucrats,"[223] many German-Americans regarded positive portrayals of these same people in the early- to mid-1940s, based on the Soviet-American alliance, as nothing but a double standard compared with depictions of Germans and German-Americans at the time. James Combs makes the following point on Hollywood's portrayal of the Soviet element in the early 1940s:

> ... the Soviet-American alliance necessitated that positive films should be made about Russia, just as negative films were being made about the Nazis. The propaganda content of the "pro-Soviet" movies was to make both the Soviet government and the Russian people acceptable as allies. In such films as *North Star* (1943) and *Song of Russia* (1944), the Russian people are portrayed as peaceable and happy peasants far removed from the grim new cities of Stalinist industrialization. Thus they could not be associated with an industrial proletariat of Marxist theory, but rather with the American myth of pastoral simplicity and democratic good sense. By contrast, the Nazi invaders were portrayed in the harshest terms, with emphasis on their penchant for outrageous atrocities. ... the political purpose was to demonstrate Nazi villainy and Soviet trustworthiness and resolve. While Nazi Germany is a grim and regimented society bent on world conquest, Soviet Russia is a friendly and peaceable place not unlike America.[224]

Thus it can be seen that Hollywood's portrayal of foreign elements was very much a relative one; those who were deemed "the bad guys," standing contrary to American interests of the moment, were singled out for harsh, often unjustified treatment and virtually stereotypical representation, particularly in the German-American community, while those seen as being on the same side as America were given preferential treatment in film depictions, to the point of distorting long-standing truths and reversing images of the past. The fickle nature of such a posture is best seen in film images of only a decade later, when German interests allied with the United States were given favorable coverage, and portrayals of the Soviet Union and its people took on increasingly negative contexts with the emerging superpower rivalry.

Conclusions

In sum, mass media in the United States played a significant role in shaping public opinion regarding the German-American community during the mid- to late 1930s and early 1940s. In Cincinnati as elsewhere, German-language newspapers, long the main voice of the German-American community, made substantial but only moderately successful efforts to distance themselves from the specter of Hitler and National

Socialist ideology, while Jewish and other anti-Nazi groups held the German-language press accountable for their every word and deed. The English-language press also exposed words and actions within the German-American community which played upon the public's fears of an upsurge in sympathy for the Nazis. Further, through editorials and by publishing letters to the editor, the English-language press provided the public with a daily outlet for viewpoints which, by virtue of being distributed by the hundreds of thousands, held significant possibilities for affecting the opinion of millions of Americans. It was inevitable that, in its haste to do a public service by calling attention to the existence of pro-Nazi activities in the United States, the English-language press would impugn the credibility of the majority of German-Americans, who were anti-Nazi in persuasion. Clearly the English-language press failed to differentiate the vast number of loyal German-Americans from those few with pro-Nazi tendencies. This failure would have a far-ranging effect on the status of the German-American community, especially after the outbreak of World War II and the subsequent American entry into the conflict against Germany.

With the growth of film production and a substantial rise in viewership, Hollywood recognized its potential for influencing public opinion and supporting politically popular and patriotic themes in movies. Through newsreels and motion pictures, major movie studios went to great lengths to attack Nazism and its proponents. Such film portrayals often did a disservice to members of the German-American community, by focusing on the exception rather than the rule. In the process, countless German legal resident aliens and German-Americans, including those who had voiced opposition openly to the Nazi regime and its aims, found their reputations tarnished and were cast into suspicion, based on the actions of a minuscule but vocal minority. Such suspicions, fostered by American newsprint and motion picture media, were seemingly not of great importance on the surface, yet would contribute to the call for action against the German-American community upon American entry into World War II, and would play a part in bringing about the arrest and internment of over 10,000 German legal resident aliens and German-Americans from December 1941 until June 1948.

Chapter IV

Alien Registration, Arrests, and
Enemy Alien Hearings

Due in large part to changing attitudes towards the German community in America, fostered by the staunch anti-Nazi and anti-German newsprint and film media, as well as changing policies within the United States Government, German legal resident aliens in America found themselves placed on the defensive by the beginning of the 1940s. Despite recovering in stature from the devastating experiences of World War I, America's German element found that its acceptance as a loyal segment of American society was directly influenced by the status of relations between Washington and Berlin. With the rise of the Nazi government in Berlin, and the fears it provoked within the United States, an increasing number of Americans called for controls to be placed on German legal resident aliens in the United States, to insure that they could not become a threat to internal security in the case of armed conflict. Such calls were prompted in part by fears for personal safety; yet just as significant in prompting requests for action against the German element in America was the outspoken pro-Nazi posture of groups such as the German-American Bund, and the intense media coverage it received.

Though the Bund and its followers represented only a tiny minority of the members of America's German-American community, it succeeded in galvanizing public opinion and provoking governmental response. While the Bund violated no law by its existence, nor did it advocate violation of existing laws, its activities, coupled with Germany's aggression in beginning World War II in September 1939, caused a significant swing of public opinion against the German-American community at the outset of the 1940s, along with prompting the registration of German legal resident aliens during the early part of the decade. While alien registration was used to develop a list of German nationals residing in the United States, beginning in December 1941 the lists would be used in part for questioning German aliens as to their loyalty, along with for who would be targeted for arrest and possible internment as an enemy alien.

In the aftermath of the bombing of Pearl Harbor on December 7, 1941, the first arrests of enemy aliens were registered, in Cincinnati and elsewhere. These arrests, and a fear of espionage and sabotage by German legal resident aliens and German-Americans in the United States, lead to the implementation of anti-sabotage measures in industry and, in some cases, public reaction against the German-American community similar to that exhibited during World War I. In response to public outcry and expressed needs for national security, federal officials quickly established special detention facilities for enemy aliens and enemy alien hearing boards, and imposed property confiscations and travel restrictions, in an effort to neutralize the threat of anti-American activity originating with German legal resident aliens and disloyal German-Americans, though relatively little evidence of wrongdoing or threats to national security interests were uncovered or disclosed.

For the purpose of this study, the role of alien registration, the arrest of aliens, and their hearings will be presented with a focus on Cincinnati, as a representative example of a traditional German-American community during the World War II era. While other German-American centers are referred to on occasion, the Cincinnati example will suffice to show the extent to which German legal resident aliens were impacted by wartime policy; comparable examples may also be noted in other areas of German-American concentration, such as Milwaukee, St. Louis, and other large cities throughout the United States.

Alien Registration

As Hitler's conquests in Europe continued into 1940, and the United States began to side more firmly with the position of the western European allies, the call to keep an eye on German legal resident aliens grew louder. By this time, though, the U.S. government had long since anticipated the need to monitor foreign nationals from the axis powers; initial steps had already been taken towards gathering information on Germans living in the United States. By early summer 1939, President Roosevelt had charged the Federal Bureau of Investigation, the War Department's Military Intelligence Division, and the Office of Naval Intelligence with responsibility for espionage, counterespionage, and sabotage, with the FBI taking on the lion's share of the burden. Anticipating the possible outbreak of hostilities in Europe, the government clearly was making a first effort to prepare the nation for a polarization of attitudes between Americans and their German and Italian neighbors. Consequently, the government began to compile lists of potentially dangerous German legal resident aliens, beginning by scanning the rosters of the German-American Bund and other overtly pro-Nazi organizations. By creating these lists, the government implicitly indicated those residents they felt posed the most serious security risks to the United States, as well as the individuals they planned to arrest first in the event of hostilities. In the Justice Department, a master list known as the "ABC List" was created by the Special Defense Unit, led by Lawrence M. C. Smith.[225] However, a list of Bundists and overt Nazi sympathizers clearly would represent only the tip of the iceberg relative to the total number of German legal resident aliens. Another method would be necessary to gain information on these Germans, as well as to keep track of their location should they need to be rounded up after the outbreak of war.

To this end, initial plans for alien registration were announced in the late summer of 1940. The legal basis for this action was provided by Public Law Number 670, Chapter 439, otherwise known as the Alien Registration Act of 1940, and was summarized as serving "to prohibit certain subversive activities; to amend certain provisions of law with respect to the admission and deportation of aliens; to require the fingerprinting and registration of aliens; and for other purposes." Initial views held that these registrations were done for the protection of the German residents, as well as to ensure that they would not encounter undue hardships from overly zealous community patriots.

To its satisfaction, the government found that popular opinion was supportive of its measures. A Gallup poll of June 10, 1940 posed the question, "Should all people who are not United States citizens be required to register with the Government?" In response, an overwhelming ninety-five percent of the respondents said "yes." From such a mandate, a logical conclusion can be drawn that many American citizens felt that the German nationals, among others, in their midst were not a welcome part of their community; additionally, a sound argument can be made that Americans as a whole held a deeply rooted fear of the foreigners, as a threat to their existence and day-to-day security.

In Cincinnati, the media served early notice that aliens would need to register, and it pointed out the steps involved in the process. As early as August 8, the *Cincinnati Enquirer* notified its readers that alien registration would be ongoing in Cincinnati, from August 27 through December 26, under the direct supervision of Assistant Postmaster Charles Heltman.

Post office employees were largely responsible for carrying out registration, while any extra workers needed would be pulled from the Civil Service Register. According to the 1930 census (1940 figures were still being tabulated), 12,500 aliens lived in Hamilton County, while reports indicated that some 3,500,000 aliens 14 and above were required to register nationally. Alien children under age 14 were registered by their parents. Further, those failing or refusing to register, or those making false statements on their registration forms, were subject to a $1,000 fine and six months' imprisonment. Registrants would be mailed receipt cards, with instructions that any change of address had to be brought to the government's attention within five days of the change. During the actual registration, questions to be asked of the aliens included how they entered the country, how long they had been in the United States, how long they planned to stay, whether they had ever served in the military, what organizations they belonged to, and whether those organizations might possibly further the interests of a foreign government.[226]

On August 23, four days before the beginning of alien registration, the *Cincinnati Post* printed an article entitled "Alien Registration: Here's How It Will Be Done: Step By Step," which in photos and text clearly illustrated how alien registration would be handled. As a first step, in registering with the Department of Justice, an alien had to go to Room 105 of the Federal Building, at the corner of Fifth and Walnut streets, where a staff of clerks under the direction of William F. Weber, Assistant Cashier, initiated the process. First, aliens had to sign and affirm registry applications with an interviewer. Those aliens who could not speak English had to furnish their own interpreters. The interviewer then checked the answers to each of the questions provided, and transferred them to a designated registration folder. The aliens would then be fingerprinted voluntarily; portable fingerprinting equipment was used, in order that aliens confined as patients (such as in hospitals and institutions) could also be registered. Authorities justified the fingerprinting, and attempted to make it more palatable for the aliens, by pointing out that "nearly all civil service employees, even J. Edgar Hoover, Department of Justice chief, have their prints on file in Washington." The registration process itself took about 15 minutes, and at the end of each day, all registration forms were placed in mail bags and sent directly to the Department of Justice.[227]

Alien registration in Cincinnati officially began at 8:00 a.m., Tuesday, August 27. The day before, Mayor James G. Stewart issued the proclamation of alien registry, again emphasizing that fingerprinting was being done on a voluntary basis, and that citizens should be both helpful and sympathetic to the aliens all the while. To help simplify the process, and to disperse the anticipated large number of registrants more evenly, registration locations were established at the main Cincinnati post office, the post office annex, and branch post offices throughout the area. The main headquarters remained at Room 105 of the Federal Building.

For the first day of registration, twenty assistants were on duty at the main office. Blank forms were distributed to aliens from the north end of the Walnut Street lobby of the post office; in turn they wrote down the information sought by the government. In case aliens wished to fill out the form and return it later, each blank bore dates for their return, so that each alien would have ample time to provide all information desired, while helping to spread out the registration and fingerprinting period until the deadline, December 26. This strategy was sound, in that the Cincinnati post office served not only those aliens living in and around the city, but also served as a clearing house for all fifty-two Ohio counties in the accounting district administering the process.[228] All things considered, things went smoothly on the hectic first day, save for a minor complication, when William Weber noticed that the American flag was not yet in place for the proceedings. Picking up the phone, he hastily told a maintenance man, "We must have one. An American flag is symbolic of what these people are missing by not becoming citizens."[229]

Over time, several small changes took place, and numbers began to illustrate the fruit of the government's labors. In early September, the registration process was slightly amended, when aliens were required to report each address change as well.[230] By late November, estimates held that 4,500 local aliens still needed to register,[231] while in early December, the post office listed 8,375 aliens registered and living in Cincinnati.[232] Finally, following the December 26 deadline, definitive figures on alien registration began to trickle in. On December 27, 10,200 aliens were estimated to have registered in Cincinnati, a substantial figure to be sure, but still 1,800 below the number which federal officials had anticipated. Several aliens, claiming ignorance of the law, reported at the Federal Building the day after registration had officially ended, thus exposing themselves to the possibility of fines and/or imprisonment. Their records were forwarded to Washington, along with notes regarding their excuses, with those of other registrants who had complied in time, with any action against the latecomers deferred to authorities at the capital. The office in town was nevertheless kept open after the deadline, especially to serve aliens reaching their 14th birthday anniversary. As the law read, children under fourteen had to be registered by their parents, but upon reaching that age they themselves had to register in person. Otherwise, so-called "interesting aliens" who had sought haven in Cincinnati from the European war were also being interviewed and photographed, by newspapers, but following a bulletin from Washington this procedure quickly came to a halt.[233]

According to Earl G. Harrison, the director of alien registration in Washington, some 5,000,000 aliens, or one out of every 26 persons in the country, had been fingerprinted and catalogued. In New York alone, a national high 500,000 aliens had registered, or one out of every 16 residents of the city.[234]

After the deadline passed, registration quickly became a thing of the past, at least as far as the media and general public were concerned. A March 1, 1941 article in the *Cincinnati Enquirer*, though, detailed the number of aliens registered in Ohio. Based on the figures, according to a report received by City Manager C. O. Sherrill from the Department of Justice, Cincinnati was second only to Cleveland in the state in total registrants. The list showed the following figures for major Ohio cities:

City	Registered Aliens
Cleveland	92,638
Cincinnati	12,271
Akron	11,351
Youngstown	11,078
Toledo	10,373
Columbus	5,402
Canton	5,332
Dayton	3,678
Springfield	598
Hamilton	433

Such figures, while impressive, paled in comparison to the national leader, New York, where a total of 951,194 were reported registered to date.[235]

*   *   *

On January 7, 1942, Attorney General Francis Biddle announced a significant change in policy in handling foreign nationals, with an eye toward keeping better track of their whereabouts and status. In the near future, reregistration of some 1,100,000 foreign nationals, primarily of German, Italian, and Japanese origin, in the United States, Puerto Rico, and the Virgin Islands would take place. Under the proposed system, the Justice Department would create and issue identification cards bearing photographs, fingerprints, and other essential data on the aliens. A similar system had been used during World War I, save for the absence of photos for identification. This differed markedly from the initial registration of aliens in 1940, when each registrant was simply given receipts showing that he or she had registered. At that time, identification cards were not provided. The new system better monitored potential changes in the status of each alien; those who planned to change residence or occupation, for example, had to appear personally before a designated officer in order to obtain approval. If approval was given, identification cards were updated to include all new information, with the government also keeping records of the changes.[236]

At 11:30 on the night of January 8, U.S. District Attorney Calvin Crawford appeared on Cincinnati radio station WLW, to explain the new procedure in alien cases. While he maintained that most resident aliens were decent, law-abiding people, and that hearing board members made every attempt "to give each alien a fair and impartial hearing," Crawford reemphasized the nation's need for protective measures in times of war. Aliens whose records were spotless, he insisted, needed have no fear of persecution or arrest. Further, he pointed out that aliens from Axis nations were able to apply for citizenship, but they had to allow for a ninety day postponement, so that a background check could be made and there would be no doubt that the applicants would be loyal American citizens. Finally, Crawford reminded Americans listening that the nation derived no good from the persecution of aliens, but rather such action would endanger the national unity vital in wartime. He requested that those citizens with any possible evidence against dangerous aliens report it promptly to a government agency, which in turn would handle the case if it believed sufficient evidence existed to justify further investigation.[237]

Specifics of the alien reregistration movement were announced on February 4 by Samuel H. Howes, the district director of the Immigration and Naturalization Bureau. According to the figures he presented, 3,600 German and Italian nationals, including 3,400 in the city of Cincinnati, had to reregister according to new regulations February 9-28. Each alien from Cincinnati was required to register at the Federal Building, in Room 105 (office of the Superintendent of Mails) just as in 1940, while axis aliens living outside of the city had to register at the post offices nearest to their homes. If absent from home during the registration period, aliens were to register at the post office nearest where they stayed, with the records to be transferred to Cincinnati. While registering, aliens would be fingerprinted, this time mandatorially. Each alien was required to carry their new card with them; if they were unable to show the card upon demand, they were subject to immediate detention. Those aliens found not to have registered could be interned for the duration of the war. The only, temporary, exemption from the procedure was for those aliens who were ill and unable to report, or those under the age of fourteen. As for the rationale of reregistration, Howes insisted that the new procedure was designed for the protection of aliens.

To prepare for reregistration, Howes advised that aliens procure three front-view photographs of themselves, each two inches square, on thin paper and with a light background. No hats were to be worn in the photographs, and each photograph submitted had to be taken within thirty days of the time they were presented to postal authorities while registering. Previous registration cards, from the first procedure, had to be taken to the post office for the reregistration.[238]

The Arrests and Hearings of Enemy Aliens

From March 1941 until December, registration of German legal resident aliens took on a low profile, as focus shifted to the increasingly hostile positions of the United States and Japanese governments. Consequently, issues concerning Japanese Americans and Japanese aliens replaced a preoccupation with German and other European aliens during mid- to late 1941. Most citizens were more involved with the immediate threat of conflict between the United States and Japan than with a war raging on another continent, which seemingly held less importance than a possible military strike on America's west coast. In the aftermath of the

December 7, 1941 bombing of Pearl Harbor, the issue of loyalties and nationalities took on a far greater meaning. Germany's declaration of war on the United States four days later inevitably cut to the quick of America's patriotic sentiment, and a renewed wave of anti-German feeling threatened the local and national German-American community. For the vast majority of Americans, alien registration was no longer enough.

Public and political outrage, in the wake of the outbreak of war, demanded that German legal resident aliens with anything less than a spotless record and reputation be held under suspicion of being a potential security threat. Consequently, numerous Cincinnati area German legal resident aliens, already registered with the government, became immediate targets of governmental roundups, for questioning, arrest, and in some cases, as will be discussed in the following chapter, even internment.

The legal authorization for the roundup of persons deemed potentially dangerous enemy aliens by the U.S. Government, dates as far back as July 6, 1798, when the Enemy Alien Act was enacted, subsequently amended on April 16, 1918, with a modern basis also found in Section 21, Title 50 of the U.S. Code. Specifically, the Enemy Alien Act provided that in wartime all enemy aliens were subject to immediate apprehension without notice, as well as detention and deportation if authorities considered such action necessary or even desirable. The existence of the so-called "ABC List," giving the names and locations of numerous Nazi sympathizers, insured that questionable German legal resident aliens would be brought in almost immediately. In fact, even before President Roosevelt undertook the formality of signing proclamations authorizing the arrests of dangerous aliens on December 7 and 8, Attorney General Francis Biddle had issued orders to arrest and detain several thousand aliens from the ABC list, with the Immigration and Naturalization Service in charge of providing detention facilities.[239]

In Cincinnati, FBI agents wasted little time in bringing in German aliens whom they deemed untrustworthy. For several years before the war, FBI sources had been secretly sitting in on meetings of German organizations in the city. While monitoring the tone of the discussions, and the degree to which they were pro-Nazi, the government began keeping tabs on those members of German clubs and others attending their social functions who spoke in positive terms of Hitler, his government, or Nazism. Consequently, the FBI began conducting background checks on numerous individuals they felt might have some pro-Nazi sympathies;

evidence gathered during this stage was heavily used in apprehending the individuals they considered most dangerous in the initial hours of the war.

In conjunction with simultaneous national raids, in which more than 400 German, Italian, and Japanese aliens were seized, local agents arrested seven German aliens (six from Cincinnati) during the night of Monday, December 8. Of the six aliens, one was from Dayton, Ohio, while one was a Cincinnati physician, and another a local baker. Three were placed in custody at the Hamilton County jail, while the remaining four were quickly taken away to a military post in Fort Thomas, Kentucky, in the custody of the Immigration and Naturalization Service.[240]

Nationally as well as locally, German resident aliens seemed to be the initial target of federal arrests; in the national drive, more than 300 of the 400 aliens rounded up overnight were said to be German, despite the fact that the Japanese had bombed Pearl Harbor and the German government had not yet declared war on the United States. Further, reports indicated that only twelve Japanese nationals were listed as living in southern Ohio, all of which were considered "reliable" by federal authorities. While the arrests had already been made, and liberties had been restricted on the seven Germans, the FBI and the Immigration Bureau stressed that no charges had yet been filed against those in custody, leaving the aliens in doubt about what offenses they may have committed and why they were being held.[241]

The next day, President Roosevelt explained publicly the rationale behind the apprehension of the foreign nationals. According to the President, there existed the threat of "an invasion or a predatory incursion" by Italy or Germany, hence his imposition of wartime restrictions upon the movements and activities of their nationals. The President had authorized the Department of Justice to round up nationals of the Axis partners considered "dangerous to American security," and thus by definition they became "enemy aliens," though no state of war currently existed. Attorney General Biddle indicated that no American citizens would be apprehended, also appealing to governors of the 48 states to keep "hands off" of the problem and to "prevent molestation of all peaceful and law-abiding foreign nationals." This lead some to minimize estimates of civilian displacement; nevertheless, spot checks indicated that, beyond the Cincinnati figures, 18 Germans and Italians had been seized in Indiana, two Germans in Springfield, Illinois, 10 Germans in Miami, 47 Germans in Wisconsin, 24 Germans in Chicago, and 60 Germans and Italians in Los

Angeles, while 86 Germans initially had been seized in New York. Among those arrested in Los Angeles were Herman Schwinn, the ousted German-American Bund leader on the west coast, and Hans Diebel, a German youth group leader. The next day, two others were added to the Cincinnati total, both coming from Huntington, West Virginia, raising to nine the number of enemy aliens held by the FBI. All nine were German, and each was described as "dangerous" by R. C. Suran, the agent in charge of the Cincinnati office of the FBI.[242]

At the same time, local authorities were taking the first steps toward housing the enemy aliens before their cases could be handled individually. Already by this early date, the government had made provisions for holding enemy aliens for an extended period of time, and in Cincinnati, temporary quarters were being established in the post office garage, located at 417 West Fourth Street, where aliens would be held until a civilian board could be appointed to hear their cases. Guards would be employed, after being trained and tested, to monitor the activities of the aliens, and living quarters were being established to accommodate some 200 people at a time, with separate quarters for men and women.[243] The day before, the *Cincinnati Post* ran a photo of the post office garage, above its story on the enemy alien arrests, showing exactly where in the building the aliens would be held and indicating that the windows would be equipped with bars before occupancy.[244]

The effect of the government's actions was felt not only by the enemy aliens, but also by those legal resident aliens seeking to become citizens of the United States. In Cincinnati, several German and Italian citizens preparing to take their final naturalization examinations at the Federal Building were told that their applications would be deferred for the time being. The deferment was in fact part of a nationwide effort, under Section 326 of the Naturalization Act of 1940, in which the government attempted to further reduce security risks to the United States based on special wartime circumstances, though again, no actual state of war yet existed between the United States and Germany and Italy. Several concerned Cincinnati area German and Italian citizens made calls to the Immigration and Naturalization Service, seeking information on their status, only to be told by Samuel B. Howes, local INS head, and his officers that, at least for the present, his officers could not naturalize any more German or Italian citizens.[245]

For the next couple of days, no further apprehensions were made in the Cincinnati area, though attempts were made to free two of the nine German aliens being held, both said to be located in the Fort Thomas military post guard house. The attempts proved futile, however, as the aliens were being held in the direct custody of Attorney General Biddle, who was unprepared to release any of the detainees at the time.[246]

The next day proved to be critical for the German aliens being held, as well as other German nationals not yet arrested or questioned. On December 11, Adolf Hitler formally declared war on the United States. Consequently, an immediate and noticeable polarization of attitudes towards German legal resident aliens living in Cincinnati, and elsewhere, became noticeable; not coincidentally, other steps were taken by federal and local officials. Such steps were designed not only to monitor the movements and actions of those Germans still living in the Cincinnati area, but, more importantly to some, also to prevent the possibility of acts of sabotage by Nazi sympathizers.

*   *   *

Shortly after the formal declaration of war had been made, the Ohio Defense Council officially gave Mayor Stewart the power to blackout the city. The only stipulation was that the mayor had to obtain permission from Governor Bricker before issuing the order. The power, for the time, remained largely theoretical, as a request made at the same time, by executive director Courtney Burton, was sent to all Ohio mayors, requesting that they not attempt to establish blackout trial runs without the governor's permission, in order to comply with defense policy. Following a day of preparations and precautions against accidents and looting, Burton forwarded to local government officials detailed instructions on how to establish blackouts.[247]

In Cleveland, the city passed an ordinance forbidding bright lights between midnight and 6:00 a.m. On June 4, the first "blackout fine" against a violator was assessed by Judge Lewis Drucker, when Sam Cowan, the owner of the Hotel Alton, was convicted and fined $100 for displaying neon signs after midnight. Also charged was hotel night manager Claire Sharp, who was fined $6.50 for the same violation, after having already been warned twice against leaving the signs on.[248]

Several Cincinnati companies and industries immediately undertook preestablished safeguards, to protect their installations and the public. Cincinnati Gas and Electric Company plants were quickly secured and deemed ready for any emergency. According to a company spokesman, "We have complied with every federal order and every advice on setting up precautions against sabotage or damage. Nothing has been left undone."[249]

On January 6, 1942, Cincinnati City Manager C. O. Sherrill awarded a contract to the Cincinnati Iron Fence Company, on a bid of $1,675, to place barbed-wire fencing and gates around key units of the California plant of the Waterworks Department, as a precaution against acts of sabotage. The same day, City Health Commissioner Carl A. Wilzbach and County Health Commissioner E. H. Schoenling called a meeting of health officers of all Hamilton County municipalities, for the purpose of preparing machinery to guard against any attempt to sabotage the city's drinking water or milk supply. Dr. Wilzbach stated that the goal of the measure was to protect such resources from contamination with impurities by saboteurs, with the proposal that frequent tests on site and a close watch of facilities be the first step in the process. To this point, there had already been an increased corps of guards stationed at all Cincinnati Waterworks branches. A second objective of the meeting was to establish plans for calling in volunteer nurses and other personnel for duty, in the event of an emergency; another meeting was slated for industrial physicians for January 9, when methods of safeguarding the health of workers in defense industries in case of emergency were discussed.[250]

The threat of sabotage did not soon fade, at least in the minds of the public and officials. In June, an intense investigation was launched into an affair in which two men, said to look Japanese, tried to photograph the Queen City waterworks pumping station. At the time, police were told that the two men were preparing to take pictures when an engineer ordered them away. They left only after being threatened with a water hose. The cautious engineer took their car's license number and then quickly summoned police, who in their haste mistakenly went to Ferguson Road, site of the water towers instead of the pumping station. The FBI was also notified and began an immediate investigation of its own. The efforts came to naught, though, as the men were soon positively identified as Ralph McKee, the official photographer of the Work Projects Administration, and Harry Graf, State Supervisor of the WPA, in Cincinnati for the purpose of photographing completed WPA projects such as the pumping station. The photos were to be used in the *WPA Writers Guide*. Work Projects Administration officials subsequently gave assurances that they would no longer attempt to take such pictures without first notifying those in charge of the property. Commenting on the affair, Cincinnati Police Chief Eugene T. Weatherly said, "They were very lucky that they were not shot."[251]

* * *

On the same day that blackout authorizations were being given, word came down that the government was ready to set up alien hearing boards, in Cincinnati as well as the other ninety-three federal judicial districts. Locally, the hearing board sat at the Fourth Street post office garage, where enemy aliens were temporarily being held.

The purpose of the boards was to enable enemy aliens that had been seized to present their appeals for release or parole. Each board consisted of five citizens, only three of whom presided over a given hearing, selected from lists submitted by local district attorneys to the Department of Justice. In the hearings, the FBI acted as prosecutor and recommended custody or release for each defendant alien. In turn, the Justice Department made a final ruling in each case, based upon the hearing board's recommendation and an FBI report.

Washington officials were quick to point out that they were, in fact, showing generosity in dealing with the enemy aliens, maintaining that the hearing boards were not being established as a matter of right for the accused, but instead to give the aliens in custody a fair chance to prove their loyalty, and to give details about their activities in the United States. According to Vern H. Wilson, chief assistant district attorney, only those aliens whose release might endanger national security and the public safety would be interned for the duration of the war.

Each board would make its recommendation in favor of one of three possible verdicts: 1) internment of the alien, based on a perceived security risk, for the duration of the war, at a specified internment center; 2) conditional parole, meaning that the alien was released due to a lack of convincing evidence of a security risk, but sufficient doubt remained that the alien had to check in with authorities on a regular basis; and 3) outright release, in which no grounds were found for suspicion of the alien, and no further contact with authorities was considered necessary.

The hearing process itself was heavily slanted in favor of the government. Aliens appearing before the board were permitted to have a relative, friend, or adviser present to vouch for character or provide insight into the alien's activities in the United States. However, they were not allowed to argue the particulars of each case, nor were they permitted to object to any line of questioning or item of evidence introduced. Further, aliens were denied legal counsel during the proceedings; each had to argue his or her own case. For their part, government officials presented all evidence they had gathered in preparing their case, and occasionally people who had accused the aliens of being enemies of the United States were called to testify. Significantly, the government was able to present accusations leveled against aliens without revealing the source, and without accusers being present for questioning. All proceedings were carried out in private, though from the beginning officials indicated that decisions would be made public, unconcerned with any potential embarrassment or public humiliation the aliens might suffer in the process.

As a gesture toward the enemy aliens, Attorney General Biddle announced that seized aliens would be given the opportunity to meet with their families and attorneys, once proper safeguards had been taken. The aliens would also be allowed to send and receive mail, although each piece would be censored; phone calls, while allowed, could only be made under close supervision.

When initial arrests of enemy aliens were made, their families were not notified of their whereabouts. To offset the fears of the families of these seized aliens, the Justice Department indicated that the whereabouts of individuals arrested could be learned at the offices of U.S. District Attorneys, the Federal Bureau of Investigation, and the Bureau of Immigration and Naturalization. No information was provided, however, on the status of businesses owned and operated by enemy aliens, some of which the Treasury Department had ordered closed. Officials simply stated that, as of December 11, no more establishments had been padlocked, but more developments might be expected momentarily.[252]

From the beginning, one of the primary goals of the U.S. government was that all enemy aliens should be given a fair and reasonable hearing, while avoiding public hysteria or overly emotional reactions, such as those seen against German-Americans during World War I. Government officials repeatedly stressed the notion of fair play for the arrested aliens, asserting that all potential measures were being taken to minimize any possible dangers, while safeguarding the aliens and their privacy. To this end, federal officials indicated on December 16 that the names of enemy aliens arrested in Cincinnati would only be released under two circumstances: 1) If determinations were made that they would be placed in internment camps for the duration of the war; and 2) if they were unconditionally paroled. Such a policy at least partially satisfied the German-American community, helping to reduce tensions between them and other community groups while giving German-Americans cause to believe that anti-German feelings would not be federally sanctioned. In the *Cincinnati Post*, an unnamed federal official indicated the government's main concern relative to the welfare of the arrested aliens:

> Names are not being released now, because a grave injustice might be done to some individuals who ultimately may be given a clean bill of health. Like all sane-thinking Americans, we are anxious to avoid hysteria, even in times like these. We don't want to stretch the democratic process so far as to be silly and careless, but we want to be just as careful in avoiding persecution. We don't want to make life unbearable for those who are sent back to their homes with a clean record.

The unnamed official indicated to concerned citizens that, while federal concerns existed that the aliens would be treated well, enemy aliens nevertheless were in custody for a specific reason:

> Not all aliens are enemies and maybe persons who have accused individuals have nothing more than "rumors" on which to base their charges. Let it be said, however, that the authorities have not arrested aliens on a mere rumor. There has been a pretty good reason for all the arrests made so far or they would not have been made in the first place.[253]

At this point, the composition of the Cincinnati alien hearing board was yet to be determined. However, officials stated that hearings would begin as soon as the board was in place.[254] A certain sense of urgency was beginning to develop, as the number of enemy aliens being held in Cincinnati and Fort Thomas had swelled from nine, on December 9, to fifteen (nine from Cincinnati) on December 12, and to twenty-six as of December 16. All of the aliens arrested to that time were males, although within a matter of days the number had grown to thirty, including the first woman detainee.

On December 18, the first steps toward forming the panel took place, as sixteen Ohioans, including five Cincinnatians, were suggested by U.S. District Attorney Calvin Crawford to the Justice Department for consideration as members. Among the Cincinnatians nominated for the board, to be known as the Enemy Control Board for Southern Ohio, were Judge Thomas H. Morrow of Common Pleas Court, attorney Edward T. Dixon, Thomas S. Burns, assistant secretary of the Kroger Grocery & Baking Company, former judge Robert N. Gorman, and attorney Burton E. Robinson. Numerous other Ohioans, of equally impeccable reputation, were recommended for the board, including James Huffman of Columbus, son-in-law of former Senator Vic Donahey, and Judge Carroll Sprigg of Dayton. Ohio had two alien hearing boards, one in Cincinnati and the other in Cleveland.[255]

Not until January 2 was the Cincinnati board officially named, when Dr. Raymond Walters, President of the University of Cincinnati, was appointed chairman and four other members, two attorneys and two businessmen, took their place beside him. Included among the other four members were two Cincinnatians: James E. Stuart, director of the Hospital Care Corporation, and the aforementioned Thomas E. Burns. Also included were Judge Sprigg and Columbus attorney Peter E. Dempsey. Hearings for the detained enemy aliens were tentatively scheduled to begin the following week.[256]

On December 18, two German aliens and an Italian were given special hearings, on the basis of hardship. In each case, continued detention of the aliens without establishment of guilt could constitute an undue hardship. Pending, but undisclosed, financial affairs of the men involved were said to require prompt and special handling of their cases. Under provisions of the special hearings, representatives of the Bureau of Immigration and Naturalization and the FBI attended, to hear the particulars of each case.[257]

*   *   *

In early 1942, several changes took place, as federal officials labored to handle increasing responsibilities and to make control of foreign nationals more efficient. On January 7, District Attorney Calvin Crawford took responsibility for enemy aliens' cases out of the hands of his chief assistant, Vern H. Wilson, while denying reports that internal friction lay behind the shakeup. According to Crawford, Wilson had been assigned to criminal cases, the heaviest load in the office, and civil case assistant Frederic W. Johnson was in a better position to handle the alien situation. That day alone, hearings for eleven suspected enemy aliens were scheduled on Fourth Street, bringing to fifteen the total number of cases heard to date, leaving twelve more to be handled. Of the eleven cases, five were heard in the morning, under the direction of board chairman Raymond Walters, along with Thomas Burns and Judge Carroll Sprigg. Another member, James Stuart, substituted for Dr. Walters in the afternoon session. According to Crawford, when hearings were scheduled, the board met from 9:30 a.m. until 12:30 p.m., and following a lunch recess reconvened from 2:00 p.m. until 5:00 p.m.[258] The next day, the efforts of the alien hearing board were recognized by Crawford, who paid tribute to its members and the job they had done after assisting them in hearing the cases of eight enemy aliens. Crawford said that he was grateful for the board members' sacrifices in handling the cases, and claimed that their work had been "thorough" and "conscientious."[259]

In March, the government made official a policy in which aliens from enemy or enemy-dominated nations could no longer be inducted into the army. The risk was simply too great, according to federal officials, that an alien sympathetic to his former country could obtain and pass on military secrets, such as armor type and strength, troop deployment and numbers, and more. In Cincinnati, the effects of the new policy were felt right away, as one registrant from Board 7, at 606 Vine Street, was recalled from the Fort Thomas induction station. The would-be soldier, Joseph Schildkraut, was a thirty-year-old furrier born in Tarnow, Poland, who had taken out his first citizenship papers in August 1940. No evidence indicated that Schildkraut held his new country in contempt or that he was a Nazi sympathizer. However, induction officers had received notice that, effective March 7, induction of aliens was to cease, and that the State Selective Service Director was to be notified of the arrival of any such inductee. Following the board's actions, Schildkraut was left unsure of his status, officially neither accepted nor rejected by the army, though both board and army officials described Schildkraut as a good potential soldier, perfectly willing to fight on the side of the United States. As for his citizenship papers, Schildkraut was informed that since the outbreak of war, no enemy aliens could be naturalized as citizens.[260]

Further actions taken by authorities illustrated their commitment to maintaining the upper hand in dealing with alien control. On June 23, law enforcement officers from Hamilton and five nearby counties attended a quarterly national defense conference at the Hotel Gibson. Along with officials of the FBI, they discussed war problems, especially with regard to enemy aliens, compared notes and strategies, and coordinated policies. Presiding over the meeting was Ray C. Suran, FBI chief in Cincinnati, while Dr. Raymond Walters spoke about his experiences as chairman of the Enemy Control Board for Southern Ohio. The conference was the final meeting in a series of five that month, all held in southern Ohio. The previous district conferences had been held in Dayton, Columbus, Zanesville, and Portsmouth.[261]

On July 1, a new supervisor for Cincinnati area enemy aliens was appointed, following the retirement of Samuel Howes. The new leader, John F. Mulcahey, had served nineteen years in the Immigration and Naturalization Service. Mulcahey began his new assignment on September 1, after moving with his wife from Boston. His responsibility was to oversee the Cincinnati district, which beyond the city included portions of Ohio, Indiana, Kentucky, and West Virginia.[262]

In the meantime, enemy alien arrests and hearings continued unabated. On January 8, the second Cincinnati female alien was arrested, to go along with two other women from Terre Haute and Nashville, making a total of thirty detainees as of that date. That same day, a hearing was scheduled for a German commercial artist who claimed he was a German nobleman, variously using the titles of "count" and "baron" in introducing himself.[263] By January 14, only four cases remained on the enemy-alien docket, with the completion of hearings predicted for the end of the week.[264]

One of the four remaining cases involved noted Cincinnati physician Otto Thuss, authorities confirmed. Thuss, who lived at 3326 Bishop Street in Clifton, was the first enemy alien taken into custody locally during the initial roundup of suspects December 8-9; his wife was not arrested until later. His was also the first name of an enemy alien made public, despite promises by authorities only to name detainees who would be interned or released outright. The action prompted the Cincinnati hearing board to ask that no further names be released until final rulings were made by the attorney general.

By early March 1942, Thuss and his wife were given interim paroles from an internment camp located near Seagoville, Texas. They were allowed to return to Cincinnati pending a final decision from the U.S.

Attorney General's office. Their daughter, Ingeborg, later claimed that Otto had wanted to return to Cincinnati and resume his medical practice, although he and his wife would be required to report daily to the Bureau of Immigration and Naturalization in the Federal Building. While in the Texas internment camp, Thuss had served as a physician for his fellow internees, while his wife worked in the camp library. Years later, shortly before his death November 14, 1973 at the age of 82, Otto claimed that he held neither bitterness nor grudges from his internment.[265]

Though public opinion at the outbreak of war, combined with a strong dose of patriotism, placed axis aliens at a strong disadvantage, on several occasions members of the community came to the support of aliens they felt beyond suspicion. On January 23, officers of Local 674, United Automobile and Aircraft Workers, announced that they had begun a fight for the reinstatement of three Norwood-based Chevrolet workers who had been dismissed as enemy aliens. The workers, including German August Baumgartner, all had served the United States loyally during World War I, and the son of one of the other aliens was soon scheduled to be inducted into the army. All three employees had been dismissed under a general policy of the company, in which citizens of nations with which the United States was at war were forbidden to work. Union Bargaining Committee chairman Ray Quinlan argued that the action stood contrary to published advice by Attorney General Biddle and President Roosevelt, that indiscriminate discharges should be avoided due to the wartime need for a stable work force at home. Quinlan further noted that there was no evidence whatsoever that any of the three workers was in any way disloyal to the United States. In an attempt to assist the workers, the union proposed that Army and Navy authorities render a final decision on the matter; management declined, and the union filed a grievance with management, demanding reinstatement and back pay for the three.[266]

Baumgartner, for his part, claimed that he thought he was a United States citizen until the matter came up. His father had filed naturalization papers when August was nineteen, but the naturalization process was not completed until he had reached the age of 25. Since he had attained majority by that time, though, August could not become a citizen legally until he filed papers for himself.[267]

Aliens were not the only people affected by governmental action; in some cases, naturalized citizens from Germany, as members of the German-American community, also were the object of federal attention. In one notable case, a Cincinnatian from Germany faced the dilemma of losing his property, job, and savings, all the while not being informed of his status. Christian Schleiermacher, 57, of 618 Straight Street, was born in Germany in 1886, and after spending some time in England came to America in 1925 with his twenty-five-year-old son. Christian was naturalized on February 24, 1931, and did not leave the country after that time. He worked for fifteen years for Procter and Gamble, saving up $1,780.53, which he deposited in a savings account at the North Cincinnati Loan and Building Company. His trouble began on January 4, 1942, when the U.S. Treasury Department, through the Federal Reserve Bank, froze Schleiermacher's bank account, under the impression that he was an enemy alien. Schleiermacher was not informed directly of this decision. On July 5 he went into the hospital for an emergency appendectomy, returning to employment on August 23. After only seven hours of work, he was told that the War Department had ordered him fired. According to Schleiermacher, there was nothing of national security interest pertaining to his job; his work was to load soap, powdered soap, and soap chips into cars. On September 25, the government filed suit in U.S. District Court in Cincinnati to cancel his certificate of naturalization, leaving him uncertain of his citizenship. Throughout the process, no one had charged him with any wrongdoing.[268]

In the aftermath of the government's action, Schleiermacher could not find another job, and while still ill from his appendectomy neither could get to the bank money he had worked for and saved nor find other means to provide for his wife. Attempts to petition the Treasury Department for release of his money were fruitless, and the bank refused to take responsibility for giving him his money without an official release. Meanwhile, the two branches of government were at odds over how to deal with Schleiermacher: The Justice Department insisted that he was in fact a citizen, and that they were intent upon revoking his citizenship. Meanwhile, the Treasury Department argued with equal vigor that Schleiermacher was *not* a citizen, and thus they tied up his funds as an alien. Schleiermacher could only ask the court for a mandatory injunction authorizing the association to turn his savings over to him.[269]

Eleven days later, following a backlash of public sentiment on behalf of Schleiermacher, the government gave in, at least partially. On September 28, Schleiermacher's cash frozen in the building association was ordered released to him, ending at least that aspect of his lengthy battle with the government. According to the building association, it had received a revocation order claiming that Schleiermacher "no longer is regarded as a national of a foreign country," with full release of the money authorized. Schleiermacher thus dismissed his suit as well.[270]

*   *   *

While cases such as that of Schleiermacher drew sympathetic support for the German-American community, other instances served to galvanize public opinion against the German element in Cincinnati, such as when aliens who had not yet attained citizenship were less than honest in making claims regarding their American citizenship. Willi Geier, a 22 year old machinist living at 3876 Paxton Road, pled guilty to a charge of representing himself falsely as a U.S. citizen, after which he was released on his own recognizance and returned to the Fourth Street detention center. According to Geier, both his father and his brother, born in Germany, were already in custody there. He believed that he was a citizen of the United States, as he had been in the country since he was five years old. While working at a manufacturing concern on Spring Grove Avenue, he had been discharged because he was not a citizen. However, Geier claimed, a foreman of the firm had told him that he should claim that he was a citizen when applying for a job.[271]

On October 25, 1944, another alien, forty-seven-year-old Richard John Bueg, was arraigned on a charge of misrepresenting his alien status. A guilty conviction carried a penalty of a $10,000 fine, in addition to a five year prison sentence, based on a federal statute. On September 18, Bueg allegedly made false claims of his status, in applying for a job as a tool and die maker at the Crosley Corporation. At the time, the company was fulfilling a contract with the Navy. Bueg pled not guilty, stating that he was in fact not a Nazi, not an alien, and had been born in Cleveland. On the contrary, he said, he was a proud purchaser of War Bonds. Nevertheless, a hearing was set for November 1, and Bueg's bond was set at $1,000. According to Charles E. Weeks, local FBI chief, Bueg actually had been born in Landow, Germany, on August 13, 1895, and that although Bueg's parents had been naturalized, he himself had never become a citizen of the United States. Further, Weeks stated that Bueg had previously applied for work at Crosley, in June 1942, at which time he had admitted that he had been born in Germany in 1903 but had become an American citizen through his father's naturalization. FBI agents cited evidence that, in applying for his marriage license on May 31, 1921, Bueg stated that he had been born in Germany in 1895.[272]

While some such cases undoubtedly were the result of an honest mistake, other cases, similar to that of Bueg, were also reported in the media, and reinforced the widespread notion that German aliens were a threat to sabotage important American industrial plants, particularly those with federal contracts. Reports focusing on more questionable enemy aliens reinforced the suspicions with which many German nationals were confronted. In mid- to late February 1942, the government announced that it would be bringing seven "dangerous" aliens to Cincinnati from the federal detention center for Axis diplomats and newspapermen in White Sulphur Springs, West Virginia. Since the outbreak of the war, five hundred German and Italian aliens had been interned there. Of the seven coming to Cincinnati, six were German, and all had been employed as waiters during their incarceration. Among them, one inmate, Hans Hensel, had a brother in the German army, and another, Gustav Amthor, had four. Both men were slated to face criminal charges of illegal entry.[273]

Though such reports contributed to some resentment of enemy aliens in Cincinnati, the *Cincinnati Post* played on a different human emotion with a story in late February, namely fear. Entitled "It Happened Here: How Nazi Agents Plotted Evil Deeds," the front-page report by Robert L. Otto chronicled Nazi intrigue and sabotage plans in the Greater Cincinnati area. Such a report, reminiscent of the anti-German hysteria of World War I, reflected the spirit of the time immediately following American entry into World War II, and threatened to incite people to take action against members of the German community as had been the case twenty-five years earlier. The principal figures were said to be among twelve or fourteen enemy aliens, including "two widely known Cincinnati physicians" among ten Cincinnatians transferred February 25 to a military camp near Sparta, Wisconsin.[274] The aliens had been loaded by six soldiers into three city police patrols, at the Fourth Street detention center, which in turn left at 2:35 p.m. and took the handcuffed men directly to a waiting train at Union Terminal.

Otto summarized the events in question as having read "like a movie thriller. One sees close contact with the German Embassy in Washington, trips abroad for conferences with Herman Goering, a clannish, more or less closely guarded Cincinnati group," including many women. Yet another part of the puzzle, according to Otto, involved "cunning operations among wives of industrialists, and here entered the love theme: The Nazi agent enchanted by the charms of beautiful women."[275]

The main figures in the plot were described with letters: "Mr. A," for example, was considered the leader, in close contact with the German Embassy, the one who provided the German government with the names of "trusted" Germans in the area upon demand, and the one who tested their "loyalty" to the cause, before he would "certify" them and find "work" for them to do. Along with family members, he boldly proclaimed the merits of Hitler and Nazism in public, arguing his points with associates, consistently defending Hitler. His home was decorated with a large picture of Hitler, in front of which normally stood fresh flowers, while he delighted in wearing jewelry with the Nazi swastika. Some years earlier, he had harbored a known German spy in Cincinnati for the night, assisting him to escape while federal agents were looking for him.[276]

"Mr. C" was known to loudly profess the joys of Nazism and its superiority to the American political and social systems. A business owner, his comments infuriated his neighbors, who in turn boycotted his business. Otto noted the hostile attitude others showed the man, stating that "he was arrested as much for his own protection as the community's."[277]

"Mr. B," as he was called, was notorious for his role as a German aviator during World War I, having flown with Herman Goering. He had since visited Goering several times and openly praised the Third Reich. Without doubt, the true identity of this mysterious "Mr. B" was Wilhelm (William) Huebener, a Clifton physician. Huebener could make one other substantial claim to fame: In later years, he was the personal physician to the exiled Kaiser Wilhelm in Doorn, before the outbreak of war. Huebener was born in northern Germany in the early 1890s, and while growing up there in the 1910s, he began to pursue medical studies. The outbreak of World War I in 1914 interrupted his studies, as in the early days of the war he set his books aside in order to join the German army. Not at all eager to fight in the trenches, he was intrigued by the glamour of flying, and set out to become a fighter pilot. Initially, Huebener served as a chauffeur, as the German army placed little faith in flying machines, which at the time were largely unreliable and as likely to crash as to complete a mission. After complaining and pestering his commanding officer long enough, Huebener was transferred to the Aviation Service, and by early 1915 he had been assigned to one of the German army's *Fliegerabteilungen*, in order to perform reconnaissance and artillery observation duties. Eventually, Huebener worked his way up to the rank of lieutenant, fighting in Verdun and eventually winning the Iron Cross. It was during his service in *Fliegerabteilung 25* that Huebener made the acquaintance of Goering, who became a skilled pilot only after faking a sick leave and going to a private flying school.

Largely because Huebener traveled to Europe to serve the exiled Kaiser, until the war began in 1939, his journeys were often covered by the press and given widespread attention, such as a December 14, 1938 *Enquirer* report. These trips and Huebener's German background, though, only serve to condemn him under different circumstances. He was interned several months before eventually being paroled, and finally attained U.S. citizenship in 1949. Like Otto Thuss, he claimed to hold no bitterness long after the fact, and following his release he lived a relatively quiet remainder of his life, returning to German soil for good in 1979 until his death on June 12, 1981, at the age of eighty-eight.[278]

During the warm summer months of 1942, enemy alien arrests continued, albeit with less frequency than in the weeks following the outbreak of war. On July 11, two German aliens were brought to Cincinnati for incarceration at the Fourth Street holding center, after being arrested on presidential warrants by FBI agents. One man who had been arrested in Portsmouth for having failed to turn in his camera protested vigorously, claiming to be a Jewish refugee from Nazi Germany. The other German, apprehended in Zanesville, was simply described as "dangerous," with no other reasons being given for his arrest.[279] The next day, two German women were also arrested by presidential warrants and brought to the downtown place of detention, joining a German married couple from Portsmouth taken into custody after contraband articles were found in their home. At the time, the alien board of review planned to hear at least four cases that week.[280]

During the summer of 1943, a notorious case involving a German-American suspected of treason played itself out in Cincinnati. Max Stephan, a German national working as a restaurateur in Detroit, was arrested for giving aid to German aviator Peter Krug, who had escaped from a prison camp in Canada in 1942.[281] For his part, Stephan was tried, convicted, and sentenced to death for treason by the Federal Court in Detroit; he was to be hanged in November 1942 at the Milan, Michigan Federal Prison. After numerous appeals, the case landed in the U.S. Sixth District Court in Cincinnati in June 1943, after a new execution date of July 2 had been set. Public reaction ran against leniency for Stephan, and the Cincinnati court verdict was equally unfavorable for him; the Sixth

District Court ruled on June 24 to uphold the sentence, leaving Stephan only the possibility of a commutation of sentence by President Roosevelt.[282]

Stephan's attorney, Nicholas Salowich, remained somewhat optimistic after the verdict, claiming that his gut feeling was that Stephan would not hang, and that the president would step in to remedy the situation. However, Attorney General Francis Biddle announced firmly that he had decided against recommending any White House action in the case, effectively ending Stephan's hopes for clemency.[283] Previously, on September 26, 1942, Mrs. Max Stephan was ordered transferred to Cincinnati's alien detention center on Fourth Street, pending a ruling on whether she would be held as a dangerous enemy alien. Her U.S. citizenship had been revoked on the grounds that she had concealed Canadian residence, as well as for not reporting arrests for liquor violations in her application.[284]

*　　　*　　　*

By the early summer of 1942, alien arrests had become less noteworthy, and failed to raise eyebrows among the general public any longer. Media coverage of alien apprehensions became more infrequent with each passing month. Most people had begun to perceive enemy alien apprehensions as being isolated or individual cases, rather than as part of a broader conspiracy against American interests; any threat these aliens may have carried was generally perceived to be small. In late July, however, news of a massive FBI manhunt for three Nazi saboteurs, whose trail ran through Cincinnati, attracted considerable attention, and the image of the "dangerous" German national received new focus. The three men, Walter Kappe, Joseph Schmidt, and Rheinhold Barth, were the subject of a nationwide manhunt, with Federal officials believing that they may have been brought illegally into the country, by submarine or by parachute. While federal officials believed that the men were not in the country, they explained that they were taking every precaution for security reasons; all three were extensively trained in the science of sabotage. Consequently, pictures, descriptions, and fingerprints of all three men were circulated throughout the country.

Of the three men, Kappe was considered the most dangerous. Likewise he held the strongest ties to Cincinnati, having worked and resided in the city for some two years during the 1930s. By 1942, he was certainly no stranger to the FBI, which held an extensive dossier on his previous activities on behalf of the Friends of New Germany and the German-American Bund. According to FBI records, Kappe had been an agent of the Ausland organization, having furnished his headquarters in Germany with a list of American newspapers favorable to the Nazi government. The FBI had full documentation of Kappe's previous arrest; on February 18, 1936, Kappe and three others were arrested in New York, charged with kidnapping J.F. Paffrath, the financial secretary of the *Deutscher Konsum Verbund*. However, charges were dismissed a week later in the City Magistrate's office, without reason being given.[285]

The other two men implicated also had extensive backgrounds as Nazi sympathizers. Joseph Schmidt, a native of Germany, came to Alberta Province, Canada, where we lived as a farmer, hunter, and trapper. In September 1939, after the war began, his farm was seized by the Canadian government. After traveling to Mexico, Schmidt returned to Germany, where he was known to have attended a sabotage school run by the Nazis. Physical strength was one of his attributes: Schmidt was said to be capable of bending heavy pieces of metal with his bare hands. Rheinhold Barth was born in Stuttgart July 14, 1907. He arrived in the United States on July 8, 1929 and worked as a draftsman with the Long Island Railroad, before returning to Germany in May 1938. Despite having filed to become a U.S. citizen in 1930, he became active in the German-American Bund, later becoming an intelligence officer in the German Army. There he also served as an instructor at a sabotage school, specializing in methods of destroying railroads and railroad equipment.

According to J. Edgar Hoover, all three men had received orders from the German high command to come to the United States and destroy vital war industries, utilizing all necessary means of sabotage in which they had been trained.[286]

Detention of Enemy Aliens in Cincinnati

With the arrest of enemy aliens, it became necessary to find a place to hold the detainees. Foreseeing a large number of aliens being arrested, perhaps for a lengthy period of time, local and federal officials turned away from widespread use of local jails for holding enemy aliens, in favor of establishing a holding facility to be used exclusively for arrested aliens.

On December 17, 1941, the government opened the doors at 417 West Fourth Street to the press, for a preview of the temporary holding facility for enemy aliens. The *Cincinnati Post* voiced approval of what it saw, describing the "alien refuge" as "clean" and "comfortable," further stating that "It isn't home, this place of detention for enemy aliens in Cincinnati, but under the circumstances it's the closest thing to home."[287] District inspector of Immigration and Naturalization Samuel H. Howes led the media tour of the facility, located on the second floor of the post office garage. Detention quarters were constructed by a team of workmen in less than a week, working night and day, and by the end of the week, all 29 aliens currently held at the Fort Thomas facility were moved to the new center downtown.

As for the internment facility itself, there were accommodations for a total of 300 men and 20 women, the quarters separated. Mattressed steel cots were made available to each internee, complete with pillows, sheets, and blankets. Internees also were provided with lockers for clothing, recreation space, plenty of light, lavatories, bathrooms, and showers. The kitchen was described in glowing terms by the *Post* reporter:

> [The facility included] a kitchen equipped with modern utensils like a hotel's. [There was] a large electric icebox with succulent hams, husky joints of beef, boxes of eggs and butter. [There was] a huge cupboard jammed with the kinds of staples the American housewife buys: large cartons of breakfast cereal, peas, carrots, beans, spinach, tomatoes, soups, fruit and vegetable juices.

Meals were served cafeteria style, three times per day. At this early date, wake up hour and bedtime were yet to be established. For those who became sick, the government provided a doctor within the compound.[288]

Despite all of the amenities, there was no mistaking the fact that it was a detention center. Stout wire grating was placed throughout the facility, and guards, whose numbers were kept a secret, were stationed at strategic locations, prepared to deal with any emergency, while handling routine monitoring of the aliens. A modern alarm system was installed, connected with the office of the immigration inspector in charge, Henry J. Boutton. If an alarm were to go off, he could tell from a glance at a box on the wall where a guard had flashed an alarm signal. For those family members wishing a supervised visit, a public entrance to the facility was located on John Street, between Third and Fourth Streets, though as yet no definite regulations had been made regarding visitation and privileges of the internees. As for the bottom line to taxpayers, Howes estimated that renovations cost a total of $8,000 to $10,000.[289]

Gerhard Fuhr was born and raised in Cincinnati, the third son of German parents residing in the city. He recalled the enemy alien detention facility, based on visits he paid there as a boy, after his parents were apprehended:

> Those floors were waxed fairly well, and they took a section of that, and had that roped off for "the Germans." There were more than just my parents in there; there were ten or fifteen or twenty that I saw, when I went down to visit. Twelve years old, you're in a hurry, you're a little embarrassed, you don't know what to do. Why your parents are there, you don't really quite understand that, but they're there.[290]

On December 20, the first transfer of incarcerated enemy aliens from Fort Thomas to the new detention center took place, as thirty aliens made the voyage across the river and became the first occupants of the post office garage facility. Special permission was given by Vern H. Wilson, Chief Assistant to the United States Attorney, for ten relatives to visit some of the thirty detainees, the first visits permitted the aliens in the up to three weeks since they had been taken into custody. Visiting hours were from 1:00 to 4:00 p.m. for those persons, at first only relatives, who had secured visiting permits from Wilson. Of the passes distributed by Wilson at that point, all but one was for relatives, the one exception being for an attorney of an internee. Each permit was good for a single visit, and to avoid overcrowding, limitations were placed on the number of visitors as well as the number of times a person could make a visit. The visitors were permitted to bring internees cigarettes, fruit, and clothing; each gift was carefully inspected before being turned over to the aliens.[291]

That Friday afternoon, the first incarcerated enemy alien was freed from the Cincinnati detention center, with two others also released by the end of the day. Each of the three had been found working in local defense industries, and were among the first foreign nationals arrested after the outbreak of the war. According to authorities, the initial detainee, an Italian, had been released "outright, with no strings attached," while the other two aliens, both Germans, were released on parole. Under conditions provided, paroled internees had to report "periodically" to their sponsors and the government.[292]

Generally speaking, Cincinnati's detained German aliens posed few if any problems for authorities. While occasionally bewildered or dissatisfied with their incarceration, the aliens tended to avoid any confrontations with their captors. Nevertheless, one incident of note occurred during the previous week, ironically involving the lone female internee. After being placed in protective custody downtown, the woman suddenly went berserk, tearing off almost all of the clothes from the matron assigned to guard her. The woman was sedated by a staff physician before being taken away to the Hamilton County jail, while the matron was listed as unharmed save for having to replace her clothing.[293]

Meanwhile, with Christmas just around the corner, authorities prepared to make special concessions to the detainees to help celebrate the season, as well as to alleviate the boredom which inevitably afflicted those incarcerated. A substantial Christmas dinner was held, with all the trimmings, and passes were liberally issued to relatives and friends. However, regulations in other areas were not relaxed: All packages brought as Christmas presents were rigidly inspected, as per instructions. Money also was an issue with the authorities, as all incoming aliens had to empty their pockets of paper money. Of the 29 men being held, some $1,400 was collected, including an astounding figure approaching $700 from a Japanese alien.[294]

Nevertheless, life in the detention center seemingly had its humorous side, at least in the eyes of an outsider. For example, one Cincinnati alien received a fruitcake during the course of a visit from his wife. Standard precautions required that the cake be examined in the kitchen for prohibited articles. After the cake had been cut into slices in a futile search for contraband and returned, the distressed internee looked askance at the cake and replied, "Take it away. I don't want it in that shape." A bewildered official only reiterated that they were simply looking for a gun. Another alien received as a gift from his wife a combination radio and phonograph player. After inspection by officials, who determined that it could not be used to transmit messages, the present was passed on, along with a stack of symphonic records included. However, as some of the aliens exhibited a distaste for classical music, the records were simply stored away in a cupboard by the alien in question. Irony was found in the fact that one of the records brought to the German alien, Tschaikowsky's "1812 Overture," had a contemporary parallel of Napoleon's retreat from Moscow in the current legions of Adolf Hitler, retreating from Soviet troops near the capital.[295]

In late April and early May, more than 600 Axis diplomats, consular officials, and their families, mostly from South America, were brought to Cincinnati, to stay in the Hotel Gibson during their time in town. The visitors were on their way to being exchanged for subjects from Allied nations, including Americans, who had been trapped in Europe when the United States entered the war. By almost all accounts, the aliens were treated well in Cincinnati, showered with attention and given every courtesy, but that did not stop the Nazi press from writing scathing criticisms of how the diplomats and others were handled. While German criticism did not mention Cincinnati specifically, and the comments made were not attributed directly to those aliens who had stayed in the city, Cincinnatians still took the comments personally, knowing that they had taken every reasonable step to insure a comfortable stay for the visitors, given the existing circumstances.

Extreme secrecy surrounded the aliens and their arrival, as government officials initially would neither confirm nor deny that the Axis diplomats were coming; newspapermen and even local officials were left uninformed until after their arrival. The first indication of the impending visit came when guests registered on the top four floors were asked to change their room assignments to other, lower floors. Only later was it learned that the Axis visitors were to stay in Cincinnati until the Swedish liner *Drottningholm* arrived in New York, to take the Germans and Italians back to their respective countries.

Upon arriving in Cincinnati aboard a special train, the visitors were taken by chartered bus to the Gibson, arriving in groups. They were conducted to two special elevators inside the hotel, bypassing the main lobby, and escorted by federal officials to the Roof Garden, where room assignments were made.[296] Few could argue the point that the Gibson was one of the most luxurious choices possible for housing the unexpected guests. Located in the heart of Cincinnati, on Fountain Square, the hotel featured 1,000 rooms, including restaurants, cafes, and various small shops. Ten Brunswick bowling lanes were available for entertaining its guests, along with one of Cincinnati's finest barber shops, a haberdashery, an epicure shop, a florist, confectioneries, an optometrist, a beauty salon, and even personal stenographers. With a guest capacity of around 1,600, plus room for 3,555 in meeting rooms and 2,483 in various dining halls, the hotel could easily accommodate the Axis visitors and afford them a degree of luxury unprecedented in other so-called "detention facilities" they might have encountered.[297]

From the moment the diplomats and their families arrived at the Gibson from New Orleans on Sunday, April 26, State Department officials insisted that all 600 plus aliens were to be given every courtesy. The hotel notified hundreds of guests on the top four floors that they would have to be moved, in order to accommodate the Axis nationals. Women were attended to by hairdressers brought in by the hotel, while men were shaved and given haircuts by professional barbers. Stenographers, capable of translating both German and English, were made available to those wishing to write letters. The spacious roof garden was made available to all of the new visitors; for children it served as a playground, and three times a day it functioned also as a dining hall. Each meal served was rated as being of better quality than the usual hotel food, since the meals were prepared in a special kitchen and arranged to suit the tastes of each individual alien. For the meals, breakfast included hot or cold cereals, ham, sausage, bacon, eggs of any style, toast, and rolls, with coffee, tea, milk, or any of a variety of juices to drink. Lunch included special food for children and a wide variety of dishes for the adults, while dinner was always on a more expansive scale. All meals were served to the aliens as a group, with their dining room remaining strictly closed off to the public for the duration of the visit. Additionally, a bar was made available to the aliens, stocking an assortment of beers, wines, and liquors. Federal officials were quick to point out that few Cincinnatians, facing rationing in a wartime economy, got better treatment or more choices of foodstuffs than the aliens had received.[298]

In late June, with the coming of summer, authorities attempted to make the season more enjoyable for its alien detainees. Samuel Howes, District Manager of the Immigration and Naturalization Service, applied to city council for permission to construct fences across an alley which separated a vacant lot from the Plaza Hotel. The goal, Howes said, was to provide outdoor recreation space for the enemy aliens, combining leisure activities with the chance to get some fresh air and sunshine. After the fences were put up, the alley was effectively closed off and secure, and the space was turned over to internees. Following clearing and grading the premises, amusement and recreation devices were installed for the aliens' benefit.[299]

In August 1943, the FBI looked into the possibility of housing enemy alien suspects in another location, one which might be more cost effective. On August 18, District Director of the Immigration and Naturalization Service John Mulcahey requested a bid on the cost of detaining aliens in the county jail. The jail recently had been made escape-proof, and thus restored to a master list of federally approved prisons. According to information provided, the department was looking to provide for the detention of aliens whose cases were being investigated until they were released or sent to an internment center. With the relative rapidity of hearings resulting from lower case numbers, detainees would be housed for only a few days at a time; thus the need for a "detention center," as was the case on Fourth Street, became less and less vital. Because of the increased cost of food and labor, including extra guards, the county decided not to contract with the federal government again, at the old rate of 70 cents per day per prisoner, the charge before the jail was removed from the preferred list for government prisoners. Instead, the new bid sent was for $1.00 per day per prisoner, inclusive of three square meals.[300]

Further Restrictions Against German Aliens

On January 1, 1942, federal authorities implemented additional measures in dealing with the enemy alien question. Beyond registration and arrests, federal authorities clearly recognized that other measures needed to be taken, in an effort to guard against a possible outbreak of sabotage or the passing of information from Nazi sympathizers to German spies and on to the German government.

To this end, immediately following an announcement from Attorney General Biddle, German, Italian, and Japanese nationals in the United States were required to surrender all firearms, radio transmitters, short wave radio receivers, and cameras to local police by 11:00 p.m. Monday, January 5. The order was an extension of a previous order which affected foreign nationals, primarily of Japanese origin, in eight states in the west coast area. Theoretically, aliens could use radio transmitters to pass on secret information; short wave receivers could be used to receive orders from Nazi agents elsewhere; and cameras could be utilized for photographing defense industries or properties of importance to the general public, such as power plants and water works.

In Cincinnati, authorities awaited further instructions on what to do with property received. Estimates held that between 4,000 and 5,000 aliens in the Cincinnati area would be affected by the action; those not complying with the orders were subject to forfeiture of property and possible internment. According to Cincinnati police chief Eugene

Weatherly, the police department was fully prepared to act upon receipt of federal instructions, with plans calling for aliens to turn in the requested items at district police stations nearest to where they lived.[301]

While the call-in was considered comprehensive by some sources, certain provisions did in fact exist by which aliens could keep some of their property. Exceptions were provided for studio or fixed cameras which could not readily be moved. Standard radio receivers also possessing short wave bands could also be kept, provided that the short wave coils were disconnected or otherwise altered so as to prevent short wave reception.

By January 3, though, local officials delayed the date for alien property to be turned in, because details of the equipment gathering and storage procedure still had to be ironed out. According to Chief Assistant U.S. Attorney Vern Wilson, the call to have the items brought in would have to be temporarily delayed, as special receipt tags were still being printed, and upon delivery they would need to be distributed to the various collection points. Further, Police Chief Weatherly stated that the police stockroom was already filled to capacity. While authorities were surveying storeroom space at the Fourth Street alien detention center, federal and local officials needed more time to continue the search for a more suitable location. Partly in an effort to alleviate the storage space problem, and to an extent as a show of goodwill, Wilson also announced that he would give permission to those aliens who used a camera for their livelihood to keep and use their photographic equipment, provided that FBI records showed no previous problems with the law and that the alien could identify him- or herself as a person of good repute within the community.[302]

By January 4, however, federal officials settled on using the second floor of the post office garage at 417 West Fourth Street, otherwise known as the alien detention center, as the holding center for firearms, short-wave radio sets, transmitters, cameras, and other prohibited equipment. While the deadline for receipt of the items was originally slated for the next day, officials conceded that proper receipt forms had yet to arrive from Washington, and that delays were inevitable. Weatherly was to inform the press and radio as soon as the forms arrived and were distributed, so that the procedure could begin immediately. He had already advised certain aliens with large, bulky, cabinet-style radios including short wave reception to arrange with technicians to disconnect the short wave part; police officials had little desire to handle and store more equipment than already was necessary, with an added benefit being that storage space at the warehouse could be saved.[303]

On January 6, the Department of Justice extended the list of items considered contraband, in addition to extending the deadline for turning in items to 11:00 p.m. January 8. In addition to the previously listed items, the following were now deemed inappropriate for possession by nationals of Axis nations:

1) Weapons or implements of war, or component parts thereof;

2) ammunition of all kinds;

3) bombs, explosives, or materials used in the manufacture of explosives;

4) signal devices;

5) codes or ciphers;

6) papers, documents, or books in which there may be invisible writing; and

7) photographs, sketches, pictures, drawings, maps, or graphical representation of any military or naval installations or equipment, or of any arms, ammunition, or implements of war.[304]

While the list of new items appeared reasonable, several items doubtless puzzled not only aliens, but even casual observers. Authorities offered no explanation of how one determined whether or not there was invisible writing inside materials to be turned in. With only a nebulous mention of forbidden signal devices and codes, some aliens were left to wonder if possession of such innocuous items as flashlights and children's games would subject them to arrest. Further, even the most hardened patriot didn't expect aliens to walk into police headquarters and say that they would like to turn in a bomb.

Indeed, the list of items initially deposited with the Cincinnati police revealed no bombs. Reports from local districts showed that, through the first day of collection, cameras were the leading item turned in:

Police District	Items Turned In
District 1 (York Street)	one camera
District 2 (Arch Street)	two radios two cameras
District 3 (Warsaw Avenue)	one camera
District 5 (Cumminsville)	one camera
District 6 (Eastern Avenue)	three cameras
District 7 (Beecher Street)	125 articles

District 7 featured one of the highest German concentrations in the city, including parts of Clifton, Hyde Park, Avondale, Bond Hill, and Walnut Hills; among the 125 articles collected there were cameras, shotguns, and radios. The police also reported that many aliens had brought in radios simply to show officials that they had had the short wave band removed. The work was acknowledged, and each alien was told that they could keep the radios, provided that they not replace the short wave band.[305] According to another report, District 7 had gathered 154 of about 200 total items turned in, as of around midday January 7.[306]

For the next couple of months, after the deadline passed, federal officials gathered information on those suspects they felt had not turned in contraband, and into April, they began to move against violators. On April 8, eleven enemy aliens from Dayton were arrested by the FBI for retaining forbidden property, as well as one more the next day. The initial eleven suspects were taken to Cincinnati during the night and placed in the alien detention center on Fourth Street. Eight of the twelve aliens were Germans, and a total of twenty residents were searched in the sweep. Among items seized were "photographs of Hitler galore," a silver swastika plaque, seventeen short wave radios, an oscillator which could be used to transmit messages, twelve cameras, six guns, and a significant stockpile of ammunition.[307] Each suspect was slated for an initial, informal hearing, where partial determinations were made. Those against whom the evidence was "slight," according to Assistant U.S. District Attorney Frederic Johnson, would likely be released, while others more suspect would be given hearings before the enemy-alien hearing board.[308]

On June 4, nine raids by federal agents on the premises of Cincinnati area aliens (the first FBI raids of this sort in the city) resulted in the arrest of six people, along with the seizure of numerous short wave radios, shotguns, rifles, revolvers, ammunition, cameras, war maps, and German propaganda. Of the six arrested, five were German nationals, and four were women. Overall, nine raids were conducted; seven were in Cincinnati, and one each occurring in Norwood and Cleves. Armed with search warrants, government officials and four Cincinnati detectives initiated the raids shortly before noon, finishing by four o'clock in the afternoon.

Police authorities quickly put together a detailed list of the seized contraband. The list read like the inventory of a German-American Bund meeting hall: five radio sets with short wave capability; five shotguns; two cameras; numerous pictures of Hitler; a plaque of the German-American Bund; various maps of the European theater of war; and many items of propaganda, largely distributed by the German Library of Information, located in New York. The plaque itself was round and made of bronze, bearing a swastika with the word *Ortsgruppe* above it and "Cincinnati" beneath it, with the words *Deutschland Bund Freunde des Neuen Deutschlands* around its circular edge. Beyond bringing in forbidden property, though, federal officials openly expressed their joy at helping achieve another objective; according to local FBI chief Ray Suran, forty-five Germans and twenty Italians in the Cincinnati area had been "taken out of circulation" since the outbreak of the war.[309]

It should be stressed that most aliens complied without complaint with the property restrictions imposed. However, while the public at large generally was set at ease by the amount of cooperation received, the reason for the initial precautions was brought home to many with the news of the trial of eight suspected German saboteurs in Washington. According to the FBI, the men came ashore from a submarine on the east coast, and brought with them enough incendiary devices, explosives, fuses, and detonating devices to maintain a two-year plan of sabotage of vital American defense plants, to compliment the sabotage training they had received in Berlin.[310]

To a lesser extent, other restrictions were also placed on enemy aliens following the outbreak of hostilities. Most notable among these in Cincinnati was the travel restriction imposed upon foreign nationals of Axis nations. Along with the property call-in announced in early January 1942, the Justice Department also explained that aliens no longer were able to travel outside of their immediate zone without first obtaining permission from the proper government officials. Aliens in question were allowed to travel freely to and from their place of work, schools, and churches within their community. All other travel was forbidden unless permission was asked and granted at least one week in advance of departure. Beyond asking permission, aliens had to state the purpose of their trip, the destination, exact route to be followed, and type of transportation to be used.[311]

Conclusions

In sum, alien registration, beginning in August 1940, assisted the government in creating master lists of German legal resident aliens who might be considered dangerous enemy aliens in the event of hostilities with Germany, and in gathering background information on people who would be arrested for posing a threat to national security interests after December 7, 1941. In Cincinnati as elsewhere, following the Japanese attack on Pearl Harbor and the outbreak of war between Germany and the United States, the government established special detention facilities for aliens from Germany and other Axis nations, where aliens would be housed until a final determination of their status was made by newly created enemy-alien hearing boards. While accommodations were far from luxurious, detention centers offered clean, decent quarters, with most of the basic amenities of home and visitation rights. Hearing boards, made up of citizens of impeccable reputation within the community, were responsible for hearing the cases of arrested aliens and, based on available evidence, determining whether detainees should be interned as dangerous enemy aliens, given conditional parole, or released outright. While conceding the need to respect the best interests of the nation, critics of enemy alien hearings pointed out that detainees received little of the legal protection guaranteed to American citizens, including the right to legal representation and the ability to confront accusers during the hearings. In early 1942, federal officials announced additional measures to safeguard Americans from the threat of espionage and sabotage activities by German aliens, including the confiscation of personal property such as cameras, short wave radios and transmitters, and maps; as well as travel restrictions which prevented German nationals from traveling beyond a limited radius without obtaining special permission beforehand.

While the majority of German legal resident aliens arrested and placed into temporary detention facilities were eventually given outright release or conditional parole, for many others alien registration and arrest was only the beginning of a lengthy period of incarceration at the hands of federal and military officials. In many cases, detainees sentenced to internment were separated from family members at a moment's notice; others were obliged to bring their families with them, to special family internment camps, for a period of several years. Seldom did detainees receive the opportunity to defend themselves fully during hearings; even more seldom were formal charges actually levied against them. By arresting and detaining thousands of reputable, respected members of America's German community, based on the words and deeds of a relative few pro-Nazi sympathizers and activists, federal authorities paved the way for the widespread internment of German legal resident aliens and, to a lesser extent, native-born German-Americans, an action which to date the United States Government has failed to recognize officially.

Chapter V

The Internment Of German Legal Resident Aliens and German-Americans

One of the most misunderstood and misrepresented aspects of the German-American situation in the World War II era is the issue of internment. Since the end of the war, spanning a time of over fifty years, the prevailing sentiment has been that German legal resident aliens and German-Americans were not interned as dangerous enemies during the war years. Far from being simply hearsay commentary, numerous sources have proclaimed that only Japanese-Americans were interned for the duration of the war, or that European-Americans and people of European heritage were never subjected to such treatment.[312] Such comments have served only to further an historical untruth; according to Arthur D. Jacobs and Joseph E. Fallon, Europeans and European-Americans made up fifty-six percent of all those interned during the war, as well as sixty-four percent of those arrested by the FBI.[313] In each case, German legal resident aliens and German-Americans constituted the largest number of those of European stock detained. Additionally, while Japanese nationals and Japanese Americans were released from internment centers by June 1946, numerous German nationals and German-Americans were held until as late as June 1948, a full three years after the end of the war in Europe. Indisputable documentation, from the United States Government and other sources, has been made available over the years, detailing not only the reasons for internment of German legal resident aliens and German-Americans, but also the locations where internment took place, the number of people detained, and the length of their incarceration. Furthermore, a limited number of detainees have made known their experiences in internment camps, providing first-hand information on living conditions for internees and how such treatment impacted upon their lives.

The arrest, detention, and internment of members of the German-American community, as dangerous enemy aliens and Americans of questionable loyalties, was not new during the 1940s. During World War I a significant number were afforded similar treatment, as an outgrowth of the anti-German hysteria of the time. In fact, some of the same camps used to hold members of the German-American community during World

War I, were also utilized during the World War II era for the same purpose.

Such camps, generally placed in remote locations for maximum security, afforded internees a reasonable standard of living, albeit with few of the comforts of home. Federal officials made significant efforts to ease the burden of internees of all backgrounds, which made internment easier to bear for those held during the war. Nevertheless, the inevitable strain of forced confinement took its toll on many of those in the camps; the emotional scars of the experience endure for many of the remaining former internees. For the purpose of this study, a detailed description will be provided of the Crystal City, Texas internment facility, as a representative example of a family internment center for German legal resident aliens and German-Americans. The description of the facility is augmented by memories of several former internees, who describe life within the Crystal City facility, life in general as an internee of German background, and the aftermath of the internment experience.

Previous Internment of Aliens in the United States

Precedent for the internment of enemy aliens goes back over two centuries in American history. In the aftermath of the Revolutionary War, American lawmakers took actions designed to detain and/or deport aliens considered to pose a threat to the security of the United States, as well as those who might further the interest of foreign powers on American soil. Enacted in 1798, the Alien and Sedition Acts originally were designed as a means to control French agents in the United States, and were later used against British subjects in America during the War of 1812. Specifically, the law stated that "all natives, citizens, denizens, or subjects of the hostile nation or government, being males of the age of fourteen years and upwards, who shall be within the United States and not actually naturalized, shall be liable to be apprehended, restrained, secured, and removed, as enemy aliens."

This initial enemy alien law had long since been forgotten until just two weeks before American entry into World War I. Discovered by Assistant Attorney General Charles Warren almost in passing, it served as the basis to intern German legal resident aliens and, to a lesser extent, German-Americans, in an effort to allay public fears about sabotage and espionage activities.[314] After American entry into the war, Congress passed the stricter Espionage Act in June 1917, along with other severe measures in October 1917 and April 1918. Consequently, some 6,500 ethnic Germans were interned during 1917-1918, in several camps located across the country.[315] Among those interned was Dr. Ernst Kunwald, the piano virtuoso and conductor of the Cincinnati Symphony Orchestra; despite being music director of the Cincinnati May Festival, a member of the Optimists Club, and being listed in *Who's Who in America* for 1918-19, he was interned for stating that his heart was with his native Germany in the war.[316] False rumors and misinformation spread by an hysterical public fanned the flames of anti-German sentiment, and played a role in the government's decision to intern those members of the German-American community it deemed threatening, even if there was no proof of wrongdoing on their part.

Four primary locations were utilized for detaining enemy aliens during World War I, including Fort McPherson, in Georgia; Fort Douglas, in Utah; Fort Oglethorpe, also in Georgia; and a converted vacation resort in Hot Springs, North Carolina. Of the four, the most notable was Fort Oglethorpe.[317] Located just southeast of Chattanooga, Tennessee, the army post was adapted, shortly after American entry into the war in April 1917, for use as an internment center for Germans and German-Americans considered most dangerous to national security. By late 1918, near the end of the war, some 4000 detainees, mostly civilians, were held at the camp, coming from a variety of other camps, immigrant detention centers, and jails. Among the inmates was a variety of German legal resident aliens and German-Americans from diverse backgrounds, including sailors and laborers, businessmen and scientists, scholars and musicians.[318] Camp facilities were divided into three categories, in which the prisoners were assigned based on their status. "Camp A" was given over to wealthier and more influential internees, who could afford to pay for their needs and, consequently, developed a higher standard of living. "Camp B" was for the remaining prisoners, offered fewer amenities than did "Camp A," and was consistently overcrowded. "Camp C" was a punishment quarters, where protesters and potential escapees, among others, were held.

While internment life was far from pleasant overall, several concessions were made to the internees, such that education, cultural activities, and recreation made life more bearable inside the complex. Particularly in "Camp A," such activities took place regularly, including university-style lectures on physics, biology, chemistry, and history. Foreign language instruction was given for Spanish, Russian, Hebrew,

Chinese, Sanskrit, and even English, among other languages, while courses in writing business letters, bookkeeping, shorthand, and mathematics were also offered. Internees kept aware of cultural developments by publishing a semi-monthly literary magazine, the *Orgelsdorfer Eulenspiegel*, which featured poetry, satire, and essays, in addition to woodcut illustrations and updates on recent developments in music, from classical to ragtime. With regard to sports, "Camp B" was the center of activity, with several playing fields and a regular schedule of soccer and baseball matches. Weekly concerts served to unify the two camps, as attendance at featured performances, including those by the Tsingtau band and the camp's own symphony orchestra, was consistently high.

When the war ended in November 1918, hopes were high that the internees would be released quickly, and allowed to return to their pre-war lives. However, a repatriation agreement, for the benefit of the stranded German seamen, was not reached until May 1919, leaving other inmates wondering what their fate would be. For many, deportation was the preferred course of action for the government, and the roughly 300 German legal resident aliens and German-Americans not deported continued to live in the camps. Not until March-April 1920 were the remaining 200 internees released, when the World War I internment camps finally were closed for good.

The Criteria for Internment of German Legal Resident Aliens and German-Americans in the World War II Era

The first steps towards the eventual internment of German enemy aliens came on September 6, 1939, just after the outbreak of World War II in Europe. At that time, the Emergency Detention Program was put into place by President Roosevelt, instructing the Justice Department to arrest and detain those persons that they deemed dangerous "in the event of war, invasion, or insurrection in and of a foreign enemy."[319] Additionally, the Federal Bureau of Investigation was given the responsibility of compiling reports on potential sympathizers with the Nazi cause, including those capable of initiating or assuming leadership roles in a public uprising. Three distinct categories of suspects were developed: 1) The "A" category, consisting of aliens who led cultural or assistance organizations; 2) the "B" category, into which slightly less suspicious aliens were grouped; and 3) the "C" category, made up of members of ethnic groups and those who donated money to them.[320] While the prime source for such information was the Alien Registration Act, as well as membership information on the German-American Bund, lists were also compiled based on those who held subscriptions to German-language newspapers, attended German Day festivities, or were leaders, or even members, of local German-American societies. In gathering such information, over two years before American involvement in the war, the government clearly was preparing for an eventual state of hostilities with Germany, and formulating policy on what to do with German legal resident aliens.

The debate over interning German legal resident aliens and German-Americans was the source of considerable friction within government and military circles. A number of local, state, and federal officials put pressure on the government to take action against the German element, in the face of European war and the negative publicity surrounding organizations such as the German-American Bund. By late 1941, a growing call had sounded to intern so-called "enemy aliens" for the duration of the war, even though the United States was not engaged in hostilities with Germany. Within the government, the leading proponent of a sweeping internment of the German element was General John L. DeWitt, the sixty-two-year-old leader of the Western Defense Command. In the view of DeWitt, by excluding all German legal resident aliens and German-Americans sympathetic to Nazi concerns or the Fatherland, national security concerns would be greatly lessened, and the threat of a domestic concern in the face of a global war would be negligible.

On the other hand, numerous political and military leaders, not to mention members of the general populace, expressed grave reservations about the prospect of a massive internment of Germans and German-Americans. According to Stephen C. Fox, several main concerns opposing internment were expressed in high-level meetings, including the following: 1) Unduly persecuting German legal resident aliens and German-Americans again, as was the case in World War I, could create unrest among just the people the government did not want to provoke; 2) beyond alienating the German nationals and German-Americans, a harsh anti-German policy might alienate the children of such people, leading to generations of discord with the government; 3) bureaucratic rivalries and strenuous differences of opinion would create factions within the government and military, potentially a greater long-term danger; and 4) most prevalent among the concerns, that the exceedingly large number of

German legal resident aliens and German-Americans in the United States made such an effort, both economically and in terms of manpower needed, virtually impossible to realize.[321]

The turning point in the internment debate came in the months subsequent to Japan's attack on Pearl Harbor, and the declaration of war between Germany and the United States. The initial reaction of the Roosevelt Administration to the Pearl Harbor bombing on December 7 was to begin rounding up, on the following day, German, Italian, and Japanese legal resident aliens considered to be security threats, based on the master lists already compiled, although there were as yet no hostilities between the United States and the European nations. Legal basis for the action was provided by Proclamation 2525, signed immediately after Pearl Harbor by President Roosevelt pursuant to the Enemy Alien Act of 1798; as amended, the order gave the government full authority to detain enemy aliens and confiscate enemy alien property at will.[322]

From the beginning of American involvement in World War II, it was clear that detention and internment proceedings would extend to American citizens, as well as enemy aliens. As reproduced by Arthur D. Jacobs and Joseph E. Fallon in volume four of a recently published multivolume work, *The German-Americans in the World Wars*, a December 8, 1941 memorandum from FBI head J. Edgar Hoover stressed that the government had already developed not only a "hit list" of people targeted for arrest, but that the majority of those to be arrested were Americans, rather than Germans. According to Hoover:

> The following figures represent the number of individuals in various categories who are being considered for custodial detention:

German Aliens	636
American Citizens Sympathetic to Germany	1,393
Persons of German Descent Whose Citizenship is Unknown:	1,694

Thus it can be seen that German legal resident aliens, as enemy aliens, were not the sole target of the U.S. Government. Rather, German-Americans, either born in this country or nationalized as citizens, constituted a larger group for arrest and potential detention.

From December 7-10, before the United States and Germany were formally at war with each other, the FBI arrested a total of 857 Germans, in thirty-five states. Additionally, in Hawaii, where the Japanese attack had polarized the conflict between the United States and the Axis powers, the entire German-American community was placed under arrest. Subsequent federal action against German enemy aliens was buoyed by public support; according to a public opinion poll from the Office of Facts and Figures, in the Office for Emergency Management, forty-six percent of those questioned considered the Germans to be the most dangerous alien group in the United States, compared with thirty-five percent who responded with the Japanese.[323]

Following the arrest of suspicious German legal resident aliens and German-Americans, establishment of alien hearing boards across the country, and recommendations of internment in selected cases, legal steps were necessary to coordinate internment policy and provide for facilities. To this end, on February 19, 1942, President Roosevelt signed Executive Order 9066, a measure designed to exclude those deemed to be "enemy aliens" and those of "enemy ancestry" from militarily strategic areas. By definition, "enemy aliens" were considered those people who were not U.S. citizens, and came from a country at war with the United States; people of "enemy ancestry" were those who in fact were citizens of the United States, whether by naturalization or by birth, of German, Italian, or Japanese heritage.[324] For the first time in American history, the government was not only attempting to exclude those it considered to be undesirable "foreigners," but also moved against its own citizens, without credible evidence of any wrongdoing on their part.

The impact of Executive Order 9066 and the actions preceding it, on ethnic Germans, Italians, and Japanese in the United States, should not be understated. Beyond excluding enemy aliens and those of enemy ancestry from strategic areas, they provided the basis for enemy alien hearings without regard for due process; for internment for some six years of people arbitrarily considered a threat to national interests; allowed for the confiscation of property and life savings without provision for compensation or reimbursement; and placed a black mark on the records of German legal resident aliens and selected German-Americans which, to date, has yet to be removed or explained officially.

However, Executive Order 9066 was not the only provision which granted the military and government the authority to exclude and intern aliens and American citizens. On March 18, 1942, as a result of another Executive Order, the War Relocation Authority was established within the Office for Emergency Management. The War Relocation Authority was formally given the task of removing, relocating, maintaining, and supervising those people excluded by order of the Secretary of War, or by military commanders within designated military security zones. In turn, the Authority created and maintained relocation centers, which housed evacuees, as well as relocation offices, which assisted displaced enemy aliens and those of enemy ancestry displaced from restricted zones. Consequently, exclusion and internment became official policies of the United States Government, beginning in the hours following the bombing of Pearl Harbor and continuing until June 1948.

Internment Camps During the World War II Era

Following the arrest of enemy aliens and people of enemy alien ancestry, suspects were transferred to temporary detention centers near the location of residence and arrest. In many cases, these were local jails or specially created holding facilities, meant to hold detainees only briefly, until a final determination of their status was made. In Cincinnati, local holding facilities, such as the jail, the Hamilton County Workhouse, and the Hotel Gibson, were used on occasion, as circumstances warranted, with the main detention center located at the old post office garage on Fourth Street. From this point, detainees were given hearings to determine their status, and whether they would be released outright, given conditional parole, or were to be placed in an internment facility. Those who were sentenced to internment were immediately sent to one of the designated internment centers across the country, based on their gender and family situation. The majority of the centers were operated by the Immigration and Naturalization Service or the Army.

Internment camps were grouped into the following four categories: 1) Adult males, females, and children, each held in separate areas; 2) adult males and females, held in separate compounds; 3) adult males only; and 4) families, in which entire families were held in individual quarters.

Two prominent camps, both of which were under the jurisdiction of the Immigration and Naturalization Service, housed adult males, adult females, and children. The first camp, Ellis Island in New York Harbor, was somewhat less conventional than other internment facilities of the day.

Often overcrowded, it served as a multi-purpose facility, used both as an intake processing center for new internees from the east coast, and a final stop for enemy aliens being repatriated or deported, frequently to Germany. Ellis Island also served as collection point for internees waiting to be relocated, after another internment facility was closed. The last of the German internees were released from Ellis Island in June 1948.[325]

The second all-purpose camp, in Seagoville, Texas, was used as a women's reformatory before it housed German legal resident alien and German-American men, women, and children. Seagoville also was somewhat distinct in internment history, in that the camp had no fence to keep internees inside the compound. Instead, the facility was surrounded by a so-called "white line" on the ground, which was patrolled by armed guards, beyond which internees were not to journey. While Seagoville was home to a mixture of men, women, and children, the primary occupants were married couples and single women; families were interned there on occasion, but not to the extent that would be the case in other, designated "family" internment camps.[326]

A relatively large number of internment camps were utilized for adult males only. Among those known to have housed German enemy aliens and German-Americans, and under supervision of the United States Army, were Fort Meade, in Maryland; Camp Forrest, in Tennessee; and Fort Oglethorpe, in Georgia, reprising its World War I role as an internment center. Under the supervision of the Immigration and Naturalization Service were Fort Lincoln, in North Dakota; and a camp in Kenedy, Texas. Still unclear is under whose authority several other camps operated, such as Camp McCoy, in Wisconsin; Fort Stanton, in New Mexico; Fort Missoula, in Montana; and a camp in Stringtown, Oklahoma.[327]

Several of the above listed all-male camps are noteworthy among internment centers. The Fort Lincoln facility was home base to internees who also were assigned to work details on the Northern Pacific Railroad and for the Forest Service. In such cases, internees often resided outside of the actual internment center, in special railroad cars, trailers, or other housing, albeit under guard, until their service was completed.[328] The Stringtown center, located within the Stringtown Correctional Facility, was one of the smaller internment camps, with a capacity of some 500 men. Activated on March 30, 1942, it was open for just over a year, before closing in June 1943. Mostly German legal resident aliens were interned within the camp, in which two died; their remains were interred at nearby Ft. Reno. Stringtown was one of three Oklahoma internment centers, including Ft. Sill (which confined mostly Japanese-Americans) and McAlester Alien Internment Camp (which primarily interned Italian aliens).[329] Camp McCoy, Fort Meade, Fort Oglethorpe, and Camp Forrest were party to a system of rotating internees, to make room for German prisoners of war from Europe. As more space was needed for an increasing number of German prisoners, the Immigration and Naturalization Service chose to consolidate its internment centers, and shift internees to other camps on occasion.[330]

The primary family internment center during the war was located in Crystal City, Texas. Opened on December 12, 1942, by December 15 the camp was home to thirty-five families, some 130 people, of German heritage. Due to an initial shortage of housing, twelve of the families were forced to share cottages until government workers had time to construct sufficient cottages for everyone.[331] Despite cramped living quarters and other hardships, living at the Crystal City facility was preferable to other camps for many of the adult male internees, since they could at least reside with their families, and maintain some semblance of a family life together.

Less well known than the internment camps was a smaller group of homes, which were used in individual cases to detain aliens with special circumstances. One noteworthy example of this, under the direction of the Immigration and Naturalization Service, were the Homes of the Good Shepherd, used as a detention center for younger women and girls not sent to internment camps. The Good Shepherd Homes, located in Buffalo, Philadelphia, Cleveland, Milwaukee, Chicago, and Omaha, provided guidance and direction for youthful or troubled female detainees of German stock, in keeping with the principles of the Homes; otherwise before and during the internment program, the Catholic Church had utilized the Homes to house unwed mothers and "wayward girls," as a means to educate and assist them.[332]

Life in the Internment Camps

For many internees, living in internment camps during World War II represented the most traumatic experience of their lives. In most cases, internees had been arrested and sentenced to internment with great haste, with no time to gather personal possessions or say good-bye to loved ones.

In many of such cases, internees were not formally advised of what crime they may have committed, and were likewise kept in the dark about their status as prisoners, where they were being taken to, and for how long. Internment represented an abrupt change in life for internees, a totally different experience from the life they had been accustomed to. For immigrants, it was seen as a repudiation of the American dream; many refugees from Nazi Germany would later observe that such treatment was what they had tried to leave behind in fleeing their native land.

Inside a typical internment facility, internees found their freedom restricted, and their ability to pursue their own individual lives lessened, given the communal nature of such a place. Nevertheless, certain amenities were made available to internees, in order to enjoy some of the comforts of home despite their confinement; according to the INS, it was "important that normal living conditions prevail,"[333] to the extent such was possible.

The Crystal City, Texas, detention facility, functioning as the primary camp for entire families, provided an enlightening perspective on what internment life was like. While most men in the Crystal City camp were forcibly interned, most of the women and children were classified as "voluntary" internees, joining the men due to family and economic hardship. Though many of the adult males were foreign-born, mostly in Germany and Japan, "practically all children and many women" internees were American born and raised.[334]

Located 110 miles southwest of San Antonio, the camp was heavily fortified with fencing and guard towers, with armed guards on patrol twenty four hours per day. By night, floodlights illuminating the perimeter of the camp were bright enough to be seen almost to the border of Mexico. Escape from the center was highly unlikely, especially in the summer months; located "in an extremely isolated spot," temperatures in the vicinity of the camp often rose to near 120 degrees Fahrenheit from June into September.[335] Compounding the problem was the huge number of insects in the area; oversized mosquitoes were a constant threat to internees, and a large scorpion population forced camp residents to shake out their shoes, and watch where they walked, with regularity.

While families often had individual cottages, privacy was otherwise very limited; only a few cottages had private bathrooms, with the majority of people using public showers and latrines. The camp laundry was designed to handle the clothing of over 4,000 internees, with a sewing shop and tailoring shop providing additional services; only the tailoring shop was permitted to charge a nominal fee for its services. For those not eating in their own cottage, a chow line was employed for feeding internees, in a cafeteria setting. With regard to mail delivery, there were few restrictions placed on the number of letters an internee could send or receive; however, censors fluent in English, German, and Spanish monitored all letters and packages, making any alterations deemed necessary before mail was passed along.

Restrictions on personal property also were common. Foodstuffs were rationed at a general store, depending on the size of the family. New arrivals to the camp had their valuables placed in a safe, in exchange for a receipt, with living quarters assigned in advance of arrival. A "very restricted variety" of clothing could be bought at Crystal City, with rationing cards or, on rare occasions, some of the plastic money or scrip used at the camp.[336]

With some 3,500 to 4,000 people living at Crystal City at a given time, health concerns took on great importance. Up to sixty internees per day were treated at camp clinics, though government officials and doctors claimed that ills were often imaginary, traceable to detention life, fences, and the changes internees underwent from their previous way of living. Five doctors, two of whom were Japanese women, were on duty or on call, to assist the over 4,000 internees; the doctors also assisted in the birth of some 250 babies while the facility was operating. Internees isolated for health reasons were provided with their own cottages, with full amenities.[337]

From the beginning of their internment, detainees were placed in charge of maintaining their own homes, and doing most of the camp work themselves. Additionally, internees were obliged to use their own personal funds to beautify, with flowers and home improvements, their cottages and allotted property. Called "morale builders" by federal officials, beautification was undertaken by many internees, particularly among those of German stock; a Japanese gardener took charge of beautifying public grounds in the camp, that much being done at government expense. An unusually high level of cooperation between internees led to remarkable efficiency in accomplishing personal and public work projects; while internees did most of their own work, officials hastened to point out that internees came to live in pleasant homes, under "traditional American standards of decent and humane treatment."[338]   Among the projects organized by internees from all backgrounds was a volunteer fire department.   In other cases, though, differences in ethnic backgrounds were more pronounced.   Ethnic Germans and Japanese generally lived on separate sides of the camp.   Chores assigned to internees were divided by ethnic groups in many cases: Japanese internees did most of the farming, as "the Germans did not like farming"; German males were largely given the responsibility of doing machine work, as well as repair work on machinery and motor vehicles at the camp.   While Japanese women were given responsibilities in cooking and medicine, German women were often left to their own devices, as "generally speaking, the German women declined to work outside of the home."[339]

However, a number of other everyday chores, such as picking up garbage and delivering ice, were done on a rotation basis, with internees of all backgrounds working a minimum number of hours each month. Internees wanting regular jobs often received them, at the rate of ten cents per hour, for twenty to thirty hours per week; such earnings became pocket money for young internees, in order to buy cigarettes or drinks, or to pay for an evening out.   The government kept careful records of payments made to internees; however, bookkeeping mistakes would occur on occasion, and would be taken up, even well after the fact.   In 1947, Gerhard Fuhr received a letter from the government, claiming that he had been overpaid $14.80 in his years of working while interned at Crystal City; he was asked to return the money, a request he chose not to acknowledge.[340]

Aliens also provided for much of their own food procurement and preparation while interned.   Numerous internees maintained small gardens at their cottages, capable of providing fresh vegetables.   A portion of Crystal City's meat, dairy, and produce came from a farm located outside of the camp, maintained by aliens under the direction of the government and the guidance of a Texas rancher.   Government authorities placed great importance on providing internees with ample food of high nutritional value, claiming that good food also was "good for morale."   The farm's cows provided at least part of the 2,500 quarts of milk needed per day in the camp, for the children whose number approximated 1,600 at one point. Food preparation was also a concern; the camp cooks, all Japanese, few of whom spoke English, struggled to learn to prepare American- and German-style food.[341]

Education was also provided for school-age internees, at several schools located within the Crystal City camp. Young children of German stock attended a kindergarten, located at the end of the Vaterland Building. A camp high school was fully accredited by the state of Texas, and provided basic courses in line with the standard high school curriculum. A library assisted students in doing their homework, as well as provided leisure reading material. Upon leaving the camp for reassignment or repatriation, internees were allowed to take with them two books, free of charge, from a selection of available titles.[342]

Recreational activities helped internees to take their minds off of their plight, and in addition provided camp residents with the opportunity to indulge some of their cultural, athletic, and hobby interests. In Crystal City, a camp orchestra was staffed largely by those of German stock, providing a chance to play and hear German classical music, in the "Vaterland Building." Lectures provided educational, cultural, and occasionally political, viewpoints. For athletic competition and exercise, many German detainees took up soccer, while others also played basketball and softball. Japanese internees not otherwise involved in those sports took turns at wrestling and a sort of horseless jousting, as means to pursue physical education. A large swimming pool, previously used as a tank for irrigating the nearby farm, helped make summer heat more bearable for all; unfortunately, seepage problems caused mudholes and unsanitary conditions, forcing the pool to close until internees could fix it with concrete, at a cost of $2,500.00 to the government.[343] The International Red Cross, as well as Swiss and Spanish legations, regularly inspected the camp, among other things making sure that internees had adequate access to sports equipment, radios, newspapers, and books.[344] Inside the camp, German internees published a weekly newspage, the *Lager-Nachrichten*. The paper provided information of interest, in German, such as camp concerns, recommendations on matters including how to send Christmas greetings (and comply with censorship regulations), dates and times of parties given for those departing the camp, library news, and dates and times of camp soccer matches, including starting lineups and team rosters.[345]

Otherwise, beyond parties for and with fellow internees, dances were held regularly for young people and school children, as a way to maintain a social life within the camp. Dances were held on Friday and Saturday nights, with big band records by Tommy and Jimmy Dorsey, among others, providing the beat. However, not all German internees took kindly to dances at the camp; according to one camp resident, "that was kind of frowned on. Because the folks would say, 'You're dancing, and the boys are dying?' They meant the German boys."[346]

Nevertheless, boredom and confinement occasionally wore on the younger internees, who in turn would organize some of their own less conventional entertainment. In one notable instance, several men built a still, in order to ferment cactus and make their own moonshine; their plans went astray when they accidentally burned down a cabin.[347]

Romance was also an issue among younger internees. For teenagers and young male internees, pursuit of the opposite sex was a natural development within the facility. However, the joy of a special relationship, struck up among people with common backgrounds and interests, was also tempered by the pain of loss, as internees often were sent to other camps or repatriated, in many cases on short notice. According to Eberhard Fuhr, "You don't really want to get involved, but you eventually wind up getting involved. You get a little hurt when you invest your love, your affection in somebody, and then they're gone."[348] However, in Eberhard's case and several others, the story had a happy ending; after Eberhard got to know Barbara, a nurse's aide, in the hospital while having his thumb treated, their casual acquaintance began to turn into a deeper friendship, ultimately to culminate in marriage in 1948.

Other Internment of Ethnic Germans in the United States

While little is known publicly of the internment of German legal resident aliens and German-Americans living in the United States, even less is known of some 2,800 ethnic Germans, brought to the United States from twelve Latin American countries for temporary internment.[349]

When the United States entered into hostilities with Germany in December 1941, a small number of American tourists and diplomats were trapped behind enemy lines, in Germany and in German-occupied nations. Given the state of war existing between the powers, the return of American citizens to their native land was out of the question without a special agreement. Recognizing the special situation, the United States Government initiated contact with the Latin American countries, with the purpose of interning those people that were deemed a threat to the security and stability of the Americas. The program was coordinated by Gen.

George Marshall, the same general who would be instrumental in rebuilding postwar Germany, through the Marshall Plan.

While the premise of the government's action was to "preserve ... the integrity and solidarity of the American continent [from] subversive activity," the government actually possessed evidence on only about 140 of the 5,000 total internees brought to America. Indeed, a later, confidential government memo stated that "the Alien Enemy Control Unit has little information concerning aliens who were brought to the United States from Latin America."[350] Far from focusing solely on high-ranking officials and people in prominent places, action taken against residents of Latin America would eventually affect numerous people otherwise out of touch with political and military strategy:

> What began as a controlled, closely monitored deportation program to detain potentially dangerous diplomatic and consular officials of Axis nations and Axis businessmen grew to include enemy aliens who were teachers, small businessmen, tailors and barbers.[351]

Upon returning to their homes, often many years later, the former internees found that matters had been made worse by the loss of all of their personal property. In some cases, looters absconded with possessions of value; in other instances, Latin American countries seized farms and businesses from the deported aliens, to sell them off and deposit the funds in national treasury accounts.

The arrest of Latin American German enemy aliens was carried out in a similar manner to that utilized against detainees in the United States, in that many arrests were carried out at night, or otherwise in an inconspicuous manner. In most cases, arrests were made by local police forces in the various Latin American countries. Local authorities in turn transferred custody of the detainees to American soldiers, who took the apprehended foreign nationals to a secure location to await processing. Deportation to the United States was conducted at a pace comfortable for both Latin American countries and the United States; for Immigration and Naturalization Service administrators, a leisurely pace seemed most suitable, in an effort to avoid overcrowding at internment facilities within the United States.[352] However, unlike in the United States, most Latin American enemy aliens were not given a hearing on their case. In almost all cases, there was no trial, no hearing, and no evidence presented against those arrested; no accusations were made against most Latin American aliens, nor were they formally charged with any crimes.

The purpose of bringing Latin American ethnic Germans to the United States was to have a ready pool of German nationals, to send back to Germany in exchange for Americans caught behind enemy lines after December 1941. In a private memo, General Marshall stated that "these interned nationals are to be used for exchange with interned American civilian nationals," a policy later brought to fruition through six prisoner exchanges with Nazi Germany. From the outset of the program, government officials were concerned with the possible repercussions of word leaking out to the general public, and that the government might be seen as the aggressor in the affair. Such concerns were expressed in a 1943 State Department memo, originating in the Division of American Republics, in which it was stated that "it is undesirable for the written record to show that the initiative for the roundup came from us."[353] In subsequent years, as evidence of the program leaked out or was disclosed through the Freedom of Information Act, criticism of the government's internment policy was expressed on various occasions, ranging from condemnation by former internees such as Arthur Jacobs, to accusations of kidnapping, by NBC on the television program *Dateline*.

The End of Internment of Enemy Aliens

With the stated goal of internment being to reduce the threat of subversive activity in the United States during World War II, internees and their families held little hope of release before the end of the war. By May 1945, with the end of World War II in Europe, German alien enemies expected to be released in short order, and allowed to return to the freedom they had experienced, and the lives they had lived, before the war. Such hopes proved unrealistic; internment continued as an official policy of the United States Government well after the conclusion of hostilities, both in Europe and the Pacific.

As the end of World War II approached in 1945, government officials began to turn their attention to the problematic issue of what to do with the enemy aliens, and how soon. As a first step towards resolving the matter, President Harry S. Truman issued Proclamation 2655, which authorized the government to deport enemy aliens considered to pose danger to the public peace and safety of the nation. In conjunction with Latin American nations, during the Latin American Conference on Problems of War and Peace, a further resolution was made to prevent wartime deportees from residing in the Western Hemisphere, should their presence be deemed undesirable by federal officials. Clearly, American policy was designed not only to influence the status of enemy aliens in the United States, but also to exercise control of the issue in other American nations.[354]

Initial action against German legal resident aliens was hindered by a disagreement between the Departments of State and Justice over exactly what security measures were best taken against internees and their families. While the Justice Department preferred to remove internees from its jurisdiction and refrain from deportation and further internment, the State Department took a more firm approach, preferring to deport detainees considered dangerous, to Germany or elsewhere outside of the hemisphere. Taking the initiative to further its aims, the State Department lobbied President Truman for support by citing a long-term plan for American security, and culminated its efforts by securing a proclamation from Truman, directing the Secretary of State to exclude enemy aliens remaining in America from the Western Hemisphere, including aliens brought in from Latin America and later considered to be not only enemy, but also illegal, aliens. Caught in the middle were children of aliens born in the United States; while not legally subject to deportation, they were not in a position to support themselves, financially or otherwise, in the United States. In many cases, without immediate family in America and not wanting to be placed in an orphanage, the children were left with no alternative but to follow their parents in deportation.

By December 1945, deportation of undesirable aliens had begun, a process which would last until July 1947. For their part, enemy aliens did not leave American shores without first putting up a fight. A group of German legal resident aliens challenged the basis of their internment, claiming that they could not be considered enemy aliens as defined by the Alien Enemy Act of 1798; according to the internees, they could not be considered natives or citizens of an enemy nation, particularly after the conclusion of the war. The effort ultimately was defeated in January 1946 in federal district court, clearing the way for the deportment of at least 897 German aliens, pending the formality of a hearing before deportation to former Axis countries.[355]

German legal resident aliens and their families being sent back to Germany were first transported to Ellis Island, New York, where they were lodged in barracks-type facilities until the time came to leave

America. In most cases, internees were allowed to take only a small portion of their possessions, while selling or leaving behind other personal belongings.

For some two years after the end of the war in Europe, repatriation of German aliens and their families continued unabated. Recognizing that the need to maintain national security interests with regard to aliens had changed over the previous two years, Senator William Langer, of North Dakota, conducted a hearing of the Senate Foreign Relations Committee in 1947 at Ellis Island, with the purpose of determining if sufficient cause existed for the deportation of aliens. Finding no basis for the policy, Langer introduced a bill in the Senate in July 1947, calling for the U.S. Attorney General to release all remaining German detainees from Ellis Island, and to suspend further deportation of enemy aliens. Within two weeks, definitive action was taken against internment as a policy of the United States Government, and the first group of internees being held at Ellis Island were dismissed from the custody of the government. Internment and deportation were phased out of American policy towards aliens, with the final release of approximately 100 German legal resident aliens, and a handful of German-Americans, coming in June 1948, over three years after the end of World War II in Europe.

A Cincinnati Enemy Alien Story: The Fuhr Family

To understand better the impact World War II, and the policies associated with it, had on the German-American community, it is worthwhile to examine the case of a Cincinnati family that was subjected to arrest, detention, and internment as enemy aliens. The experience of the Fuhr family is representative of that which many other German-American families, as well as individual German legal resident aliens and German-Americans, endured during the 1940s.

Carl Fuhr grew up in a small town in northern Germany, later working in chemical factories near Cologne before he emigrated to the United States in 1927. In 1922 he took a wife, Anna, in Germany; in 1924, they had their first child, Julius, and their second, Eberhard, in 1925. When Carl Fuhr emigrated to the United States in 1927, he went alone, but after establishing himself as a baker in his new country, he sent for the rest of the family in 1929. Later that year, a third son, Gerhard, was born. Despite a growing anti-German sentiment during the 1930s, the

Fuhrs chose not to seek citizenship; in fact, no serious consideration was ever given to the idea.[356]

In 1940, the Fuhr family registered according to the Alien Registration Act, and continued to comply with all restrictions placed on enemy aliens after the outbreak of war in December 1941. Without warning, in August 1942, Carl and Anna Fuhr were arrested as enemy aliens and, within a short time, sent to the Seagoville, Texas, internment facility, before being transferred to the Crystal City camp. Gerhard, at the time twelve years old, went into internment with his parents, classified as a "voluntary" internee; had he not chosen to go with them, he would have been sent to an orphanage instead. He recalled his experience in going to, and living in, the Seagoville camp:

> Everything was in limbo. They took us in a van to the Union Terminal, [we] got on a train, rumbled off to St. Louis ... and headed off to Seagoville, Texas, my first internment camp. You ate in a communal dining room, you ate and you went back to your little room, with a bed, a desk, a light, and a chair. The dimensions were probably about six by eight feet. We could open up the bars in the windows. We grew some crops, we had a school, we had an auditorium where I saw "Bambi."[357]

The internment of his parents and younger brother came as a complete surprise to Eberhard, who found out the news upon his return from summer camp in North Carolina: "I didn't know about this until I walked in the door and said, "Where's Mom and Pop?" Julius said, "They were interned two weeks ago. We didn't want to get you upset, because you couldn't do anything about it anyway."[358] When Julius went away to college in the fall, with a football scholarship, Eberhard was left alone at home, paying for groceries with money earned from a *Cincinnati Enquirer* paper route. After the football season, Julius left college and returned home to assist in maintaining the Fuhr home, taking a job in a local brewery to help pay the bills.

Eberhard had his first encounter with federal authorities in November 1942; they asked him to come downtown with them, late at night, to answer questions about his family and his loyalties in the event that he would be drafted at age eighteen. In the course of the interrogation, Fuhr was repeatedly confronted with "evidence," preceded with phrases such as "Somebody said that ..." and "Some neighbors said ...". Eberhard believes that the people who discussed him with federal authorities were fellow German-Americans, or even family members, who wished to deflect attention away from themselves; and that some people with a grudge against German legal resident aliens took advantage of opportunities to get them into trouble:

> All [the authorities] presented was raw FBI data, which is maybe somebody calls in and says, "You know, this guy's got bombs in his house," or something, and the FBI puts it down. Or "He's got Nazi propaganda in his house." And it's not true. But it becomes fact.[359]

On March 23, 1943, Eberhard was taken out of his English class at Woodward High School by his principal, and without warning was apprehended by two federal authorities. The arrest was a blow to Eberhard and his school plans; two months away from graduation, he was deprived of the opportunity to graduate with his classmates. After the seventeen-year-old high school senior was handcuffed outside the building; the authorities then took him to the brewery, where Julius also was apprehended, and then to the police station for booking on suspicion. After spending an hour in a jail cell, the two were sent to the Workhouse, the old Hamilton County prison. Held in primitive conditions, including a metal bucket to be used for a toilet, the brothers were kept far away from each other. No secret was made of the reason for their presence in prison; a guard proclaimed for other inmates and authorities to hear, "Hey, we've got a couple of Nazis here. These guys want to fight for Hitler."[360]

The next morning, federal authorities questioned the brothers at the federal building in downtown Cincinnati. The interrogation touched upon aspects of the family's life as German legal resident aliens and members of the German-American community, including questions such as "Five years ago did you say that Hitler was good for Germany?"; "Did you go to a German Day at Coney Island?," after which they showed pictures of the family members in attendance; and "Your cousin from Germany ... just came up the Ohio River in a submarine and wants you to put him up. What are you going to tell him?"[361]

After the hearing, the brothers were driven home, told to pick up two changes of clothes, and then driven back to jail. The next morning, they were driven to Chicago, to a detention center there, without the opportunity to secure their home in Cincinnati or take any personal possessions with them. According to Eberhard, the family lost everything, and was never compensated:

> When my older brother and I were taken away, they said, "Take two
> changes of clothing, because if you go [to Chicago], you'll come back to
> the house and close it up." And that was it. That was the last time I
> saw the house. It was gone. Everything in it was gone.[362]

The sudden upheaval in an otherwise routine life left Eberhard
shaken; the German enemy alien considered himself far more American
than German:

> Up to that point I was a happy-go-lucky high school jock. I didn't do
> too well in school with my grades. I just played football, baseball, and
> had a lot of fun. I wanted to be a professional baseball player. I wanted
> to be the best catcher that ever played for the Cincinnati Reds.[363]

As boys growing up in America, Julius and Eberhard always felt
themselves to be American, even though others pointed out that they were
German by birth and citizenship. According to Eberhard, "I grew up
knowing I was a German, because everybody in the neighborhood
reminded me of it. As a matter of fact, I couldn't even speak German ... I
think things became exacerbated after 1938, 1939, when people realized
there was a problem over there in Europe."[364] In the case of Gerhard,
born and raised in the United States, stereotypes dominated even the
children's games he would play with friends: "Up to about [the age of]
eleven, twelve, thirteen, fourteen, I think those things are important ... I
went from a Hun to a Nazi in the war games we played."[365]

In Chicago, Julius and Eberhard were held at 4800 S. Ellis Avenue,
in a converted mansion. The twenty-five to thirty detainees rotated chores
such as scrubbing the floors, tending a small outdoor garden, and kitchen
duty; in their free time, detainees had little to do but read, talk, or play
cards. Armed guards patrolled the grounds, but according to Eberhard,
security was not as tight as might have been expected. In one case, he
stumbled upon an unlocked closet full of munitions: "This thing was
loaded with rifles. Ammunition and the whole bit. It was totally unlocked.
We could have blasted our way out. But we didn't." On another occasion,
Eberhard was bribed to steal away from the center to buy beer: "And like
a jerk I did it. I didn't get caught. My problem was to sneak back in."
With regard to why he didn't try to escape while out, he stated that the
thought crossed his mind, "But the problem was, any identity papers were
taken away from you. And, you see, I was down to my last pair of pants
and they had holes ... I didn't have any socks on, because I ran out. I
quickly said, 'Hey, what am I going to do when I get away?'"[366]

In July 1943 Julius and Eberhard were sent by train to join their parents and their brother Gerhard at the INS family camp in Crystal City. The Fuhr family resided there until April 1947, when they were sent back to Cincinnati to prepare for possible deportation. The family resided in a four-room multifamily unit, with cooking facilities and a small garden to grow vegetables; the brothers slept in a nearby barracks with other males of their age. According to Eberhard, camp conditions were adequate, far from a concentration camp, if also not with all the amenities of home:

> I think you have to separate the living conditions from the other things that make it a place of prison. From a standpoint of living conditions, you couldn't really get better. Because I compare it to, say, the Hamilton County Workhouse, which [was] terrible. At Crystal City, you could get out, you could see the sun shine, you were with your family. We had movies twice a week, there were dances there. The educational system was kind of crappy, but you'd make the best of it.[367]

Despite the acceptable accommodations at Crystal City, internees felt the stigma of their situation, particularly on rare occasions when family and friends visited internees at the camp. Eberhard's wife Barbara recalled the difficulty of such a situation:

> The only time I felt [shame], my grandparents came to visit us one time. They lived in Texas, and they came to visit us. That was the only time I felt ashamed, embarrassed, imprisoned. I felt ... it was worse than detention sitting in high school ... That was the only real time that I felt humiliation.[368]

By 1943, some of the Crystal City internees were being repatriated to Germany; by the end of the war, some 4,450 Germans and their families had been deported. Though Eberhard was largely unfamiliar with Germany, he signed up to be repatriated in 1944; his girlfriend Millie and her family were being deported, and he wanted to follow them.[369] According to Eberhard:

> I did try to sign up to be repatriated to Germany, but they wouldn't let me go. But I think there were three, more or less exchanges between citizens ... from the United States to Germany and vice versa. But the last one, I think, was in January 1945.[370]

Like many people, Fuhr had had enough, and saw repatriation as the best way to get away from internment life: "[Officials asked,] 'Why did I really want to go back? Did I want to kill Americans, or did I just want some freedom?' I was military age, but then they sent some other guys there that were military age too. I just wanted to get out."[371]

After his internment ended in 1947, Eberhard went to college, and eventually took a job as a salesman for Shell Oil. After becoming a student at Ohio University in 1949, he applied to become a United States citizen, and was naturalized in 1955. In 1958, Shell transferred him to Cincinnati; it was a move which Eberhard made with reluctance:

> I never really wanted to come back to Cincinnati, because I really felt that the Germans that were [in Cincinnati], a lot of those were responsible for my plight, to cover their own little tails. Of course, Gerhard came back ... I told him never to come back.[372]

Though Eberhard did not choose to be apprehended, detained, and interned by the government, he insists that the country had a right to intern him as an enemy alien. According to Fuhr, it is necessary to take precautions in times of war, even if personal freedoms occasionally must be sacrificed:

> I've always felt this, as an alien born in Germany, that ... even though I was underage, I believe any nation at war can intern the citizens of another country they're at war with, but when the war is over, it should revert to the status prior to the war.[373]

Years after his internment, Eberhard insisted that he sought neither monetary compensation nor an apology for his internment as a German legal resident alien; his goal was formal recognition of the internment of members of the German-American community, particularly after the war had ended:

> I don't think [German legal resident aliens] necessarily should be compensated, [though] ... guys like [Gerhard] should be compensated. He's a native; because his parents are considered dangerous enemy aliens, and his brothers are considered dangerous enemy aliens, he's bearing this terrible guilt and he shouldn't have to. I do think there should be recognition that the Germans were indeed interned, and it really wasn't necessary to have these phony hearings where no witnesses were permitted and counsel was denied. They really didn't have a right to keep us interned after the war was over.[374]

Conclusions

To summarize, while internment of German legal resident aliens and a smaller number of German-Americans served to lessen security risks for the United States during a time of war, it also proved to be a controversial strategy among American political and military leaders at the highest levels. The issue of internment brought into focus the clash of two fundamental ideals in American society: The right of people in the United States, whether Americans or not, to live in freedom, under the presumption of innocence of wrongdoing until proven guilty; and the needs of the nation to respect national security interests and safeguard its people in a time of international warfare.

The indiscriminate and secretive manner in which German legal resident aliens and German-Americans considered threatening were arrested and, in some cases, interned, overestimated the extent to which such people posed a threat to American interests. Documentation only recently declassified by the government, and exhaustively compiled in the newly published multivolume work *German-Americans in the World Wars*, clearly shows that federal officials, in charge of formulating and carrying out internment as a wartime policy, were unsure of how to approach the issue, and often reacted more out of caution than on the basis of proof of wrongdoing. Subsequent governmental denial of responsibility, and a general unwillingness to address the desire of former internees to have their permanent records cleared, would reflect poorly on the expressed desire of the federal government to make a full accounting of the wartime treatment of enemy aliens and Americans of enemy ethnic background.

In later years, the United States Government would acknowledge the internment of America's Japanese element and give them redress. However, the German-American community would find its efforts to receive equal treatment go unrewarded, implying the German legal resident aliens and German-Americans were not interned during the World War II era. Such a position directly contributed to the widely held, and mistaken, impression that America's German element was not arrested, detained, and interned during that critical time in American history. On the contrary, recently uncovered, declassified federal documents have provided indisputable factual information about the internment of German legal resident aliens and German-Americans.

Chapter VI

German-American Internees in the Post-World War II Era

With the release of German-American internees from their World War II internment camps, detainees were left with the difficult task of putting back together lives disrupted, and permanently changed, up to six years earlier. Those internees fortunate enough to be released outright went away with only the possessions they had with them, in search of families and friends they could go back to. Returning to their previous homes often was not an option, as in many cases individual houses had long since been ransacked, or foreclosed by banks, with personal possessions left behind having been sold to pay bills, if they hadn't been stolen by looters beforehand. Also of concern was the internees' need to find employment in beginning a new life, made more difficult by having to explain, or artfully evade the issue of, where and why they recently had been interned. Others were not so fortunate, as individuals and even entire families were often repatriated to postwar Germany, to be placed in prison camps until their fate could be determined, or to be left to fend for themselves in a country they no longer knew. For German-Americans born in the United States, particularly the women and children who made up the majority of those sent to Germany, the adjustment was especially difficult.

While the vast majority of internees were able to resume their lives and make necessary adjustments, the federal government proved unwilling to address the issue of the internment of America's German element. Government officials repeatedly refused requests by German-American former internees to have their records cleared of wrongdoing, though no evidence of wrongdoing existed, and to give formal recognition to their internment; meanwhile, a variety of laws were passed, designed to compensate Americans of Japanese descent for their arrest and internment during World War II. To date, while Japanese-Americans have been given legal protection, formal recognition, and monetary compensation for their wrongful arrest and internment, America's German element has failed to receive equal treatment, despite governmental documentation clearly showing the basis for redress.

Such a failure is not due to a lack of effort to rectify the situation by interested parties. In recent years, former internees Arthur Jacobs and Eberhard Fuhr, among others, and organizations such as the German-American National Congress and the Steuben Society, have called for the government to address the German-American question in earnest. Scholars have unearthed long-unseen documents, federal and otherwise, which place the events of World War II in a new light. Further, an increasing number of former internees have shown a willingness to discuss, openly and frankly, the details of their experience. It is their desire to set the historical record straight, more than to receive personal gain, and to come to terms with the widespread feelings of guilt and shame that many have felt for the past half century.

German-American Internees Immediately After World War II

As the remainder of the 10,905 German-American internees were released from custody beginning in late 1945, the government was faced with the dilemma of what to do with the people it had considered to be dangerous to national security. Far from simply choosing to release internees outright after the end of the war with Germany, the government chose to delay action on releasing internees until it could determine the best course of action. Consequently, detainees who had felt that the end of the war in Europe would mean the beginning of freedom, found instead that it marked the beginning of a new period of uncertainty and isolation.

In the face of uncertainty about how to handle the internees, the government chose to delay action until a clear set of objectives was formulated. Within six months, federal officials decided upon two basic plans for handling internees: 1) Release outright those deemed non-threatening to American postwar concerns, namely those seen as least likely to speak out against or strike back at, and as a result cause difficulties for, governmental and military authorities; and 2) maintain in detention those felt to constitute a continued threat to American interests, within or outside of America's German community. In the meantime, internees were given the responsibility of preparing internment centers for dismantling and reconfiguration. In Crystal City, Texas, as elsewhere, camp buildings were taken down as internees were sent to other camps or deported; divided into sections and numbered, buildings were shipped to border patrol stations elsewhere, or placed at the disposal of army and governmental officials as the need arose.[375]

For those the government decided to deport, it was first necessary to transfer them to a centralized location, in preparation for final disposition of cases and transport by ship to Germany. Federal officials transferred internees to Ellis Island, New York, in preparation for final deportation, with entire families often designated for relocation to Germany. As with initial internment actions, many wives and children were obliged to follow husbands and fathers into deportation, due to economic hardship in America, as well as the fact that, in the case of voluntary internees, many of those who chose to enter internment camps to be with family members, were not allowed to reverse their decision.

Unlike camps such as Crystal City, which provided internees with at least some semblance of comfort and freedom, the Ellis Island center was condemned as being far more oppressive. According to Cincinnati internee Eberhard Fuhr:

> At least at Crystal City we had a big perimeter we could walk around, so there was a certain feeling of freedom. At Ellis Island you were confined to this big room. It was a real, total bore. We did a lot of talking and a lot of card playing and a lot of waiting. I painted for ten cents an hour because I needed that for cigarettes, but above all because you needed to keep yourself busy. Otherwise you'd go daffy.[376]

At Ellis Island, internees were granted just one visitor per week, for one hour. As in other camps, internees held only limited possessions, usually only as much as they could store within a highly confined space.[377]

Following a nine-day voyage by ship, deportees arrived in port in northern Germany, where they were met by armed guards and prepared for transport to established prisoner camps, such as in Hohen Asberg, a high-altitude, high security facility for those deemed most dangerous by American officials. Prisoners were separated by gender; despite its designation as a camp for the most threatening of those deported, a significant proportion of detainees were women and children.

Ironically, the end of the deportation of German-Americans and German nationals was brought about not by government officials, but rather by internees in the Crystal City camp. In late 1945, a group of internees organized a committee designed to prevent their deportation upon release from the camp. Internees donated pocket change to raise money for a lawyer, who would use the test case in an attempt to show that the deportation of internees to Germany was unconstitutional. Though the test case was dismissed from the U.S. Court of Appeals in May 1946, INS officials apparently feared a Supreme Court appeal enough to instruct Crystal City administrators to refrain from attempts to deport internees until further notice.[378] Another effort to assert the legal rights of aliens failed in August 1946, and in the U.S. Circuit Court of Appeals in early 1947, when internees argued that they had the right to have lawyers present and examine witnesses at their repatriation hearings; following the setbacks, the Department of Justice proceeded to issue deportation orders against over 300 German aliens and their family members. However, the court action served its purpose by attracting attention to the enemy alien issue; in June 1947, the Langer hearings into the deportation cases effectively ended the repatriation of Germans and German-Americans by undermining the basis for the action. According to Eberhard Fuhr:

> From the first question you knew it was over. Because the guy asked rational questions. He didn't talk about submarines coming up the Ohio River and stuff like that. It was obvious that it was geared not to find fault but to find reason why you shouldn't be allowed to stay. The first question was "You never intended any disloyalty to the United States?" I said, "Absolutely not." When I walked out I told my brother, "We're out of here. This is all over."[379]

Within a month, in July 1947, Langer introduced his bill in the Senate calling for the immediate release of the remaining 207 internees at Ellis Island. Two weeks later, most of the Ellis Island detainees were indeed freed. Despite the legal authority behind their newfound freedom, some internees took nothing for granted. According to Eberhard Fuhr, the Fuhr brothers left as soon as possible, lest the authorities might have a change of heart:

> [The director of Ellis Island] said, "You're free to go. We'll have your train tickets tomorrow morning to go back to Cincinnati." I said, "When's the next ferry to the mainland?" He said, "Twenty minutes." I went up to my mother and said, "I think they're going to let you go too, but I'm leaving on the next ferry. Goodbye, Mom." Julius made the same ferry. I left my dirty laundry there. I didn't care, because I was gone. I didn't want them to change their minds.[380]

Upon release, the Ellis Island internees faced a similar situation to that encountered by German enemy aliens previously given their freedom. After being confined, in most cases, for a period of years, internees were unable to go back to the lives they had previously lived, in that their previous way of existence was no longer available to them. Many internees did not have a home, as it had been taken away by the authorities, with its contents either sold or stolen over time. In the case of the Fuhr family, parents Carl and Anna Fuhr returned to Cincinnati to find that their home and its contents were no longer available to them. Most of their personal property had been ransacked by burglars after brothers Julius and Eberhard had been taken away by the FBI in 1943.[381] For many internees, it was difficult, if not impossible, to return home, due to the bad memories that inevitably were provoked. According to Barbara and Eberhard Fuhr, Eberhard's brother Gerhard was placed in just such a situation upon returning to Cincinnati:

> He had a hard time dealing with the internment. Except in the last couple of years he's come to terms with it. I think one of the reasons he had trouble dealing with it was he stayed in Cincinnati. All of his memories are there. He'd go by the old house and say, "Hey, we lost that sucker and everything in it."[382]

The jobs internees had held before their departure had long since been filled by others; many of those in search of work were placed in the awkward, and disadvantageous, position of having to account for their whereabouts during the previous several years. For many German detainees, finding a job was made more difficult by the desire not to speak of having been interned.[383] In many cases friends, and even some family members, turned away from the former internees, fearing reprisals from zealots in the manner of the World War I anti-German hysteria, or otherwise suspecting the detainees of disloyalty or anti-American acts, under the belief that the government, despite reassurances from the returning German-Americans, could not possibly have been mistaken in its decisions.

Another victim of enemy alien arrests and internment was the German-American community itself. Collectively, German-American societies witnessed declining membership from the early 1940s onward, due to the wartime situation and declining cohesiveness among their members. For many members of the German-American community, resentment developed towards local and regional German-American societies, based on the feeling that the clubs did not support the German-American community at a time of crisis. On an individual level, many of those arrested and interned felt that they were victimized by fellow German-Americans; far from blaming solely the United States government for their situation, some internees of German descent would blame other German-Americans for having been placed under suspicion, and for having been arrested. A number of former internees have claimed that many who had something to hide, chose to deflect blame onto someone else in the community instead. According to Eberhard Fuhr, his mother Anna felt she was a victim of such treatment:

> My mother was more bitter than my father. He could take most anything, I think. He would have been satisfied just to have a good bakery job. She thought that everything was unfair. She'd lost her house. She'd lost everything in it. It kind of broke her spirit. She'd compulsively acquire things - if she got a hold of anything she just squirreled it away. She was never really close again with some of the people she had been, because I think the suspicion was that they were some of the people that told things to the FBI.[384]

Consequently, many German-Americans returning from internment after World War II came to feel stigmatized as a result of their experience. They faced the prospect of a life forever changed, living under new and completely different circumstances. While the German-American community would continue to exist in America, and former internees began the difficult process of adjusting to a changed existence, many interned German-Americans would experience great difficulty in coming to terms with their ordeal, having to balance their desire to set the record straight and live productive lives in America, with the reality of their situation as having been classified enemy aliens in a time of war. Fifty years after the fact, Eberhard Fuhr has characterized his feelings on internment in the following way:

> I still feel stigmatized. For people forty-five, fifty years old, at their career stage, you can really visualize some horrendous career possibilities. For a guy like [Gerhard], who was literally deprived of an education during that time, he had to use his free time, his release time, to literally catch up again. It was tough.[385]

German-American Internees and the Postwar Mindset in America

For members of the German-American community returning from internment after World War II, mental adjustments to a new life were just as important as physical ones. Internees coming home were forced to confront feelings of confusion, guilt, and shame, as well as anger, bitterness, and resentment, in an effort to make sense of their ordeal and put their lives back together; the burden of having to explain their internment to relatives, friends, and potential employers, caused considerable strain, and contributed significantly to a variety of emotional, and even physical, complications. Federal authorities would concede the hardship experienced by internees of all backgrounds, in hearings conducted on wartime relocation and internment during the early 1980s:

> The exclusion, removal and detention inflicted tremendous human cost. There was the obvious cost of homes and businesses sold or abandoned under circumstances of great distress, as well as injury to careers and professional advancement. But, most important, there was the loss of liberty and the personal stigma of suspected disloyalty for thousands of people who knew themselves to be devoted to their country's cause and to its ideals but whose repeated protestations of loyalty were discounted.[386]

Foremost among the feelings internment generated in many of the German-American internees was anger. Such anger was directed at many sources, including the American government, the German nation, and the German-American community, based not only on the internment itself and its material consequences, but also the time and opportunities lost that could never be replaced. Foremost among the opportunities lost were career plans; German-American internees from the age of forty to fifty-five during the 1940s suffered the most, having lives ripped away from them, and deprived of their means of making a living.[387] Among many other people, internment had significant consequences for the entire Fuhr family. After marrying Barbara in the summer of 1948, Eberhard began college at Gustavus Adolphus in Minnesota, before transferring to Ohio University to take business courses:

> I figured I couldn't afford the luxury of a liberal arts education. I didn't figure I had any more time to lose. I figured I had to come out of school qualified to do something. The last thing I wanted to be was a salesman, but that's all I could get a job at.[388]

Similarly, Barbara's father, previously a writer, was unable to return to his career choice after being interned. While her mother found a job in New York selling pots and pans at a department store, her father was reduced to shoveling coal; according to Barbara, "His career by that time had been wrecked totally. He tried to write articles, but he just never got anywhere."[389] Almost fifty years after the internment of Tilly Busse and her parents, Jakob and Ottilie Reseneder, Tilly expressed resent about the internment of Jakob, the family's obligation to follow him into internment for financial reasons, as well as the fact that they had been ignored when the government gave formal recognition to the internment of Japanese-Americans:

> Meine Mutter hatte keine Arbeit, ohne Vater hätten wir uns nicht über Wasser halten können. Das ist einfach nicht gerecht. Mir wurde keine ordentliche Ausbildung zuteil. Unsere Familie wurde getrennt. Und das war doch alles nicht mein Fehler.[390]

> (My mother didn't have a job. Without my father, we wouldn't have been able to get by. That's just not fair. I wasn't blessed with a proper education. Our family was separated. And none of that was my fault.)

Shame was another emotion felt strongly by the former internees. While internees knew that they had done nothing wrong before being interned, the stigma of having been arrested, coupled with the embarrassment of explaining their internment, and the skepticism and disbelief they expected to encounter, caused German-American internees to maintain an awkward silence about their past. This was particularly true of the Fuhr family; for many years, Eberhard Fuhr found himself laughed at and disbelieved on the rare occasions when he told his story.[391] Accordingly, the vast majority of German-American former internees chose to avoid the subject, refusing to discuss the it for many years even with their closest friends and relatives; Carl and Anna Fuhr never talked about the internment issue with their family, while son Gerhard began discussing the topic openly only after some fifty years had passed, and Julius Fuhr chose not to mention his internment to his children until many years later.[392] Gerhard is one of many former internees who, despite considerable accomplishments after release from internment, continued to feel shame, and struggled with the need to suppress such feelings: "We suppressed all those feelings that we had about internment. Some of us were ashamed to even talk about it. I never talked about it."[393]

Other former internees throughout the nation faced similar feelings of shame and anxiety. One of them, named John,[394] was born in Philadelphia to German parents in 1932, but forced to join his parents in internment camps, in New Jersey and later also Crystal City, beginning in 1943. According to John, speaking years later from his home near San Jose, California, guilt was felt not only because of the internment experience, but also because of his parents' background: "We [children] always felt guilty for what happened in Germany. We felt like we deserved this punishment because our parents were German. Looking back now, that bothers me. My parents were good, simple people."[395] John also echoed a complaint that other internees have expressed, one which prevents many from speaking publicly of their ordeal, namely that many people who hear of the experience refuse to believe it; according to John, who had sought counseling at a veterans' hospital some years later, "I told the shrinks that I had been in a U.S. internment camp. They called me a liar. They said I was making it up."[396] Such an experience, and the shame factor those interned have felt, does not surprise other internees; fellow Crystal City internee Arthur Jacobs has researched the topic extensively, and found numerous similar experiences:

> What you're seeing in John is just the tip of the iceberg, a person who has walked around in some sort of shroud for 50 years, reluctant to speak out. Many of the older people have gone silently to their grave with this feeling of shame.[397]

Consequently, it becomes clear that German legal resident aliens and German-Americans were deeply affected by their internment experience, both tangibly and emotionally. As a result of internment, friendships were lost, families were separated, possessions were taken away, and jobs and careers were eliminated or placed in jeopardy. Emotionally, internees were forced to confront feelings of shame, guilt, anger, and resentment in the postwar years, a process which took years for most internees to realize fully, compounded by a disbelieving public and a government which would not formally recognize their arrest and internment.

Formal Recognition of Japanese-American Internment and German-American Efforts To Receive Equal Treatment

Before the end of the internment of enemy aliens in July 1948, key federal authorities had begun to have misgivings on the necessity for internment, and doubts as to the way in which alien arrests and internments had been carried out. In postwar discussions of the enemy alien question, Henry L. Stimson came to see that "to loyal citizens, this forced evacuation was a personal injustice"; Francis Biddle would express the view that "the program was ill-advised, unnecessary, and unnecessarily cruel"; Justice William O. Douglas, who had found forced evacuation to be constitutionally permissible, stated that the case "was ever on my conscience"; and even Chief Justice Earl Warren went on record saying that "I have since deeply regretted the removal order and my own testimony advocating it, because it was not in keeping with our American concept of freedom and the rights of citizens."[398]

Almost from the minute the government began to phase out internment and evacuation of enemy aliens and citizens of enemy alien heritage, Japanese-Americans were the focus of efforts to give redress to complaints of unfair arrest and internment, and provide compensation to those who were subjected to such treatment. Citing public comment and press statements by prominent figures such as Gen. John DeWitt, that only after Japanese-Americans were detained and/or excluded would German legal resident aliens, German-Americans, and others be dealt with; and that some German and Italian aliens would be altogether exempt from detention and exclusion,[399] federal authorities gave full attention to members of the Japanese-American community, in an effort to right the wrongs committed during the war. Legitimacy for such a viewpoint was provided years later at the highest level; on February 19, 1976, President Gerald Ford officially revoked Executive Order 9066, proclaiming that "we know now what we should have known then: Not only was that evacuation wrong, but Japanese-Americans were and are loyal Americans."[400] No reference was made to any other ethnic group.

According to Joseph E. Fallon, in a 1995 unpublished manuscript entitled "Hostages of Hate: German-Americans and the Home Front in the Two World Wars," beginning in early July 1948, shortly before the final enemy alien, a German-American, was released from custody, the government passed nine separate laws to provide financial compensation and formal apologies to Japanese-American former internees. Each of the nine laws was written specifically to benefit only Japanese-American former internees; none of the laws address the issue of European-American internees, nor make provisions for redress, should former internees of that background choose to challenge the authority:

Public Law	Title	Date
No. 80-886	American-Japanese Evacuation Claims Act	July 2, 1948
No. 82-116	Amendment to Claims Act of 1948	Aug. 17, 1951
No. 82-545	Benefits for Certain Federal Employees of Japanese American Ancestry	July 15, 1952
No. 84-673	Amendment to Claims Act of 1948	July 9, 1956
No. 86-782	Credit for Periods of Internment for Certain Federal Employees of Japanese American Ancestry	Sep. 14, 1960
No. 92-603	Social Security Amendments of 1972 (Sec. 142)	Nov. 17, 1972
No. 95-382	Japanese American Civil Service Retirement Credit for Periods of Internment	Sep. 22, 1978
No. 100-383	Civil Liberties Act of 1988	Aug. 10, 1988
No. 102-371	Amendment to Civil Liberties Act of 1988	Sep. 27, 1992

The most important of the nine laws was the Civil Liberties Act of 1988, signed into law by President Ronald Reagan, after he had previously proclaimed that it would end "a sad chapter in American history in a way that reaffirms America's commitment to the preservation of liberty and justice for all."[401]   In the Cincinnati area, the congressional vote was divided along party lines; of nine members of the House of Representatives voting near Cincinnati, in Ohio, Kentucky, and Indiana, all four Democrats voted "yes," with Rep. Willis Gradison of Cincinnati the only Republican joining them.[402]

As stated by Public Law 100-383, the goal of the United States government was sevenfold:

1) "To acknowledge the fundamental injustice of the evacuation, relocation, and internment of United States citizens and permanent resident aliens of Japanese ancestry during World War II";

2) "apologize on behalf of the people of the United States";

3) "provide for a public education fund to finance efforts to inform the public about the internment of such individuals so as to prevent the recurrence of any such event";

4) "make restitution to those individuals of Japanese ancestry who were interned";

5) "make restitution to Aleut residents ... while those Aleut residents were under United States control during World War II";

6) "discourage the occurrence of similar injustices and violations of civil liberties in the future"; and

7) "make more credible and sincere any declaration of concern by the United States over violations of human rights committed by other nations."[403]

Under the act, some 60,000 Japanese-American former internees and their families were eligible to receive a lump-sum payment of $20,000 per person, with a total of $1.25 billion appropriated for disbursement; elderly former internees would be given priority over younger, with relatives of internees who died after the signing of the bill coming next. No payments were to be made to the families of those who died before the bill was signed, accounting for the discrepancy between the roughly 60,000 recipients and the over 120,000 estimated Japanese-Americans interned and evacuated during the war era. The government was given ten years to make all payments, with the first compensation checks to be mailed out in January 1990.[404]

The basis for Public Law 100-383 was the report of the Commission on Wartime Relocation and Internment of Civilians, established by Public Law 96-317 in 1980 with the expressed purpose of reviewing the relocation and internment of American citizens; after conducting research and hearings from 1980 to 1982, its findings were published in *Personal Justice Denied*, considered by the government to be the definitive account of wartime internment and evacuation of legal resident enemy aliens and Americans of enemy alien heritage. While the report included sections on German-Americans, Latin Americans of enemy alien citizenship or heritage, and other groups, the focus was squarely placed on the Japanese-American situation, to the exclusion of factual documentation on other ethnic groups; among the questionable and undocumented claims made by the commission was that "no negative assumption was made with regard to citizens of German or Italian descent during the Second World War."[405]

The passage of the Civil Liberties Act provoked significant response from the German-American community. German-American former internees and activists were quick to point out a number of inconsistencies, inaccuracies, and injustices in commission hearings and *Personal Justice Denied*. Though the commission had been in existence for over two years, it held only twenty days of public hearings on the matter. The committee sought testimony from Japanese-Americans and Aleutians on their arrest and internment, but made no effort to take, and did not allow, testimony from former European legal resident aliens and European-Americans, including internees. The commission made no attempt to contact national German-American organizations or scholarly societies of German-American Studies in its fact-finding investigations; such organizations were not aware of the commission's existence or of its efforts to determine the facts behind internment and evacuation efforts. Japanese-Americans and others who testified before the committee were not placed under oath, thus removing them from the possibility of perjury charges were they found to have lied. High-level officials involved in internment proceedings, such as Edward Ennis, former Director of the Alien Control Unit of the Department of Justice, and James Rowe, former Assistant Attorney General, stated during hearings that Japanese-Americans were not treated differently than German-Americans, implying that the Japanese-American case was identical to that of the German-Americans, and that German-

Americans were entitled to equal recourse under the law; their testimonies were not included in the official report, *Personal Justice Denied*.[406]

Of similar interest to German-American former internees and activists was Public Law 102-371, the Amendment to the Civil Liberties Act of 1988, enacted in September 1992. Because of the amendment, European legal resident alien and European-American spouses of Japanese-American internees who had voluntarily gone into internment were made eligible for financial compensation; European legal resident alien and European-American spouses of European-American internees were denied compensation.[407]

In keeping with one of the stated goals of the Civil Liberties Act of 1988, namely to provide for a public education fund which would finance efforts to educate and inform the public on Japanese-American internment in World War II, the Civil Liberties Education Fund was established by the government, with an allocation of $500 million for research projects, public displays, and museum exhibits. Such funds were utilized in the late 1980s and early- to mid-1990s to help finance projects dedicated to the Japanese-American internment, often in connection with fiftieth anniversary commemorations of World War II activities. Many subsequent displays gave extensive attention to the Japanese-American community during the war, including detailed discussions of internment and relocation, with little, if any, mention of similar situations for German legal resident aliens and German-Americans. In Cincinnati, traditional home of the German element, the Cincinnati Historical Society, with the cooperation of the Japanese American Citizens League, sponsored "U.S. Detention Camps: 1942-1946," a free exhibit designed to show through ninety photos and text "the reality of life for approximately 120,000 West Coast Japanese Americans who were sent to detention camps during World War II." In the museum preview of the exhibit, no mention was made of the German-American community or of the German experience during the war.[408] In Chicago, the American Library Association, in cooperation with the Smithsonian Institution National Museum of American History, was awarded a $40,000 planning grant in 1992 to develop a traveling exhibition on the internment of Japanese-Americans, and their subsequent efforts to reestablish their constitutional rights. Entitled "A More Perfect Union," initial plans called for the display to travel to at least fifty libraries across the United States and its territories from May 1994 to April 1996. Like the Cincinnati exhibition, no mention was made of German legal resident alien and German-American internment.[409]

A separate law, Section 202, Title II of Public Law 102-248, addressed plans to identify and commemorate former internment camps. Proposed on March 3, 1992, the Japanese-American National Historic Landmark Theme Study Act required the Secretary of the Interior to locate internment centers and designate them as national historic landmarks, in consultation with Japanese-American groups in the area. When Arthur Jacobs attempted to testify before Congress during hearings on the bill, in an effort to insure fair representation for the German-American community, he was denied permission to do so; only through persistent efforts was he able to have a written testimony included in the published record of the proceedings.[410] Such efforts to obtain equal time have met with some success in recent years; when a memorial was dedicated to Japanese-American internees in March 1994 in San Jose, California, former German- and Italian-American internees were able to make mention of their experiences during the war. The month before, the Santa Clara County Human Relations Committee acted upon complaints from German- and Italian-American internees that their plight had been ignored, urging education officials to correct textbooks that claimed that European legal resident aliens and European-Americans were neither interned nor relocated.

Conclusions

In sum, German legal alien residents and German-Americans leaving internment were placed in a difficult situation in the immediate postwar years. While some internees were freed to go home and try to pick up the pieces of their lives, others were faced with the prospects of deportation to Germany, including some who had been born in America, had never been in Germany, and did not speak German.[411] Compounding the burden was the difficulty in finding employment in the aftermath of internment, having to admit to, or lie about, internment in matter concerning one's livelihood. Coming to terms with feelings of shame, guilt, anger, and bitterness proved especially challenging for the former internees; while some were able to make a satisfactory emotional adjustment to having been interned, many other would silently take their feelings to their graves.

With the end of the war, high-level governmental authorities began to question openly the wartime internment policy, and its justification as a policy of the government and military. As internment formally came to an end, the first of nine laws was passed designed to compensate Japanese-Americans for their suffering during the war, and to issue formal apologies for their internment and exclusion. Of the nine laws passed through 1992, each was designed to benefit exclusively members of the Japanese-American community and those of Japanese descent; none of the laws addressed the presence of German legal resident aliens and German-Americans in internment camps during the same period, nor their exclusion from areas deemed strategically important. Additional legislation, designed to fund exhibits on Japanese-American internment and erect memorials to Japanese-American internment, has also failed to address the internment of Germans and German-Americans during World War II. While German-American former internees and activists have since pointed out contradictions and inadequacies in the various public laws enacted since 1948, to date the government has failed to take up the issue formally, and address the concerns raised by an increasing number of German-Americans, who wish to provide a full and balanced account of the internment and relocation of enemy aliens and those of enemy alien heritage from December 1941 until July 1948.

Chapter VII

Conclusion

This study has shown the changes the German-American community endured during the World War II era, from a prewar position of respect and honor following recovery from the traumatic experience of World War I, to having loyalties questioned with the rise of a vocal minority of pro-Nazi German-Americans, to attaining enemy alien status upon American entry into World War II in 1941. Further complicating the wartime experience for German legal resident aliens and German-Americans was the difficulty of adjusting to postwar life, particularly for those interned as enemy aliens and sympathizers during the war, and the unwillingness of the federal government to acknowledge the injustices done to selected members of America's German community, while providing Japanese-Americans with compensation and apologies for their evacuation and internment.

At the heart of the German-American experience during the World War II era is the fact that little of the changing perception of America's German element, and its subsequent problems, was the result of wrongdoing or illegal activity. Even the most vocal pro-Nazi organization of the late 1930s and early 1940s, the German-American Bund, broke no laws by its existence or activities, and despite the bad press the group generated, its members represented only a tiny fraction of the entire German-American community. At the highest level of government and military planning, actions were considered, and later implemented, based on the train of thought that aliens of an enemy nationality were *deemed* to be *potentially* dangerous;[412] perception, rather than evidence, was the determining factor in how German legal resident aliens and German-Americans would be treated during the World War II era.

As a result of misleading, incomplete, and inaccurate information, many misperceptions have become commonly accepted beliefs about Japanese-American, as well as German legal resident alien and German-American, internment and evacuation during World War II. Such misperceptions have triggered intense debate, and considerable controversy, among scholars in a variety of fields of specialization, most notably with regard to aspects of racism; internment as opposed to evacuation; and the extent to which German-Americans, as citizens of the United States, were interned alongside German legal resident aliens and Japanese-Americans.

In recent years, in the aftermath of the Civil Liberties Act of 1988 which awarded Japanese-Americans, but not German legal resident aliens and German-Americans, an apology and compensation for internment, members of the German-American community and scholars have made a concerted effort to clarify some of the misperceptions which formed the basis for governmental action, and fueled heated debate on the issue. Freelance writer Joseph Fallon has researched the issue extensively, and has cited the following areas which have been misrepresented with regard to the German-American community, in discussing the ethnicity of persons interned and evacuated during World War II:

1) Fifty-six percent of all internees were Europeans and European-Americans, indicating that Japanese-Americans did not make up the majority of those interned;

2) sixty-four percent of those arrested by the FBI from December 7, 1941 to June 30, 1945 were Europeans and European-Americans, including seamen of foreign ships in American ports, arrested as early as April 1941;

3) the arrest of German legal resident aliens and German-Americans began on December 7, 1941, four days before the United States was at war with Germany;

4) while Japanese-Americans were released from internment by June 1946, Europeans and European-Americans were interned until July 1948;

5) in passing laws designed to apologize to and compensate former internees, Congress solicited testimony from Japanese-Americans affected by wartime detention, relocation, and internment procedures, but not from any European legal resident alien and European-American former internee;

6) *Personal Justice Denied*, the official government position on wartime internment, included no testimony from European and European former internees; did not include testimony from high-ranking federal officials during the war who stated

that Japanese-Americans were not arrested in mass or because of race; and

7) former internment camps, which have become historic landmarks according to Public Law 102-248, are identified officially as having interned only Japanese-Americans.[413]

Summary of Key Points

In order to summarize the German-American experience during the World War II era, it is worthwhile to ask, and answer, some of the prominent questions that German legal resident aliens and German-American have been forced to come to terms with, and what those affected by wartime restrictions against the German-American community wish to achieve in making known their difficulties during the past half century.

One of the main complaints German legal resident alien and German-American detainees and internees have expressed about their predicament is that the German-American community did not come to their assistance, failing to offer support and present a united front in the face of adversity. One explanation for this is the experience of the German-American community during World War I. After suffering extensively at the hands of nativist hysteria, when anything German was subject to hostile and even violent treatment, few German-American individuals or societies were inclined to make known their presence, or assert their German character publicly. Another reason for the failure of the German-American community to support its members can be found in the lack of cohesiveness of the community itself; in the wake of the rapid assimilation process which took place after World War I, German-American institutions suffered declining memberships and support, resulting in weakened bonds within the community and a relative lack of strength as a whole. Third, ethnic harassment contributed to the lack of support that German legal resident aliens and German-Americans received from their community. Faced with ethnic slurs, anonymous threats, and intimidation, such as the vandalizing of the German House in Cleveland,[414] many members of the German-American community became convinced that silence was the best response to a difficult situation.

A second question of importance is the extent to which pro-Nazi German legal resident aliens and German-Americans, although a decided minority, influenced public perception of all members of the community, and caused the arrest and internment of selected individuals from 1941 to 1948. Stephen C. Fox has maintained that the threat of American Nazi activity was overstated by the government, and that in some circles government officials believed that, rather than punishing the German-American community for pro-Nazi activities, federal officials would be better served to court the favor of the nation's largest ethnic group:

> Stories existed, wildly exaggerated to be sure, of the "fifth column" activities of German-born aliens, especially of the several thousand pro-Nazi, German American Bundists. Some in Washington and elsewhere speculated that if these people continued to support Nazism or fascism, they might influence their millions of American-born children to do the same. Should not the government do something positive to promote the aliens' loyalty rather than undermining their allegiance by classifying all of them as "enemies"?[415]

However, Susan Canedy related the issue to the rise and fall of the German-American Bund, the largest and most influential pro-Nazi group in the United States:

> The image of Nazism presented by the Bund brought the reality of German Nazism to American shores, and while not a contributing factor to the United States' entrance into the war, the Bund certainly helped determine the American perception of the Third Reich. Due to the basic freedoms guaranteed to all, German Americans were free to gather together under the banner of American Fascism. The German American Bund's fate stands as a classic example of what happens to a group when it abuses those liberties.[416]

Through governmental examination in the House Un-American Activities Committee as early as January 1939, and continuing into 1941, activities of the Bund and other pro-Nazi groups and individuals were closely monitored, widely reported, and certainly were fresh in the minds of the American people when the nation went to war in December 1941. Inevitably, the German-American community, was faced with the unpleasant consequence of guilt by association; as Canedy stated in *America's Nazis*, "The group as a whole was punished for crimes committed by the few due to the solidarity which the group portrayed."[417]

A third concern of many German legal resident aliens and German-Americans is the reason some detainees and internees received unfair, and possibly illegal, interrogations and judgments during alien registration, enemy-alien hearings, and internment and deportation procedures during the 1940s. According to Arthur Jacobs, many aliens, and possibly some citizens, faced hearings which, while consistent among detainees, were slanted heavily in favor of the prosecution:

> ... *boards*, not courts, heard the case as presented by the *alien* (without attorney) but witnesses were allowed to testify on behalf of the alien. After hearing the case, the Board would make a recommendation ... to the U.S. Attorney General. Ultimate *power* to accept or reject the decision of the Board rested in the Attorney General of the United States. The reader should note that this process did *not* discriminate by *race* ... The process applied to *all* aliens of enemy nationality.[418]

Fourth, and in many ways foremost, among the questions posed by the German-American community in the aftermath of its World War II experiences is why they have met with only limited success in having their wartime grievances addressed, despite clear documentation of their arrest and internment, and despite their strength of being America's largest ethnic group. To answer this complex question, it is necessary first to review the basis for internment, and what factors contributed to recent federal legislation on behalf of Japanese-American former internees.

In formulating its policies for interning enemy aliens and sympathizers in the World War II era, governmental and military officials based their decisions on precedent set in the Alien Enemy Act of 1798. In the case of war, the President was authorized to detain, remove, and/or intern enemy aliens above the age of fourteen, in the interest of maintaining public safety. Such actions were not considered to violate due process of the law, in that legal residents of the United States holding enemy citizenship were not guaranteed the same protections offered to American citizens under the Constitution. The legality of the government position was upheld by the Supreme Court, in *Johnson v. Eisentrager*, in which the distinction between citizenship and resident alien status was addressed:

> The rights of ... enemy aliens all flow from and must be vindicated within the framework of the system established for the occupation of their country, and they cannot properly call upon the protections and rights stemming from our domestic or internal law, unless Congress has expressly granted such rights to them.[419]

While such rulings acknowledged that enemy aliens were not within their rights to demand equal protection under the law, they did not address the concerns of American citizens who also were arrested, detained, and interned during World War II. Almost thirty-five years after the final internee, a German-American, was released from custody in July 1948, the Commission on Wartime Relocation and Internment of Civilians took up the issue of the internment of American citizens, as well as legal resident aliens, in its report *Personal Justice Denied*. The Commission cited the unique character of such an action in American history, in finding fault with wartime policy:

> The personal injustice of excluding, removing, and detaining loyal American citizens is manifest. Such events are extraordinary and unique in American history. For every citizen and for American public life, they pose haunting questions about our country and its past.[420]

The Commission concluded that there was no need for Executive Order 9066, authorizing exclusion of enemy aliens from restricted zones, and the detention and internment of legal resident aliens and citizens, without proof of wrongdoing:

> The promulgation of Executive Order 9066 was not justified by military necessity, and the decisions which followed from it (including) detention, ending detention and ending exclusion ... were not driven by analysis of military conditions. A grave injustice was done to American citizens and resident aliens ... who, without individual review or any probative evidence against them, were excluded, removed and detained by the United States during World War II.[421]

The Commission's findings, while a confirmation of former internees' position on the matter, nevertheless were contested by members of the German-American community, who maintained that the report primarily addressed the arrest, detention, exclusion, and internment of Japanese-Americans during World War II, while virtually ignoring the German-American experience of the same period. A careful reading of the report illustrates the validity of such a viewpoint; repeated references to the Japanese-American community, without a discussion of similar experiences encountered by German legal resident aliens and German-Americans, and the fact that the majority of the report's sections deal with the treatment of ethnic Japanese during the war, show a clear disposition that Japanese-Americans were not only the primary, but virtually the only, victims of wartime mistreatment.

The Commission based many of its findings on first-hand commentary from former internees and evacuees; German legal resident alien and German-American former internees have since stated that their testimony was never sought. Governmental documents also were utilized by the Commission in its fact-finding efforts, though for unexplained reasons the vast majority cited Japanese-American internee experiences, to the exclusion of, or minimization of, discussion on the German-American experience. In one case, the Commission cited an exchange in a Congressional committee between an official named Bates and Gen. John DeWitt, a leading figure in the wartime internment and evacuation movement, discussing wartime policy:

> *Gen. DeWitt*: It makes no difference whether he is an American citizen, he is still a Japanese. American citizenship does not necessarily determine loyalty.

> *Mr. Bates*: You draw a distinction then between Japanese and Italians and Germans? We have a great number of Italians and German and we think they are fine citizens. There may be exceptions.

> *Gen. DeWitt*: You needn't worry about the Italians at all except in certain cases. Also, the same for the Germans except in individual cases. But we must worry about the Japanese all the time until he is wiped off the map. Sabotage and espionage will make problems as long as he is allowed in this area - problems which I don't want to have to worry about.[422]

Such passages, as cited by the Commission and appearing with relative frequency, illustrate the justification for Japanese-American redress in the postwar years, but do not do justice to German-American claims. The prominence of comments such as those by Gen. DeWitt stand in contrast to other, less frequent and less visible, references in the report to the German-American community; in one instance, the Commission cited a public opinion poll from the Office of Facts and Figures in the Office for Emergency Management, in which Germans were listed as "the most dangerous alien group" by forty-six percent of respondents. Thirty-five percent responded with the Japanese.[423]

In sum, the lack of attention given by the Commission to the similar difficulties encountered by German legal resident aliens and German-Americans to those of Japanese-Americans, served to understate legitimate claims to redress made by the German-American community. This shortcoming would have consequences for German legal resident alien and German-American former internees in Public Law 100-383, the Civil Liberties Act of 1988, when the government provided a formal apology and monetary compensation to Japanese-American former internees, based directly on the Commission report *Personal Justice Denied*, but denied German legal resident alien and German-American former internees equal treatment.

Despite the one-sided nature of the report, one passage concerning the German-American community makes clear that the Commission found reason for claims against the government by German legal resident aliens and German-Americans:

> The history of the First World War bears a suggestive resemblance to the events of 1942: rumors in the press of sabotage and espionage, use of a stereotype of the German as an unassailable and rapacious Hun, followed by an effort to suppress those institutions (such as) the language, the press and the churches ... that were most palpably foreign and perceived as the seedbed of Kaiserism. There were numerous examples of official and quasi-governmental harassment and fruitless investigation of German Americans and resident German aliens. This history is made even more disturbing by the absence of an extensive history of anti-German agitation before the war.[424]

The Commission made clear its finding that, as in the World War I era, many German legal resident aliens and German-Americans who were loyal to the United States, or at least not aligned with German interests, were the victim of an anti-German sentiment, expressed through widespread stereotypes, in public forums such as newspapers, and through governmental action.

The Quest for Equal Redress in the German-American Community

With the enactment of Public Law 100-383, the Civil Liberties Act of 1988, and the 1992 passage of Public Law 102-371, the Amendment to the Civil Liberties Act of 1988, members of the German-American community noted the benefits given exclusively to Japanese-American former internees, and began efforts to gain both unofficial and official redress for perceived inequities in the law. On an unofficial level, German legal resident and German-American former internees and others strove to awaken public awareness to the events of the past, by providing the media, scholarly institutions, and German-American groups with additional information, including many previously unseen government documents, personal mementos, and contemporary news accounts. On an official level, former internees and others have pursued legal action and petitioned the government to have their stories heard, in order to present previously classified federal documents and to modify previous legislation.

The primary activist in the German-American community seeking equal provisions for German legal resident alien and German-American former internees has been Arthur Jacobs, the former internee and retired major in the United States Air Force. In recent years he has collected some 10,000 documents, many from government sources, related to the detention and internment of German legal resident aliens and German-Americans from December 1941 to June 1948; the documents include personal reminiscences from former internees and their families, declassified federal briefs and memos, and publications concerning the arrest and internment of members of the German-American community.

Jacobs has expended considerable time and personal resources in his efforts to obtain equal treatment for German legal resident alien and German-American former internees. A large part of his efforts has been geared towards raising public awareness of the internment of members of the German-American community, and illustrating the injustice of Public Law 100-383. To this end, Jacobs has written to numerous scholarly publications and newspapers, both German- and English-language, detailing the facts of internment in articles and letters; presented his father's internment story at professional conferences; and made television appearances discussing the ordeal of his family and of other internees.[425] More formally, on December 6, 1991, Jacobs argued his case before the United States Court of Appeals, District of Columbia Circuit, challenging the federal statute providing compensation to Japanese-Americans on the grounds of equal protection; in an earlier hearing, a United States District Court judge held that Jacobs had no standing to pursue legal action.

In the case of Jacobs' appeal, Chief Judge Mikva noted that the district court had confused standing questions with defenses on the merits of the case; according to Mikva:

> The fact that Mr. Jacobs says he was interned ... is enough to establish injury for standing purposes; he is not required to allege at the outset that he was interned for the same reasons as the Japanese and Aleuts, as the district court suggested. Since we think Mr. Jacobs has adequately alleged injury, we turn to the remaining tests for standing, which he passes easily.[426]

With regard to the merit of the case, the Court of Appeals found in favor of the original decision, that Jacobs was not able to show that he was interned because of racial prejudice, and that no sufficient basis existed to overturn the criteria which led to the enactment of the Civil Liberties Act of 1988, specifically that no mass exclusion or detention was ordered against American citizens of German or Italian descent. In the view of the Court of Appeals:

> We do not know ... whether children like Mr. Jacobs were ordered to accompany their fathers as a matter of course. But this much is clear: Congress' finding that "no mass exclusion or detention ... was ordered against American citizens of German or Italian descent" is broad enough to cover children as well as adults, and it leaves no room for the unlikely suggestion that German American children were the victims of prejudice, while their fathers were not.[427]

In conclusion, the Court of Appeals vacated the District Court holding that Jacobs had had no standing to bring his suit, but stood by the original decision as to merit. While Jacobs was vindicated in his ability to bring suit, the rulings on behalf of the defendants gave judicial recognition to the Civil Liberties Act of 1988, and the viewpoint that the legislation does not deprive German-Americans of equal protection of the law.

Despite the Court of Appeals verdict, Jacobs and others interested in the case continued their efforts to clarify the internment issue, and establish the basis for a revision of the Civil Liberties Act in favor of German-American former internees. Following the Court of Appeals decision, Jacobs compiled a four-page response to the verdict, responding to individual aspects of the judgment with factors which had not been taken into account in formulating the Appeals Court ruling. In his first-pass critique of the findings, Jacobs reiterated several points which he believed the Court had not adequately taken into account:

> 1) To the best of his knowledge, not one German-American who had been "interned, relocated, paroled, and/or interned-at-large" was invited to testify, in Jacobs' case as recently as July 25, 1991, on the matter;

> 2) the Commission on Wartime Relocation and Internment of Civilians solely utilized documents related to the case of the Japanese-Americans, with second-hand sources utilized with regard to the German-American community;[428]

3) the report lacked specific definitions of key terminology, such as what constituted "small numbers" of German-American internees; and "evidence" introduced without oath in hearings, which Jacobs stated was a representation of "hearsay, anecdotes, and even untruths"; and

4) in contrast to Congressional and legal comments to the contrary, by December 9, 1941, two days before the United States went to war with Germany, twenty-six German-Americans were arrested in the state of Washington, and between December 7, 1941 and June 30, 1945, 115 German-Americans were arrested in the same state.[429]

Another former internee who in recent years has called attention to German-American internment during the World War II era is former Cincinnatian Eberhard Fuhr. In addition to providing an account of his family's internment to Chicago-area newspapers and German-American scholars, Fuhr has written to Congressmen, and even President George Bush on at least two occasions. Speaking on behalf of European-American former internees, Fuhr requested of the President that they receive "the same reconciliation accorded Japanese"; short of that, Fuhr requested that his internment be deleted from his permanent record, "because it was used against me at various stages of my employment."[430]

While he has openly discussed his wartime experiences, Fuhr admits that he still possesses a paranoia about the events of the past, and feels the need to show his loyalty:

> I don't go to German American days in Chicago. I don't belong to the German American National Congress in Chicago. I don't belong to any German groups. Because those things get on your record. I don't join anything. I did join the Simon Wiesenthal Center for a while. I want it on my record that I belonged for three years. And I belong to the Republican Party ... I just send them twenty-five bucks a year.[431]

While former internees such as Jacobs and Fuhr have presented vital information on the issue of internment, and provided valuable insights to scholars, their example has been followed by relatively few other former internees. For most, even fifty years after the fact, the issue remains a sensitive one; the majority of those who remain are unwilling to discuss their arrest and internment publicly, with those few willing to speak of their experiences often using only a first name, initials, false names, or otherwise speaking anonymously. Eberhard Fuhr has expressed the difficulty he has encountered in getting fellow former internees to speak publicly of their past:

> [I still have friends who say] "I believe in what you're doing, but I don't want to go public." You say, "Hey, we ought to get together on this." They say, "No. Forget it." They're afraid. "You'd have all that stuff on your record, and your record's going to come up again sometime." I don't want to overstate it, but I don't want to understate it either. There's a real paranoia out there.[432]

Family members, such as the children of internees, often have little to add, because their parents either did not tell them about internment or would not go into detail about the experience. Still other family members, noting the wishes of their relatives not to publicize their role as German legal resident alien and German-American detainees and internees, choose not to discuss the matter, respecting the former internees' wishes for privacy. Either way, the result is that less information is available to legislators and scholars, those who would otherwise provide a fuller account of the German-American experience during the World War II era.

The Goal of German-American Former Detainees and Internees

A remaining issue of importance in analyzing the German-American community in the aftermath of World War II is what goals German legal resident aliens and German-Americans possess in speaking out about their experiences before, during, and after the war. Beyond seeking formal recognition of their status as having been detained and interned, and the same treatment given the Japanese-American community, several former internees have expressed a desire which goes beyond the German-American community.

Beyond the goals already presented, one area of concern stands out among former internees. Many former internees fear that, in another era of war or anger towards a given ethnic group, the same fate awaits others, that the lessons of the past have not been learned. In discussing his experiences as an internee, Eberhard Fuhr compared his situation to that which others might encounter:

> This was a political internment, and it could happen again. I'm really afraid it could happen again. Next time, it could be Arab Moslems,

Lutherans - who knows? What happened to me and thousands of others is old history, but the next time it could be any other group, which is then not "politically correct," or out of favor for any other reason.[433]

In correspondence with others, including letters to members of Congress, Fuhr included an appeal in his personal internment story: "Internment and incarceration could happen again. This time to another group not then in good favor. You could name some *undesirable group here* (fill in the blank). Please add your voice now to prevent this."[434]

Others, including non-internees, have echoed a similar sentiment. M.U. Eninger, in an editorial on the internment issue, urged readers not to forget the events of the past, so as not to experience them again:

Today, we keep hearing the cliché that those who forget the injustices of history are doomed to reexperience them. Indeed there are those who, having paid a heavy price in the historical drama of this century, now almost make it a cult to remember their ethnic experience of man's inhumanity to man. They are the practitioners of remembrance. They are the activists who pour their own version of the historical experience that needs to be remembered over everyone's heads, willing or not.[435]

Ultimately, the German-American community will carry forward the legacy of the World War II experience in the same manner as it did after World War I, by coming to terms with the past and pointing out instances where the full truth has yet to be told. There is no way to undo what was done in the past, to alter the suspicions that befell countless members of the German-American community from the mid-1930s to the mid-1940s, and allowed for the arrest, detention, and internment of over 10,000 German legal resident aliens and German-Americans. However, by learning about, and understanding, the events of the past, it becomes less likely that such events will repeat themselves, and more likely that those who suffered such treatment will be afforded a more complete opportunity to have the full story of their experience told.

Bibliography

Alien Enemy Detention Facility. Film. United States Immigration and Naturalization Service, 1947.

American Israelite. Anonymous articles: 18 Jan. 1934; 1 Feb. 1934; July 20, 1934.

American Library Association. "ALA plans exhibition on WWII internment of Japanese Americans." Press release. June 1992.

Arndt, Karl J.R., and May E. Olson. *The German Language Press of the Americas.* New York: K.G. Saur, 1980.

Bavarian Mutual Support Organization. Meeting report. Cincinnati: 22 July 1941.

Bell, Leland V. "The Failure of Nazism in America: The German American Bund, 1936-1941." *Political Science Quarterly* 85.4 (1970): 585-599.

---. *In Hitler's Shadow: The Anatomy of American Nazism.* New York: Kennikat Press, 1973.

Blair, Mike. "Cruel Odyssey of Family in FDR's Concentration Camps." *Spotlight* 20 May 1991.

Bosworth, Allan R. *America's Concentration Camps.* NewYork: Bantam Books, 1968.

Brinkley, Alan. *Voices of Protest: Huey Long, Father Coughlin and the Great Depression.* New York: Alfred A. Knopf, 1982.

Burton, Shirley J., and Kellee Green. "Oaths of Allegiance, Acts of Treason: The Disloyalty Prosecutions of Max Stephan and Hans Haupt." *Prologue* 23.3 (1991): 236-247.

Canedy, Susan. *America's Nazis: A Democratic Dilemma.* Menlo Park, CA: Markgraf Publications, 1990.

Carlson, John. *Under Cover.* New York: E.P. Dutton, 1943.

Chancellor, John. *NBC Nightly News.* Commentary: 5 December 1991.

Cincinnati Enquirer. Anonymous articles: 29 Aug. 1935; 29 Aug. 1937; 2 Mar. 1938; 6 Mar. 1938; 9 Mar. 1938; 17 Mar. 1938; 25 Mar. 1938; 26 Mar. 1938; 9 July 1938; 8 Aug. 1940; 27 Aug. 1940; 1 Mar. 1941; 4 Apr. 1941; 5 June 1941; 10 Dec. 1941; 11 Dec. 1941; 20 Dec. 1941; 1 Jan. 1942; 3 Jan. 1942; 4 Jan. 1942; 7 Jan. 1942; 8 Jan. 1942; 14 Jan. 1942; 24 Jan. 1942; 4 Feb. 1942; 11 Feb. 1942; 26 Feb. 1942; 20 Mar. 1942; 9 April 1942; 10 April 1942; 28 April 1942; 5 June 1942; 24 June 1942; 11 July 1942; 12 July 1942; 21 July 1942; 26 July 1942; 19 Aug. 1942; 27 Sep. 1942; 24 Mar. 1943; 25 Mar. 1943; 25 June 1943; 17 Sep. 1943; 29 Sep. 1943; 26 Oct. 1944; 11 June 1947; 14 June 1947; 13 Feb. 1949; 14 Feb. 1965; 15 Nov. 1973; 21 June 1981; 5 Aug. 1988.

Cincinnati Historical Society. "New Exhibit Presents A Different Perspective of WWII." *History Express: News From the Cincinnati Historical Society* January-March 1994: 2.

Cincinnati Post. Anonymous articles: 25 Nov. 1938; 23 Aug. 1940; 27 Dec. 1940; 9 Dec. 1941; 12 Dec. 1941; 13 Dec. 1941; 16 Dec. 1941; 17 Dec. 1941; 18 Dec. 1941; 19 Dec. 1941; 20 Dec. 1941; 22 Dec. 1941; 23 Dec. 1941; 29 Dec. 1941; 7 Jan. 1942; 9 Jan. 1942; 10 Jan. 1942; 27 Feb. 1942; 3 Mar. 1942; 6 Mar. 1942; 12 Mar. 1942; 14 Mar. 1942; 11 Apr. 1942; 20 May 1942; 15 July 1942; 2 Aug. 1942; 3 Aug. 1942; 6 Aug. 1942; 7 Aug. 1942; 30 Dec. 1942.

Cincinnati Times-Star. Anonymous articles: 6 Sep. 1940; 25 Nov. 1940; 14 Jan. 1941.

Cincinnatier Freie Presse. Anonymous articles: 4 Feb. 1934; 18 Sep. 1939; 12 Apr. 1942.

Combs, James. *American Political Movies: An Annotated Filmography of Feature Films.* New York: Garland, 1990.

Commission on Wartime Relocation and Internment of Civilians. *Personal Justice Denied.* Washington: U.S. Government Printing Office, 1982.

Congressional Record. *Public Law 100-383: Wartime Relocation of Civilians.* Washington: U.S. Government Printing Office, 1988.

Craig, E.M. "A Doctor Comments On Appeal For Enemy Aliens." *Cincinnati Post* 11 March 1942.

Daniels, Roger. *Coming to America: A History of Immigration and Ethnicity in American Life*. New York: HarperCollins, 1990.

Davis, Gerald H. "'Orgelsdorf': A World War I Internment Camp in America." *Yearbook of German-American Studies* 26 (1991): 249-`265.

Dennis, Lawrence. *The Coming of American Fascism*. New York: AMS Press, 1977.

Deutsche Zeitung. Anonymous articles: 4 Jan. 1934; 14 Apr. 1934.

Deutscher Weckruf und Beobachter. Newspaper: 18 May 1939.

Diamond, Sander A. *The Nazi Movement in the United States, 1924-1941*. Ithaca: Cornell UP, 1974.

Dies, Martin. *The Trojan Horse in America*. New York: Dodd, Mead, and Co., 1940.

Eninger, M.U. "The Way I See It." *German American Journal* January 1994.

Epstein, Benjamin. Letter. 9 December 1940. American Jewish Archives Manuscript Collection. Hebrew Union College, Cincinnati.

Every Friday. Newspaper: 20 July 1934.

Fallon, Joseph E. "The Facts About Internment." Unpublished manuscript, n.d.

---. "Hostages of Hate: German-Americans and the Home Front in the Two World Wars." Society for German-American Studies 19th Annual Symposium. Louisville, 7 April 1995.

---. "Summary of the Fate of German-Americans in the Two World Wars." Unpublished manuscript, n.d.

Farago, Ladislas. *The Game of the Foxes: The Untold Story of German Espionage in the United States and Great Britain During World War II*. New York: David McKay Company, 1971.

Fielding, Raymond. *The American Newsreel, 1911-1967.* Norman: U Oklahoma P, 1972.

"The Foreign Language Press." *Fortune* 22 (November 1940).

Foreman, Cul. J. "Leniency To Spies An Insult To Soldiers." *Cincinnati Post* 9 July 1942.

Fox, Stephen. "General John DeWitt and the Proposed Internment of German and Italian Aliens During World War II." *Pacific Historical Review* 57.4 (1988): 407- 438.

---. *The Unknown Internment: An Oral History of the Relocation of Italian Americans During World War II.* Boston: Twayne Publishers, 1990.

Fuhr, Barbara. Personal interview. 27 Mar. 1993.

Fuhr, Eberhard. Personal interview. 27 Mar. 1993.

---. "An Internment Story." Unpublished manuscript, n.d.

---. "To President George Bush." Letter. *Amerika Woche* 21 November 1992.

Fuhr, Gerhard. Personal interview. 27 Mar. 1993.

Galicich, Anne. *The German Americans.* Philadelphia: Chelsea House, 1989.

Gathright, Alan. "Memories of Injustice." *San Jose Mercury News* 2 January 1991.

Gesensway, Deborah, and Mindy Roseman. *Beyond Words: Images From America's Concentration Camps.* Ithaca: Cornell UP, 1987.

Glancy, H.M. Rev. of *Confessions of a Nazi Spy*, ed. Nicholas Thomas. Vol. 1 of *International Dictionary of Films and Filmmakers.* Chicago: St. James, 1990.

Hatfield, Dianna. "The Internment of Germans and German- Americans During World War II: The Untold Story." *Society for German-American Studies Newsletter* 14.2 (1993): 12-14.

Hennessey, Charles F. "On Spies," *Cincinnati Post* 14 July 1942.

"Inside Nazi Germany." *The March of Time*. Time, Inc., 1938.

Jacobs, Arthur D. Personal interview. 8 Apr. 1995.

---. "Circuit Court of Appeals (D.C. Circuit) Decision Dated March 27, 1992, in the Case of Arthur D. Jacobs." Unpublished manuscript, 30 March 1992.

---. "The Facts About Internment," *Newsletter of the Institute for German American Relations* 3.7 (1993): 2-4.

---. "Fifty Years of Silence: All Quiet on the Arrest and Internment of German Americans in the United States during World War II." *Society for German-American Studies Newsletter* 12.2 (1991): 10-11.

---. "History Quiet on the Arrest and Internment of German Americans in the United States during World War II." *Society for German-American Studies Newsletter* 12.3 (1991): 18-19, 23.

---. "Synopsis of *Factual* Events/Actions on the 'Internment Affair.'" Unpublished manuscript, n.d.

---. "Untruths and Truths About the Evacuation, Relocation, and Internment in the United States During World War II." Unpublished manuscript, 5 January 1990.

"Jacobs v. Barr." Case summary. n.p.: Westlaw, 1992.

"Johnson v. Eisentrager." *Cases Argued and Decided in the Supreme Court: October Term, 1949*. Book 94, Lawyers' Edition. Rochester: Lawyers Co-Operative Publishing Company, 1950.

Jones, Kenneth Paul, ed. *U.S. Diplomats in Europe, 1919- 1941*. Oxford: Clio Press, 1981.

Kahn, David. *Hitler's Spies*. New York: Macmillan, 1978.

Kelly, W.F. Letter to A. Vulliet. 9 August 1948. Uncredited photocopy made available to the author.

King, Bill. "The Triumph of Pluralism In Cincinnati: 1930-1945." Unpublished manuscript, 28 May 1991.

190

Korte, Martin. "Internierte Deutsche fordern Gerechtigkeit." *Nordamerikanische Wochen-Post* 14 April 1990.

Krause, Kitry. "Dangerous Enemy Alien." *Reader* 22.48, 3 September 1993.

Lager-Nachrichten: Wöchentliches Mitteilungsblatt der Deutschen Gruppe, *Crystal City, Texas.* Nr. 42. 24 November 1945.

Langman, Larry, and Ed Borg. *Encyclopedia of American War Films.* New York: Garland, 1989.

Luebke, Frederick C. *Bonds of Loyalty: German-Americans and World War I.* Dekalb: Northern Illinois UP, 1974.

Maujean, Paul. "Would Send Nazi Spies To Firing Squad." Letter. *Cincinnati Post* 2 July 1942.

Millikin, Mark. "Would Give Nazi Spies A Lesson In Democracy." Letter. *Cincinnati Post* 3 July 1942.

Nash, Jay Robert, and Stanley Ralph Ross, *The Motion Picture Guide: C-D, 1927-1983.* Chicago: Cinebooks, 1985.

Vol. 3 of *New Encyclopaedia Brittanica: Micropaedia.* Chicago: Encyclopaedia Brittanica, 1989.

New York Times. Anonymous articles: 22 May 1934; 24 May 1934; 19 Feb. 1939; 20 Feb. 1939; 21 Feb. 1939; 26 Feb. 1939; 13 Mar. 1939; 13 May 1939; 21 June 1939; 5 July 1939; 7 July 1939; 1 Sep. 1939; 6 Sep. 1939; 7 Sep. 1939; 8 Sep. 1939; 3 Oct. 1940; 5 Oct. 1940; 23 Nov. 1940.

Oberndorf, Ludwig. "The German Press in the United States." *The American-German Review* 6 (December 1939).

Otto, Robert L. "It Happened Here: How Nazi Agents Plotted Evil Deeds." *Cincinnati Post* 26 February 1942.

Page, Clarence. *McNeil-Lehrer News Hour.* Commentary: 6 December 1991.

Pells, Richard. *Radical Visions and American Dreams: Culture and Social Thought in the Depression Years*. Middletown, CT: Wesleyan UP, 1977.

Rippley, LaVern J. *The German Americans*. Boston: Twayne, 1976.

"Roundup." Narr. Stone Phillips. *Dateline*. National Broadcasting Corporation. November 1994.

Sennett, Vernon. "Urges Firm Hand Upon Our 'Internal Enemies.'" *Cincinnati Post* 6 February 1942.

Sheridan, Peter B. "The Internment of German and Italian Aliens Compared With the Internment of Japanese Aliens in Analysis." Research Report. Government Division, Congressional Research Service, Library of Congress, 24 Nov. 1980.

Swing, Raymond G. *Forerunners of American Fascism*. Salem, NH: Ayer Co. Publishers, 1935.

Theoharris, Athan. *Spying on Americans: Political Surveillance from Hoover to the Huston Plan*. Philadelphia: Temple UP, 1978.

Tolzmann, Don Heinrich. *The Cincinnati Germans After the Great War*. New York: Peter Lang, 1987.

---, ed. *German-Americans in the World Wars*. 5 vols. Munich: K.G. Saur, 1995.

United Banater Society. Meeting report. 21 July 1941. American Jewish Archives Manuscript Collection. Hebrew Union College, Cincinnati.

United States Code Service, Lawyers' Edition: 50 USCS, War and National Defense. Rochester: Lawyers Co-Operative, 1981.

U.S. Congress. "Propaganda in Motion Pictures," *Hearings Before a Subcommittee of the Committee on Interstate Commerce: United States Senate, Resolution 152*. 77th Congress. First session, 9-26 September 1941. Washington: United States Government Printing Office, 1942.

U.S. Congress, Special Committee on Un-American Activities. *Investigation of Nazi and Other Propaganda.* Washington: U.S. Government Printing Office, 1935.

Warner, Richard S. "Barbed Wire and Nazilagers." *The Chronicles of Oklahoma* 64.1 (1986): 46-47.

Webster's Third New International Dictionary of the English Language, Unabridged. Springfield: Merriam-Webster, 1993.

Wittke, Carl. *German-Americans and the World War.* New York: J.S. Ozer, 1974.

---. *The German Language Press in America.* Lexington: U Kentucky P, 1957.

Wood, Richard, and David Culbert, ed. *Film and Propaganda in America: A Documentary History.* 2 vols. New York: Greenwood, 1990.

Vol. 4 of *World Book Encyclopedia.* Chicago: World Book, 1990.

Endnotes

Chapter I: Introduction

1. Peter B. Sheridan, "The Internment of German and Italian Aliens Compared With the Internment of Japanese Aliens in the United States During World War II: A Brief History and Analysis," Government Division, Congressional Research Service, Library of Congress, 24 November 1980: ii. In claiming that over 100,000 Japanese-Americans were interned during the war era, Sheridan misleadingly includes those individuals subject to evacuation, a process legally distinct from internment as per Executive Order 9066 of February 1942; in reality non-renunciant Japanese legal resident aliens and Japanese-Americans numbered 11,229 internees, compared with a total of 10,905 German legal resident aliens and German-Americans.

2. Commission on Wartime Relocation and Internment of Civilians, *Personal Justice Denied* (Washington: U.S. Government Printing Office, 1982) 3. While true on the surface, in that a relatively small number of "American citizens" of German and Italian heritage were interned compared with Japanese-Americans, the report is misleading, in that it does not take into account the number of German-born, non-naturalized internees, nor does it define what is meant by the term "ethnic Japanese."

3. John Chancellor, *NBC Nightly News*, 5 December 1991; Clarence Page, *McNeil-Lehrer News Hour*, 6 December 1991.

4. quoted in Deborah Gesensway and Mindy Roseman, *Beyond Words: Images From America's Concentration Camps* (Ithaca: Cornell UP, 1987) 155.

5. Allan R. Bosworth, *America's Concentration Camps* (New York: Bantam Books, 1968) vi-vii.

6. W.F. Kelly, Assistant Commissioner, Immigration and Naturalization Service, letter to A. Vulliet, 9 August 1948, as received in photocopy form by the author without further documentation. Not included in the Japanese internment figures are 5,620 renunciants, Japanese-American native-born American citizens who publicly renounced their allegiance to the United States after December 7, 1941 and were not initially interned as aliens. No such examples of German-American

renunciants are known to exist. Also not included in internment figures are some 6,000 German merchant seamen, taken into custody in American ports during 1940 and 1941 and later placed in internment facilities.

7. Kitry Krause, "Dangerous Enemy Alien," *Reader* 22.48, 3 September 1993. Corroborating evidence can be found in a *Cincinnati Enquirer* article of March 24, 1943. In the words of the *Enquirer*, the two Fuhr brothers "will be given a hearing today before the Civilian Alien Hearing Board, then transferred to a temporary internment center at Chicago until action is taken by the United States Attorney General's office." ("Brothers Want To Help Hitler," *Cincinnati Enquirer* 24 March 1943) The *Enquirer* comment strongly suggests that the case of the Fuhr brothers was decided in advance of their opportunity to clear themselves, and that the appeal was regarded by federal officials as merely a formality.

8. Stephen C. Fox, "General John DeWitt and the Proposed Internment of German and Italian Aliens During World War II," *Pacific Historical Review* 57.4 (1988): 410.

9. Arthur D. Jacobs, "Untruths and Truths About the Evacuation, Relocation, and Internment in the United States During World War II," unpublished manuscript, 5 January 1990. Jacobs utilized the personal testimony of former internees, and numerous, many previous classified, government documents in compiling his list, as well as a collection of over 10,000 items relating to the internment of members of the German-American community.

10. Joseph E. Fallon, "Hostages of Hate: German-Americans and the Home Front in the Two World Wars," paper presented at the Society for German-American Studies 19th Annual Symposium, 7 April 1995: 2. Fallon has worked extensively with Arthur Jacobs, drawing his information from Jacobs' collection of documents and from his own research.

11. *Cases Argued and Decided in the Supreme Court: October Term, 1949*, Book 94, Lawyers' Edition (Rochester: Lawyers Co-Operative Publishing Company, 1950) 1255.

12. *Supreme Court of the United States, October Term 1949* 1261.

13. *United States Code Service, Lawyers' Edition: 50 USCS, War and National Defense* (Rochester: Lawyers Co-Operative, 1981) 11.

14. *50 USCS, War and National Defense* 11-12.

15. *World Book Encyclopedia*, vol. 4 (Chicago: World Book, 1990) 926-927.

16. *New Encyclopaedia Brittanica: Micropaedia*, vol. 3 (Chicago: Encyclopaedia Brittanica, 1989) 513.

17. *Webster's Third New International Dictionary of the English Language, Unabridged* (Springfield: Merriam-Webster, 1993) 469.

18. Krause "Dangerous Enemy Alien" 14.

19. While a detailed discussion of the German-American experience during World War I is beyond the scope of this work, it has been the subject of extensive analysis in previous scholarship. Recommended for an overview of the German-American community during this time period are Carl Wittke, *German-Americans and the World War* (New York: J.S. Ozer, 1974); Frederick C. Luebke, *Bonds of Loyalty: German-Americans and World War I* (Dekalb: Northern Illinois UP, 1974); and Don Heinrich Tolzmann, ed., *German-Americans in the World Wars, vol. 1: Anti-German Hysteria of World War One* (Munich: K.G. Saur, 1995). For a detailed account of the Cincinnati German-American community in the years immediately following World War I, see Tolzmann, *The Cincinnati Germans After the Great War* (New York: Peter Lang, 1987).

20. Tolzmann *The Cincinnati Germans* 14-15.

21. Tolzmann *The Cincinnati Germans* 15-16.

22. Tolzmann *The Cincinnati Germans* 15. Such tendencies were seen in numerous German-American centers of the day, most notably in the Midwest, where the core of German-American population was located. One notorious case in the Midwest where a German-American lynching did take place, was that of Robert Paul Prager, on April 5, 1918 in Collinsville, Illinois. Prager had been accused of hoarding explosive powders for subversive purposes, a charge later proven to be untrue. Prager was jailed by the mayor of Collinsville, only to be removed by an enraged mob and hung from a tree outside of town. In June 1918, the perpetrators were found not guilty of the lynching. For details of the incident, see Franziska Ott, "The Anti-German Hysteria: The Case of Robert Paul Prager," *German-Americans in the World Wars*, ed. Don Heinrich Tolzmann, vol. 1 (Munich: K.G. Saur, 1995).

23. Tolzmann *The Cincinnati Germans* 16.

24. Anne Galicich, *The German Americans* (Philadelphia: Chelsea House, 1989) 84. For a better understanding of the National German-American Alliance, and the Senate hearings concerning it, see "The U.S. Senate Hearings Against the National German-American Alliance," *German-Americans in the World Wars*, ed. Don Heinrich Tolzmann, vol. 2 (Munich: K.G. Saur, 1995).

Chapter II: American Nazi Activities and Their Effect on the Status of German-Americans

25. cited in LaVern J. Rippley, *The German Americans* (Boston: Twayne, 1976) 198. Sufficient information is lacking to determine the number of German-born in America who had obtained citizenship by this time. It is widely assumed that the majority had not yet done so; beginning with the process of assimilation immediately following World War I, doubtless more Germans in America sought citizenship than had been the case before the war.

26. A more detailed discussion of the *Teutonia* group can be found in Sander A. Diamond, *The Nazi Movement in the United States, 1924-1941* (Ithaca: Cornell UP, 1974) 91-99.

27. Susan Canedy, *America's Nazis: A Democratic Dilemma* (Menlo Park, CA: Markgraf Publications, 1990) 38-40.

28. Canedy *America's Nazis* 50. While a number of factors beyond American Nazi groups influenced relations between Germany and America during this period, the ideological difference between the two governments often proved most difficult to reconcile, particularly with regard to public relations. A fuller account of American-German diplomatic relations during this time period can be found in Kenneth Paul Jones, ed., *U.S. Diplomats in Europe, 1919-1941* (Oxford: Clio Press, 1981) 113-126.

29. Canedy *America's Nazis* 50.

30. Canedy *America's Nazis* 53.

31. Canedy *America's Nazis* 51.

32. "Mob of 1,000 Raids Jersey Nazi Rally," *New York Times* 22 May 1934.

33. "Newark Bans Rallies," *New York Times* 24 May 1934.

34. Canedy *America's Nazis* 53.

35. Rippley *The German Americans* 199. For a brief discussion of *Das neue Deutschland*, see Tolzmann, ed., *German-Americans in the World Wars*, vol. 4, 1659.

36. Canedy *America's Nazis* 56.

37. Rippley *The German-Americans* 199.

38. Canedy *America's Nazis* 62.

39. Canedy *America's Nazis* 62.

40. cited in Canedy *America's Nazis* 63. See also *Deutsche Zeitung* 4 January 1934, 14 April 1934.

41. Canedy *America's Nazis* 64.

42. Rippley *The German Americans* 199.

43. Canedy *America's Nazis* 63. The full report of the Dickstein-McCormack Committee can be found in U.S. Congress, Special Committee on Un-American Activities, *Investigation of Nazi and Other Propaganda* (Washington: U.S. Government Printing Office, 1935).

44. Canedy *America's Nazis* 64.

45. Canedy *America's Nazis* 55.

46. Canedy *America's Nazis* 77-81. A more detailed account of Fritz Kuhn's background and his role in the German-American Bund can be found in Leland V. Bell, *In Hitler's Shadow: The Anatomy of American Nazism* (New York: Kennikat Press, 1973); and Diamond *The Nazi Movement in the United States* 21-31. See also John Carlson, *Under Cover* (New York: E.P. Dutton, 1943) 111.

47. Canedy *America's Nazis* 81.

48. Canedy *America's Nazis* 81.

49. Canedy *America's Nazis* 82-83. An in-depth discussion of the pro-Nazi movement and its role in American Fascism can be found in Raymond G. Swing, *Forerunners of American Fascism* (Salem, NH: Ayer Co. Publishers, 1935); Richard Pells, *Radical Visions and American Dreams: Culture and Social Thought in the Depression Years* (Middletown, CT: Wesleyan UP, 1977); and Lawrence Dennis, *The Coming of American Fascism* (New York: AMS Press, 1977).

50. Martin Dies, *The Trojan Horse in America* (New York: Dodd, Mead, and Co., 1940) 306.

51. "Bundsmen Linked to Defense Plants," *New York Times* 3 October 1940.

52. Rippley *The German Americans* 204.

53. A lengthy list of known units of the Bund and their locations can be found in Bell, *In Hitler's Shadow* 20-21.

54. Dies *Trojan Horse* 306.

55. "Bundsmen Linked to Defense Plants," *New York Times* 3 October 1940.

56. Canedy *America's Nazis* 83.

57. Rippley *The German Americans* 205.

58. "Link German Bund to Army Officers," *New York Times* 8 September 1939.

59. "Bundsmen Linked to Defense Plants," *New York Times* 3 October 1940.

60. Dies *The Trojan Horse* 310-311. A summary of Coughlin's importance to the Bund is provided in Alan Brinkley, *Voices of Protest: Huey Long, Father Coughlin and the Great Depression* (New York: Alfred A. Knopf, 1982). For a discussion of *Social Justice* and *Liberation* respectively, see Tolzmann, ed., *German-Americans in the World Wars*, vol. 4 (Munich: K.G. Saur, 1995): 1651, 1654.

61. Dies *The Trojan Horse* 311-312.

62. Rippley *The German Americans* 204.

63. Dies *The Trojan Horse* 311.

64. cited in Dies *The Trojan Horse* 308-309. For a brief discussion of the *Weckruf* as a pro-Nazi publication, see Tolzmann, ed., *German-Americans in the World Wars*, vol. 4, 1660.

65. cited in Dies *The Trojan Horse* 308-309.

66. cited in Dies *The Trojan Horse* 309-310.

67. Rippley *The German Americans* 205-206.

68. Rippley *The German Americans* 204.

69. "Bund Is 'Audacious' Effort to Foist European Hatreds Upon America, Vet Asserts," *Cincinnati Enquirer* 2 March 1938. In subsequent years, radio and news magazine coverage stressed the controversial nature of the Bund, and provided detailed reports on group activities, reinforcing the anti-American image of the Bund for a large national audience. For contemporary news magazine reports on the Bund in America, see the articles "Nazi Eye View of San Francisco," *Time* 12 May 1941; "Roundup and Rally," *Newsweek* 26 May 1941; and Curt Reis, "The Nazis Carry On," *Cosmopolitan* June 1944.

70. "Crowd Storms Bund Meeting; Score Hurt In Resultant Riot," *Cincinnati Enquirer* 25 March 1938.

71. "Clubhouse Destroyed, St. Louis, Mo.," *New York Times* 7 September 1939.

72. "Link German Bund To Army Officers," *New York Times* 8 September 1939.

73. cited in "'Peewee Hitlers' Found In America," *New York Times* 1 September 1939. Incidents regarding the German-American Bund were widely and regularly reported in America's English-language newspapers, particularly in those areas with a high German-American concentration. For the purpose of this study, the *New York Times* is used as a representative example of newspaper reporting and editorial comment on the Bund, in a major metropolitan area with a traditional German-American presence.

74. cited in "'Peewee Hitlers Found In America," *New York Times* 1

September 1939.

75. "Link German Bund to Army Officers," *New York Times* 8 September 1939.

76. "Bundsmen Linked to Defense Plants," *New York Times* 3 October 1940.

77. quoted in "Says Bund Mapped Wall St. Hangings," *New York Times* 5 October 1940.

78. "Says Bund Mapped Wall St. Hangings," *New York Times* 5 October 1940.

79. "Bund Rally to Get Huge Police Guard," *New York Times* 19 February 1939.

80. "Anti-Nazi Outbreak Feared," *New York Times* 20 February 1939.

81. "22,000 Nazis Hold Rally In Garden; Police Check Foes," *New York Times* 21 February 1939.

82. "Bund 'Party' Egged On Coast," *New York Times* 26 February 1939.

83. "St. Louis Germans Snub the Bund," *New York Times* 26 February 1939.

84. "Young Bund Members Drill In Brooklyn; Police Guard Almost Outnumbers Children," *New York Times* 13 March 1939.

85. "Bund Defies Jersey Ban on Its Uniform; Leader Denies Link to a Foreign Nation," *New York Times* 5 July 1939.

86. "Jersey Bund Loses Its Liquor Permit," *New York Times* 7 July 1939.

87. Canedy *America's Nazis* 198-203.

88. Canedy *America's Nazis* 204-205.

89. Leland V. Bell, "The Failure of Nazism in America: The German American Bund, 1936-1941," *Political Science Quarterly* 85.4 (1970): 587.

90. Bell "The Failure of Nazism" 588.

91. Canedy *America's Nazis* 221-222.   Despite concern over fifth column activities in the United States, before and during World War II, there is no evidence to suggest that German officials recruited Bundists to be spies or saboteurs; see David Kahn, *Hitler's Spies* (New York: Macmillan, 1978). Regarding individual spies on behalf of Germany, see Ladislas Farago, *The Game of the Foxes: The Untold Story of German Espionage in the United States and Great Britain During World War II* (New York: David McKay Company, 1971).

92. Canedy *America's Nazis* 225.

93. Canedy *America's Nazis* 225-226.

94. Kitry Krause, "Dangerous Enemy Alien," *Reader* 22.48, 3 September 1993.

95. Bill King, "The Triumph of Pluralism In Cincinnati: 1930-1945," unpublished manuscript, 28 May 1991: 3.

96. King "The Triumph of Pluralism" 10.

97. "Cincinnati Nazi Salutes Hitler," *American Israelite* 18 January 1934.

98. "Cincinnati Nazi Salutes Hitler," *American Israelite* 18 January 1934.

99. "'Amerikanische Buergerliga' Prints Blacklist," *American Israelite* 1 February 1934.

100. cited in King "The Triumph of Pluralism" 13.

101. King "The Triumph of Pluralism" 16.

102. "German League Makes Light Of "Nazi" Affair Criticism; 'Incident Closed,' Vote Says," *Cincinnati Enquirer* 29 August 1935.

103. "Two Features Announced For 'German-American Day'," *Cincinnati Enquirer* 29 August 1937.

104. "Bund Is 'Audacious' Effort To Foist European Hatreds Upon America, Vet Asserts," *Cincinnati Enquirer* 2 March 1938.

105. "Bund Is 'Audacious Effort'," *Cincinnati Enquirer* 2 March 1938.

106. "Bund Is 'Audacious Effort'," *Cincinnati Enquirer* 2 March 1938.

107. "Bund Is 'Audacious Effort'," *Cincinnati Enquirer* 2 March 1938.

108. "German Bund Head Resigns; Plans Address To Veterans 'To Reaffirm Americanism'," *Cincinnati Enquirer* 6 March 1938.

109. "German Bund Head Resigns," *Cincinnati Enquirer* 6 March 1938.

110. "New Blow Struck At Bund; Veterans Condemn All Isms; Zimmer Fails To Show Up," *Cincinnati Enquirer* 9 March 1938.

111. "New Blow Struck At Bund," *Cincinnati Enquirer* 9 March 1938.

112. "New Blow Struck At Bund," *Cincinnati Enquirer* 9 March 1938.

113. "New Blow Struck At Bund," *Cincinnati Enquirer* 9 March 1938.

114. "Bund Rapped By Veterans' Council," *Cincinnati Enquirer* 17 March 1938.

115. "Duffy Demands Full Data On Bund Activities In Ohio, Including Cincinnati Camp," *Cincinnati Enquirer* 25 March 1938.

116. "New Blow Struck At Bund," *Cincinnati Enquirer* 9 March 1938.

117. "County Free Of All Camps Of Bund," *Cincinnati Enquirer* 26 March 1938.

118. "County Free Of All Camps Of Bund," *Cincinnati Enquirer* 26 March 1938.

119. "County Free Of All Camps Of Bund," *Cincinnati Enquirer* 26 March 1938.

120. "Post Demands Publicity For Bund Members," *Cincinnati Enquirer* 26 March 1938.

121. "Protest On Bund Is Slated," *Cincinnati Enquirer* 9 July 1938.

122. "Protest On Bund Is Slated," *Cincinnati Enquirer* 9 July 1938.

123. "Protest On Bund Is Slated," *Cincinnati Enquirer* 9 July 1938.

124. "C.I.O. Officer Communist, Bund Strong In Cincinnati, Leader Of

Legion Declares," *Cincinnati Enquirer* 4 April 1941.

125. "Bund Strong In Cincinnati," *Cincinnati Enquirer* 4 April 1941.

126. "Bund Strong In Cincinnati," *Cincinnati Enquirer* 4 April 1941.

127. "Bund Strong In Cincinnati," *Cincinnati Enquirer* 4 April 1941.

Chapter III: Media Perception and Coverage of the German-American Community

128. For a more comprehensive discussion of the German-language press and its function, see Carl Wittke, *The German Language Press in America* (Lexington: U Kentucky P, 1957); Karl J.R. Arndt and May E. Olson, *The German Language Press of the Americas* (New York, K.G. Saur, 1980); Ludwig Oberndorf, "The German Press in the United States," *The American-German Review* 6 (December 1939); and "The Foreign Language Press," *Fortune* 22 (November 1940).

129. Wittke *The German Language Press in America* 282.

130. Wittke *The German Language Press in America* 282.

131. Wittke *The German Language Press in America* 282.

132. Wittke *The German Language Press in America* 283.

133. Wittke *The German Language Press in America* 283. The unwillingness of German-American newspapers to take on mainstream opinion in a controversial setting, perhaps is best illustrated by the arrest, conviction, and execution of Bruno Hauptmann for the kidnapping of the Lindbergh baby. Wary of public backlash in the face of support for Hauptmann, many German-language newspapers understated coverage of the trial, some even choosing not to run editorial comment on the case. Beyond the scope of this study, a noteworthy recent account of the Hauptmann affair can be found in Gert Raeithel, "Bruno Hauptmann: Neue Theorien zur Entführung des Lindbergh-Babys," *Deutsch-Amerikanischer Almanach* 3 (1994-1995): 6-18.

134. Wittke *The German Language Press in America* 284. The tendency of German-language newspapers, and German-American

organizations in general, to quickly and emphatically stress a pro-American posture was seen in small towns as well as urban areas. In Winona, Minnesota, for example, Emil Leicht, a publisher of German-language newspapers, wrote a strongly pro-American editorial shortly after the attack on Pearl Harbor, and the Winona German Society changed its name to the American Society in mid-December 1941. (*Winona Daily News* 6 December 1991)

135. "*Freie Presse* Editor Given Decoration By Hitler," *Cincinnati Post* 25 November 1938.

136. "Obituaries," *Cincinnati Times-Star* 14 January 1941.

137. "Obituaries," *Cincinnati Times-Star* 14 January 1941.

138. "Obituaries," *Cincinnati Times-Star* 14 January 1941.

139. "Our Platform For German-Americans," *Cincinnati Freie Presse* 18 September 1939.

140. "Paper Disdains Responsibility," *New York Times* 23 November 1940. For a description of the Trans-Ocean News Service as an organization for the dissemination of Nazi propaganda, see Tolzmann, ed., *German-Americans in the World Wars*, vol. 4 (Munich: K.G. Saur, 1995): 1636, 1656.

141. cited in *Cincinnati Post* 2 August 1942.

142. cited in *Cincinnati Post* 2 August 1942. Despite the patriotic overtones voiced by German-American newspaper and community leaders, suspicion continued to run high regarding their loyalties, particularly after American entry into the war. A wartime public opinion survey of east coast residents, cited by the Bureau of Intelligence, found that some twenty-five percent wanted to stop publication of all German-language newspapers. About fifty percent of those polled also felt that German-language radio broadcasts should be banned for the duration of the war.

143. "Local Nazis Gloat Over Hitler Killings," *American Israelite* 20 July 1934.

144. "Local Nazis Gloat Over Hitler Killings," *American Israelite* 20 July 1934.

145. *Cincinnatier Freie Presse* 4 February 1934.

146. *Every Friday* 20 July 1934.

147. "Local Nazis Gloat Over Hitler Killings," *American Israelite* 20 July 1934.

148. Benjamin Epstein, letter, 9 December 1940, American Jewish Archives, Hebrew Union College, Cincinnati.

149. *Cincinnatier Freie Presse* 12 April 1942.

150. "Warning Issued Against Solicitor," *Cincinnati Post* 30 December 1942.

151. United Banater Society, meeting report, Cincinnati, 21 July 1941.

152. Bavarian Mutual Support Organization, meeting report, Cincinnati, 22 July 1941.

153. "Nazi Agents," *Cincinnati Post* 27 February 1942.

154. B.E., "A Protest," *Cincinnati Post* 12 March 1942. The issue of the treatment of suspected spies and saboteurs generated considerable concern, and discussion, on both sides. Many letter writers used initials or false names in their correspondence, not wishing to disclose their true identity for fear of reprisals.

155. F.L.C., "Says We Must Act Against the Rumor Mongers," *Cincinnati Post* 6 March 1942.

156. Vernon Sennett, "Urges Firm Hand Upon Our 'Internal Enemies,'" *Cincinnati Post* 6 February 1942.

157. "Treachery," *Cincinnati Post* 3 March 1942.

158. Dr. E.M. Craig, "A Doctor Comments On Appeal For Enemy Aliens," *Cincinnati Post* 11 March 1942.

159. Paul Maujean, "Would Send Nazi Spies To Firing Squad," *Cincinnati Post* 2 July 1942.

160. Mark Millikin, "Would Give Nazi Spies A Lesson In Democracy," *Cincinnati Post* 3 July 1942.

161. R.H., "A Comment On 'Nice Treatment' For Spies," *Cincinnati Post* 8 July 1942.

162. Cul. J. Foreman, "Leniency To Spies An Insult To Soldiers," *Cincinnati Post* 9 July 1942.

163. "Those Spies," *Cincinnati Post* 3 August 1942.

164. Charles F. Hennessey, "On Spies," *Cincinnati Post* 14 July 1942.

165. B.G., "In Praise Of," *Cincinnati Post* 17 December 1941.

166. "Our Enemy Aliens," *Cincinnati Post* 13 December 1941.

167. "No War-Hysteria," *Cincinnati Post* 19 December 1941.

168. "Assurance To Aliens," *Cincinnati Post* 29 December 1941.

169. "Those Spies," *Cincinnati Post* 15 July 1942.

170. "German Name," *Cincinnati Post* 23 December 1941.

171. "German Language," *Cincinnati Post* 10 January 1942.

172. "Exile's Plea," *Cincinnati Post* 6 August 1942.

173. "Enemy Alien," *Cincinnati Post* 11 April 1942.

174. "German Books," *Cincinnati Post* 14 March 1942.

175 "From An Exile," *Cincinnati Post* 7 August 1942.

176. Richard Wood and David Culbert, ed., *Film and Propaganda in America: A Documentary History*, vol. 1 (New York: Greenwood, 1990) xv.

177. Larry Langman and Ed Borg, *Encyclopedia of American War Films* (New York: Garland, 1989) 547.

178. Langman and Borg 547.

179. Langman and Borg 547.

180. Langman and Borg 547.

181. Raymond Fielding, *The American Newsreel, 1911-1967* (Norman:

U Oklahoma P, 1972) 115.

182. quoted in Fielding 116.

183. Fielding 123.

184. quoted in Fielding 123.

185. Fielding 278.

186. Fielding 253.

187. "Inside Nazi Germany," *The March of Time*, newsreel, Time, Inc., 1938.

188. "Inside Nazi Germany," *The March of Time*.

189. "Inside Nazi Germany," *The March of Time*. Ultimately, the Bund camp was banned in Southbury due to zoning code restrictions. Such legalities were often invoked by local authorities in bowing to vocal anti-Nazi camp opponents, while wishing not to offend the sizeable local German community. In Southbury, as elsewhere, local officials also turned to stricter enforcement of liquor laws, in efforts to deny Bund camps licenses or camp permits. Perhaps not coincidentally, when the Bund camp was overturned in Southbury due to zoning laws, two people were also arrested and charged with violating liquor laws in Southbury.

190. James Combs, *American Political Movies: An Annotated Filmography of Feature Films* (New York: Garland, 1990) 29.

191. Combs 31-32.

192. Combs 32.

193. Combs 32.

194. Jay Robert Nash and Stanley Ralph Ross, *The Motion Picture Guide: C-D, 1927-1983* (Chicago: Cinebooks, 1985) 472.

195. H. M. Glancy, rev. of *Confessions of a Nazi Spy*, *International Dictionary of Films and Filmmakers*, vol. 1 (Chicago: St. James, 1990) 205.

196. Glancy 205.

197. Langman and Borg 122.

198. Glancy 205.

199. Nash and Ross 472-473.

200. *Deutscher Weckruf und Beobachter* 18 May 1939.

201. "Kuhn Sues For $5,000,000," *New York Times* 13 May 1939.

202. "Nazi Film Banned in Cuba," *New York Times* 21 June 1939.

203. "Kuhn Fails to Get Film Writ," *New York Times* 21 June 1939.

204. "News of the Screen," *New York Times* 21 June 1939.

205. Glancy 205.

206. "Bund Here Called Agency of Reich," *New York Times* 6 September 1939.

207. "Bund Ending Film Suit," *New York Times* 3 October 1940.

208. "Kuhn Drops $5,000,000 Suit," *New York Times* 23 November 1940.

209. Richard Wood and David Culbert, ed., *Film and Propaganda in America: A Documentary History*, vol. 2 (New York: Greenwood, 1990) xix. The full testimony of Warner and other noteworthy Hollywood film executives, illustrating the mindset of American filmmaking on the eve of American entry into World War II, can be found in this volume as well.

210. U.S. Congress, "Propaganda in Motion Pictures," *Hearings Before a Subcommittee of the Committee on Interstate Commerce: United States Senate, Resolution 152*, 77th Cong., first session, 9-26 September 1941 (Washington: United States Government Printing Office, 1942) 339.

211. U.S. Congress "Propaganda in Motion Pictures" 344.

212. U.S. Congress "Propaganda in Motion Pictures" 345.

213. U.S. Congress "Propaganda in Motion Pictures" 350.

214. U.S. Congress "Propaganda in Motion Pictures" 362.

215. Langman and Borg 545.

216. Combs 34.

217. Nash and Ross 50.

218. Combs 37.

219. Nash and Ross 385-386.

220. Langman and Borg 547.

221. Langman and Borg 545.

222. Combs 36-37.

223. Combs 34.

224. Combs 35.

Chapter IV: Alien Registration, Arrests, and
Enemy Alien Hearings

225. Stephen R. Fox, *The Unknown Internment: An Oral History of the Relocation of Italian Americans During World War II* (Boston: Twayne Publishers, 1990) 152.

226. "Aliens' Registry To Start In Cincinnati August 27," *Cincinnati Enquirer* 8 August 1940.

227. "Alien Registration: Here's How It Will Be Done, Step By Step," *Cincinnati Post* 23 August 1940. According to existing documentation, each alien was required to answer fifteen primary and twenty-seven secondary questions during the registration process. For an overview of the registration process, and further details on how it was carried out, see the June 1944 "Report of the Delegation of the Emergency Advisory Committee for Political Defense Which Made the Consultative Visit to the United States of America," reproduced in Tolzmann, ed., *German-Americans in the World Wars*, vol. 4: 1677-1736.

228. "Cincinnati Postoffice Is Ready For Alien Registration Today," *Cincinnati Enquirer* 27 August 1940.

229. *Cincinnati Post* 27 August 1940.

230. "Aliens Required To Report Each Address Change," *Cincinnati Times-Star* 6 September 1940.

231. "4,500 Aliens Still To Be Registered," *Cincinnati Times-Star* 25 November 1940.

232. "Post Office Lists 8,575 Aliens In Cincinnati," *Cincinnati Times-Star* 10 December 1940.

233. "10,200 Aliens Estimated To Have Registered Here," *Cincinnati Post* 27 December 1940.

234. "10,200 Aliens Estimated To Have Registered Here," *Cincinnati Post* 27 December 1940.

235. "Aliens Total 12,271," *Cincinnati Enquirer* 1 March 1941.

236. "Denies Friction Behind Alien Work 'Shakeup,'" *Cincinnati Post* 7 January 1942. Evidence of the new procedure can be seen in the certificate of identification Cincinnati registrant Eberhard Fuhr was required to carry at all times. Among information required upon demand of authorities, and contained inside the certificate, were the alien registration number; birth location; citizenship; length of residence in the United States; current residence, height, and weight information; and physically distinctive marks. On the back cover were seven admonishments to certificate holders, including reminders of exclusionary areas and restricted items of possession; a requirement to obey all regulations; and the need to keep federal officials updated as to name, address, and place of employment changes. Violation of any of the listed statutes constituted grounds for detention and internment for the duration of the war.

237. "German Woman Arrested Here As Enemy Alien," *Cincinnati Post* 9 January 1942.

238. "County Has 3,600 Axis Aliens To Register February 9-28," *Cincinnati Enquirer* 4 February 1942.

239. Fox *Unknown Internment* 153. According to a 1990 report by Arthur Jacobs, based on declassified Department of Justice documents, FBI apprehensions of German legal resident aliens and German-Americans

from December 7, 1941 to June 30, 1945, were most common along the east and west coasts. The pattern was prompted by the attack on Pearl Harbor and the perceived need to secure American shores from aerial and naval attack, and invasion. According to Jacobs, New York showed the most German legal resident alien and German-American apprehensions by state, with 2,291, followed by New Jersey with 756. California ranked third with 572 apprehensions, with Oregon (133) and Washington (115) also ranking in the top ten nationally. Among midwestern states representing the core group of German-American settlements, Ohio (139) ranked second in FBI arrests, behind only Illinois (318). Wisconsin, with 110 detentions, placed a distant third.

240. "Nine Cincinnati Aliens Held, Including Physician, Baker," *Cincinnati Enquirer* 10 December 1941. Regarding the total number of enemy alien arrests made in the Cincinnati area during World War II, declassified Department of Justice documents show that ninety-five aliens were detained between December 7, 1941 and June 30, 1945. Of those, sixty-nine were of German background, with twenty-five Italian-Americans arrested and one Japanese alien incarcerated. These figures are equal to or lower than many other midwestern cities, including Chicago, Cleveland, Detroit, and Milwaukee, indicating that Cincinnati had relatively few problems with enemy aliens and their control. Only St. Louis, with forty-five ethnic German and fifty-six total arrests, showed lower figures than Cincinnati among the major midwestern cities. For complete statistics on FBI alien arrests by field offices, see Tolzmann, ed., *German-Americans in the World Wars*, vol. 4 (Munich: K.G. Saur, 1995): 1740-1749.

241. "Six German Aliens Seized Here By FBI," *Cincinnati Post* 9 December 1941.

242. "G-Men Seize Enemy Aliens As Roosevelt Reveals Threat Of Invasion By Axis Partners," *Cincinnati Enquirer* 10 December 1941. The early, vigorous rate of arrest of enemy aliens of all nationalities continued into January 1942; a January 14, 1942 memo to J. Edgar Hoover stated that, as of January 8, 1,243 Germans had been arrested, along with 1,206 Japanese and 235 Italians. For the full content of the memo, see Tolzmann, ed., *German-Americans in the World Wars*, vol. 4 (Munich: K.G. Saur, 1995): 1577.

243. "Nine Cincinnati Aliens Held," *Cincinnati Enquirer* 10 December 1941.

244. *Cincinnati Post* 9 December 1941.

245. "Nine Cincinnati Aliens Held," *Cincinnati Enquirer* 10 December 1941.

246. "Attempts Made To Free Two Enemy Aliens Picked Up In Cincinnati By Federal Men," *Cincinnati Enquirer* 11 December 1941.

247. "Mayor Stewart Gets Power To Blackout City," *Cincinnati Post* 12 December 1941.

248. "Blackout Fine $100; First In Cleveland," *Cincinnati Enquirer* 5 June 1942.

249. "Mayor Stewart Gets Power To Blackout City," *Cincinnati Post* 12 December 1941.

250. "Barbed Wire To Be Placed About Units Of Waterworks To Guard Against Sabotage," *Cincinnati Enquirer* 7 January 1942.

251. "'Twas WPA, Not Japanese, Tried To Photograph Pumps," *Cincinnati Enquirer* 5 June 1942.

252. "Government To Set Up Alien Hearing Boards," *Cincinnati Post* 12 December 1941.

253. "U.S. to Protect Innocent Aliens," *Cincinnati Post* 16 December 1941. The secrecy behind the hearing boards and alien status also was designed to protect the board, and the government itself. According to a confidential February 2, 1942 Justice Department memo to all United States attorneys, a listing of German organizations deemed "dangerous," including the Friends of New Germany and the German-American Bund, was to be kept strictly private. According to the memo, "Public disclosure of the views set forth in this memorandum might lead to controversies which would be of no advantage at the present time and might also lead to the unwarranted inference that the organizations mentioned herein are the only dangerous ones." (*German-Americans in the World Wars*, vol. 4: 1578-1579)

254. "U.S. to Protect Innocent Aliens," *Cincinnati Post* 16 December 1941.

255. "Five in City Urged for Alien Hearing Board," *Cincinnati Post* 18

December 1941.

256. "Dr. Walters Is Chairman Of Alien Hearing Board," *Cincinnati Enquirer* 3 January 1942.

257. "Five in City Urged for Alien Hearing Board," *Cincinnati Post* 18 December 1941.

258. "Denies Friction Behind Alien Work 'Shakeup,'" *Cincinnati Post* 7 January 1942.

259. "Tribute Is Paid By Attorney To Men Hearing Alien Cases," *Cincinnati Enquirer* 8 January 1942.

260. "Enemy Aliens Now Barred From Army," *Cincinnati Enquirer* 20 March 1942. In recent years, evidence has surfaced that a number of German-American soldiers were subjected to loyalty interrogations during the early years of the war, despite having been born in America and lacking any ties to Germany save for German parents. In a July 14, 1994 letter in the possession of the author, one German-American former soldier, Werner C. Kaatz, discussed his experience while in the Army. According to Kaatz, who served without incident in the National Guard from 1933-1939 and in the Army beginning March 1, 1942, he was questioned twice with regard to his loyalties during 1942, at Camp Sibert Gadsden, Alabama. No reason was given to him for the interrogations, nor was any evidence of wrongdoing presented during or after the questionings.

261. "Alien Control Discussed In Conference With FBI," *Cincinnati Enquirer* 24 June 1942.

262. "New Inspector Arrives To 'Boss' Enemy Aliens," *Cincinnati Enquirer* 21 July 1942.

263. "German Woman Arrested Here As Enemy Alien," *Cincinnati Post* 9 January 1942.

264. "Only Four Cases Remain On Enemy Alien Docket," *Cincinnati Enquirer* 14 January 1942.

265. "Obituaries," *Cincinnati Enquirer* 15 November 1973. Documentation of the Thuss family's internment experience still exists, including August 1942 letters concerning the transfer of Otto to the

Seagoville internment camp; and post-internment letters from Cincinnati, dated March 1945, from Otto and Hetty Thuss to Camp Warden Dr. Amy Stannard. See Tolzmann, ed., *German-Americans in the World Wars*, vol. 4: 1872-1873, 2039-2040.

266. "Union Protests Discharge Of 'Enemy' Alien Workers," *Cincinnati Enquirer* 24 January 1942.

267. "Union Protests Discharge Of 'Enemy' Alien Workers," *Cincinnati Enquirer* 24 January 1942.

268. "Problems Are Multiplied For German-Born Resident," *Cincinnati Enquirer* 17 September 1943. A Department of Justice memo outlining Treasury Department policies on blocking internees' assets, and by extension those of select non-internees such as Schleiermacher, can be found in Tolzmann, ed., *German-Americans in the World Wars*, vol. 4: 1662-1666.

269. "Problems Are Multiplied For German-Born Resident," *Cincinnati Enquirer* 17 September 1943. The perspective of the Treasury Department on blocking the assets of internees and select other aliens, can be found in a July 1944 memo from J.W. Pehle, reprinted in Tolzmann, ed., *German-Americans in the World Wars*, vol. 4: 1966-1969.

270. "Frozen Cash Released To Native," *Cincinnati Enquirer* 29 September 1943.

271. "Young Alien Pleads Guilty Of Claiming Citizenship," *Cincinnati Enquirer* 4 February 1942.

272. "War Worker Is Alien, FBI Charge," *Cincinnati Enquirer* 26 October 1944.

273. "Seven Aliens To Be Brought Here," *Cincinnati Enquirer* 11 February 1942.

274. "Transfer Of 12 Aliens From Cincinnati To Wisconsin Concentration Camp Is Reported," *Cincinnati Enquirer* 26 February 1942.

275. Robert L. Otto, "It Happened Here: How Nazi Agents Plotted Evil Deeds," *Cincinnati Post* 26 February 1942. The fear factor such articles catered to was noticed by the federal government as well, with public opinion polls serving as a factor in, and rationale for, many decisions

regarding the treatment of German aliens. An undated wartime memorandum, from the Bureau of Intelligence to Archibald MacLeish, disclosed that forty-three percent of east coast residents believed that few or no German aliens were loyal to the United States, with only half that amount, twenty-two percent, responding that all or most were loyal. Of those polled, forty percent felt that German aliens represented the most dangerous alien group in the country, compared with only one percent stating the same of Italian aliens. Sixty-three percent were of the opinion that governmental treatment of German aliens had not been strict enough to date, while only one percent held that their treatment had been too strict.

276. Otto "It Happened Here," *Cincinnati Post* 26 February 1942.

277. Otto "It Happened Here," *Cincinnati Post* 26 February 1942.

278. "Obituaries," *Cincinnati Enquirer* 21 June 1981. For a more detailed discussion of Huebener's relationship with the Kaiser, see "Former Kaiser Really Kind, His Personal Physician Says," *Cincinnati Enquirer* 5 June 1941; and "My Years With the Kaiser," *Cincinnati Pictorial Enquirer* 14 February 1965.

279. "Two Aliens Arrested," *Cincinnati Enquirer* 11 July 1942.

280. "Two Women Are In Custody Here As German Aliens," *Cincinnati Enquirer* 12 July 1942.

281. A more detailed account of the Max Stephan case can be found in Shirley J. Burton and Kellee Green, "Oaths of Allegiance, Acts of Treason: The Disloyalty Prosecutions of Max Stephan and Hans Haupt," *Prologue* 23.3 (1991): 236-247.

282. "Supreme Court Denies Stephan Plea," *Cincinnati Enquirer* 25 June 1943.

283. "Supreme Court Denies Stephan Plea," *Cincinnati Enquirer* 25 June 1943.

284. "To Hold Wife Of Traitor In Cincinnati Alien Camp," *Cincinnati Enquirer* 27 September 1942.

285. "Former Cincinnatian Is Sought, Along With Two Others, By FBI As Saboteurs For Nazi Germany," *Cincinnati Enquirer* 26 July 1942.

286. "Former Cincinnatian Is Sought," *Cincinnati Enquirer* 26 July 1942.

287. "Alien 'Refuge' In City Clean, Comfortable," *Cincinnati Post* 17 December 1941. Detention centers under the jurisdiction of the Immigration and Naturalization Service, such as the one in Cincinnati, were subject to extensive guidelines on the proper treatment of detainees, including specific rules regarding sanitation, exercise and fresh air, food requirements, bedding and towels, religious services, and visitation rights, among others. The full INS memo is reprinted in Tolzmann, ed., *German-Americans in the World Wars*, vol. 4: 1580-1589.

288. "Alien 'Refuge' In City Clean, Comfortable," *Cincinnati Post* 17 December 1941.

289. "Alien 'Refuge' In City Clean, Comfortable," *Cincinnati Post* 17 December 1941.

290. Gerhard Fuhr, personal interview, 27 March 1993.

291. "Aliens Are Moved From Fort," *Cincinnati Enquirer* 20 December 1941; "Alien Held Here Released By U.S.," *Cincinnati Post* 20 December 1941.

292. "Woman Detained Here As Enemy Alien Goes Berserk, Rips Dress From Matron," *Cincinnati Post* 22 December 1941.

293. "Woman Detained Here As Enemy Alien Goes Berserk," *Cincinnati Post* 22 December 1941.

294. "Woman Detained Here As Enemy Alien Goes Berserk," *Cincinnati Post* 22 December 1941.

295. "Woman Detained Here As Enemy Alien Goes Berserk," *Cincinnati Post* 22 December 1941.

296. "Diplomats, Families Are Held At Hotel Gibson Waiting Ships For Homes In Europe, Japan," *Cincinnati Enquirer* 28 April 1942.

297. "A Veritable City In Itself," *Cincinnati Enquirer* 13 February 1949.

298. "Aliens Treated Well Here But Nazis Criticize," *Cincinnati Post* 20 May 1942.

299. "Recreation Lot Proposed For Use By Enemy Aliens," *Cincinnati Enquirer* 24 June 1942.

300. *Cincinnati Enquirer* 19 August 1942.

301. "Cameras And Radios Called In," *Cincinnati Enquirer* 1 January 1942.

302. "Storage Place Sought In Cincinnati," *Cincinnati Enquirer* 3 January 1942.

303. "Place Found To Store Equipment," *Cincinnati Enquirer* 4 January 1942.

304. "Bombs Are Added To Lists Of Contraband As Aliens Relinquish Radios And Cameras," *Cincinnati Enquirer* 7 January 1942.

305. "Bombs Are Added To Lists," *Cincinnati Enquirer* 7 January 1942.

306. "Denies Friction Behind Alien Work 'Shakeup,'" *Cincinnati Post* 7 January 1942.

307. "F.B.I. Nabs 11 Enemy Aliens For Holding Banned Goods," *Cincinnati Enquirer* 9 April 1942. Confiscation of pro-German and pro-Nazi materials continued in Cincinnati to a lesser extent for the duration of the war, often based on tips relayed by patriotic-minded neighbors and coworkers. In March 1943, some fifty pounds of pro-German literature, medals, and Nazi propaganda, as well as photographs of Hitler, were seized in a series of raids on Cincinnati area residences. ("Nazi Activities Investigated By FBI," *Cincinnati Enquirer* 25 March 1943)

308. "Seized Aliens Brought To Cincinnati," *Cincinnati Enquirer* 10 April 1942.

309. "G-Men Net Six Aliens In Cincinnati Raids; Contraband Is Seized," *Cincinnati Enquirer* 5 June 1942.

310. "Former Cincinnatian Is Sought," *Cincinnati Enquirer* 26 July 1942.

311. "Storage Place Sought In Cincinnati," *Cincinnati Enquirer* 3 January 1942.

Chapter V: The Internment of German Legal Resident Aliens and German-Americans

312. Noteworthy among many such references are *Time* magazine, which stated in an article that there had been no camps for German-Americans, and a December 5, 1991 commentary by John Chancellor for NBC, commemorating the fiftieth anniversary of Pearl Harbor, in which he stated that no Germans or Italians had been interned during the war. Extensive records continue to be maintained by the federal government, in print, microfilm, and microfiche form, detailing the scope and extent of the internment of members of the German-American community, the basis for their internment, locations and conditions of the camps in which they were held, and individual case records. One of many representative examples of such matter can be found in *Federal Records of World War II* (Washington: General Services Administration, National Archives and Records Services, 1950), a multivolume overview of available source materials and governmental involvement in wartime internment.

313. Arthur Jacobs, a retired United States Air Force officer, was interned at the age of twelve with his family from February 1945 until February 1946, in Ellis Island, New York, Crystal City, Texas, and, following deportation, in Hohen Asberg, Germany. Jacobs returned to his native United States with his brother in November 1947. In recent years he has been the leading activist on behalf of German and German-American former internees, assembling a collection of thousands of documents relating to the enemy alien internment program. Such documents, along with his personal experiences, have formed the basis of numerous publications and presentations, as well as legal action, aimed at informing others of the situation of internees during the World War II era, and at gaining official recognition of the internment of native Germans and German-Americans from 1941 to 1948.

314. Gerald H. Davis. " 'Orgelsdorf': A World War I Internment Camp in America," *Yearbook of German-American Studies* 26 (1991): 251-252. This article remains to date one of the best sources for information on the World War I internment experience of German-Americans.

315. Of the more than 6,500 detainees during World War I, some 1,400 were soldiers of the German navy, interned after being forced into American ports by superior British forces. On several occasions before

April 1917, and under terms of the Hague Conventions of 1907, the United States was obliged to prevent hostile naval forces from using its harbors regularly; German ships and their crews in American harbors not departing within forty-eight hours were subject to internment. While the crews were permitted to live on board their ships while the United States was neutral, the detainees were formally interned after relations between Germany and America were broken off in February 1917, later to be declared prisoners of war.

Another 2,300 internees came from German merchant ships stranded in American ports after the British had seized control of the shipping lanes. The German merchantmen initially were able to leave their ships, find work in German-American communties, and even marry American women, but were quickly rounded up upon American entry into the war, at which point they were sent to the internment camps as enemy aliens. Ultimately, the majority of German naval prisoners of war were sent to Fort McPherson, with Fort Douglas and Fort Oglethorpe detaining mostly civilian Germans and German-Americans.

Ironically, German sailors would undergo a similar experience in the late 1930s and early 1940s, when they were trapped in American ports while evading British sea forces. The Germans initially were detained as illegal aliens, before they were classified as enemy aliens and sent to internment facilities. For a contemporary account of their experience, see the article "A Camp for Aliens," *Time* 27 January 1941. For a detailed account of the experience of the German seamen, including interviews with former internees, see also John Christgau, *"Enemies": World War II Alien Internment* (Ames: Iowa State UP, 1985).

316. Davis 257.

317. A detailed discussion of Fort Oglethorpe as a World War I internment facility can be found in Davis, "'Orgelsdorf': A World War I Internment Camp in America," *Yearbook of German-American Studies* 26 (1991): 249-265.

318. Davis 254. Of the approximately 4,000 internees, the vast majority were German legal resident aliens; a significantly lesser number of German-Americans deemed to be security risks were also held, as well as some 150 ethnic Austrians, and a small number of detainees of other nationalities.

319. Athan Theoharris, *Spying on Americans: Political Surveillance*

from Hoover to the Huston Plan (Philadelphia: Temple UP, 1978) 40. Further information on the origin of internment as American policy during the World War II era, and the legal aspects thereof, can be found in Jacobus ten Broek et al., *Prejudice, War and the Constitution* (Berkeley: U California P, 1954), an early but thorough analysis of this complicated issue.

320. Commission On Wartime Relocation and Internment of Civilians, *Personal Justice Denied* (Washington: United States Government, 1982) 54.

321. Stephen C. Fox, "General John DeWitt and the Proposed Internment of German and Italian Aliens during World War II," *Pacific Historical Review* 57.4 (1988): 409-410.

322. *Personal Justice Denied* 54.

323. *Personal Justice Denied* 112.   Other figures recently made available show the extent to which members of the German-American community were targeted for detention in early December 1941.   A December 15, 1941 memo from W.F. Kelly stated that, to date, 1,757 arrest warrants had been issued against German legal resident aliens and German-Americans, compared with only 700 against ethnic Japanese and eighty-five against ethnic Italians.   The full memorandum, including all relevant figures, is reproduced in Tolzmann, ed., *German-Americans in the World Wars*, vol. 4: 1572.

324. cited in Dianna Hatfield, "The Internment of Germans and German-Americans During World War II: The Untold Story," *Society for German-American Studies Newsletter* 14.2 (1993): 13.

325. Arthur Jacobs, "History Quiet on the Arrest and Internment of German Americans in the United States during World War II," *Society for German-American Studies Newsletter* 12.3 (1991): 18.   The Immigration and Naturalization Service has preserved its records of enemy alien internment facilities of World Wars I and II, as well as relevant records from its central and field offices.   A directory of these materials was compiled in January 1965, and is available, from the National Archives and Records Administration Library, under the title of "Preliminary Inventory of the Records of the Immigration and Naturalization Service."

326. Jacobs "History Quiet" 18-19.

327. Jacobs "History Quiet" 18.

328. Jacobs "History Quiet" 19.

329. Richard S. Warner, "Barbed Wire and Nazilagers," *The Chronicles of Oklahoma* 64.1 (1986): 46-47.

330. Jacobs "History Quiet" 19.

331. Jacobs "History Quiet" 19.

332. Jacobs "History Quiet" 19.

333. *Alien Enemy Detention Facility*, film, United States Immigration and Naturalization Service, 1947. In 1947, the Department of Justice, and specifically the Immigration and Naturalization Service, produced this film, centered on the Crystal City facility. The documentary began and ended with the playing of "My Country 'Tis of Thee," and featured an introductory commentary by Immigration and Naturalization Service Commissioner Argyle R. Mackey. Designed to show that the Government treated internees in a decent and humane manner, while maintaining national security interests, the film exists in a color print; former internees who have watched it say that they have also seen a black-and-white version, indicating that the production may have been colorized at some point. If in fact the color is original, it was a rarity for the time. It remains unclear to whom the film was shown and distributed, and why exclusively the Crystal City camp was featured.

334. *Alien Enemy Detention Facility* film. A description of the essential features of the Crystal City facility was provided by the Immigration and Naturalization Service, while the camp was still open. This information has been reproduced for contemporary scholars in Tolzmann, ed., *German-Americans in the World Wars*, vol. 4: 1758-1761.

335. *Alien Enemy Detention Facility* film.

336. *Alien Enemy Detention Facility* film. While certain items could be purchased at the camps, internees preferred to bring their own items from home whenever possible. Among items internees were permitted to bring with them were clothing of choice; necessary toilet articles; handicrafts for women; small toys for children; and small photographs. Items not allowed to be brought in by internees included pets of any type; household furnishings; and any type of transportation, including roller skates,

bicycles, and/or wagons. (*German-Americans in the World Wars*, vol. 4: 1864) Further details on clothing and financial allowances for internees, including what clothing the camp provided for internees; how monies and objects of value were stored for internees; and what internees were paid for work performed, may be found a document reprinted in the above listed source, volume 4: 1980.

337. *Alien Enemy Detention Facility* film.

338. *Alien Enemy Detention Facility* film. Many former internees willing to speak for the record have stated that their treatment in the internment centers indeed was humane; relatively few have opined that they were treated in an unduly harsh manner. To its credit, the Department of Justice went to great lengths to ensure that camp officers and employees respected the rights and privileges of the internees. A confidential memo of April 28, 1943 is noteworthy in this regard; its contents stress the need for harmony and a spirit of cooperation; that all internees would be given a voice in internee affairs; and that suggestions for improvement were encouraged from the internees. The memo is reproduced in its entirety in Tolzmann, ed., *German-Americans in the World Wars*, vol. 4: 1667-1670.

339. *Alien Enemy Detention Facility* film. A list of specific kitchen and house cleaning chores for German internees, and house rules in general, dated October 29, 1943, can be found in Tolzmann, ed., *German-Americans and the World Wars*, vol. 4: 1914-1916.

340. Gerhard Fuhr, personal interview, 27 March 1993.

341. *Alien Enemy Detention Facility* film. That Japanese and German alien internees had trouble adapting to American eating habits, is shown clearly in comments which surfaced at the Seagoville facility in July 1943. A group of Japanese internees requested that less meat be served, and in particular no ground meat or lamb. Instead, they requested more fish, rice, and fresh vegetables. German internees, for their part, complained of inferior meat quality, particularly with lamb. Among their requests were one hot meal per day; chicken and bread on a regular basis; and more fresh vegetables and milk in their rations. (*German-Americans in the World Wars*, vol. 4: 1903) Extant menus for internees in the Seagoville facility show a daily diet including fruit and cereal for breakfast; meat, bread, and vegetables for lunch; and soups and vegetables for the lighter evening fare. Specific examples of such menus are reprinted in Tolzmann,

ed., *German-Americans in the World Wars*, vol. 4: 1905-1906, 1982-1984.

342. *Lager-Nachrichten: Wöchentliches Mitteilungsblatt der Deutschen Gruppe, Crystal City, Texas* 42, 24 November 1945.

343. *Alien Enemy Detention Facility* film.

344. Kitry Krause, "Dangerous Enemy Alien," *Reader* 3 September 1993. Camp inspections were conducted regularly, with reports prepared following each visit. Among the areas critiqued by the visiting representatives were housing; washing and toilet facilities; food and cooking areas; medical facilities; the canteen; and recreation and education possibilities. Another section of each report addressed internee complaints and requests, ensuring that internee voices would be heard in the camp evaluation process. Several inspection reports concerning the Crystal City facility have been preserved, and have been reprinted in Tolzmann, ed., *German-Americans in the World Wars*, vol. 4: 2045-2076.

345. *Lager-Nachrichten* 24 November 1945.

346. quoted in Krause "Dangerous Enemy Alien."

347. Krause "Dangerous Enemy Alien." Legal alcohol was made available to internees of age, through the purchase of beer and wine at the camp canteen. Strict regulations were posted governing conduct while and after drinking, including a prohibition on gambling. Names of rule violators were publicly posted, in the canteen and housing units, and those in violation had their drinking privileges revoked. (*German-Americans in the World Wars*, vol. 4: 2001-2003)

348. quoted in Krause "Dangerous Enemy Alien."

349. To a lesser extent, ethnic Japanese, Italians, and other enemy aliens were also brought to the United States from Latin America for internment purposes. According to the NBC television program *Dateline*, in a November 30, 1994 report entitled "Roundup," over 2,800 ethnic Germans were brought to the United States for detention, compared with some 2,200 ethnic Japanese, representing the the majority of the over 5,000 people brought to America under the program.

350. "Roundup," *Dateline*, NBC, 30 November 1994. The full transcript of the *Dateline* report, including interviews with former internees, is available as show transcript number 150, from Burrelle's

Information Services (Livingston, NJ).

351. *Personal Justice Denied* 305.

352. *Personal Justice Denied* 309.

353. cited in "Roundup," *Dateline*, NBC, 30 November 1994. The *Dateline* report used a video clip showing detainees disembarking from a ship, claiming the clip to be from a rare film of Latin Americans about to be traded for interned Americans. A revealing State Department memo dated November 15, 1943 illustrates the extent to which such activities were meant to be kept as secret as possible. After the U.S. Embassy in Costa Rica sent a formal note to the Costa Rican foreign office, with a list of enemy nationals there approved for internment in the United States, an unnamed State Department writer described the embassy note as "the kind of thing which I have been fearing and which in my opinion may well rise to damn us when the present crisis is over." Further, the author of the memo advised that the State Department should call attention internally "to the dangers of this course," urging that the State Department "rap the Embassy sharply over the knuckles for such [an] indiscreet act." (cited in Tolzmann, ed., *German-Americans in the World Wars*, vol. 4: 1671.)

354. Despite American efforts to exclude German enemy aliens from the hemisphere, some aliens were allowed to return to their Central and South American countries of origin. During 1945-46, almost 600 German nationals would be returned to Latin America, while many others were sent back to Germany. (*Personal Justice Denied* 313)

355. *Personal Justice Denied* 312.

356. Krause "Dangerous Enemy Alien."

357. Gerhard Fuhr, personal interview, 27 March 1993. In 1947, before all of the Fuhr family save for Gerhard was scheduled for deportation, mention finally was made of the reasons for the apprehension, detention, and internment of Carl and Anna Fuhr. According to Enemy Alien Hearing Board findings in Cincinnati in August 1942, the Fuhrs had refused to state which side they wished to win the war; had been active members in the Friends of New Germany; intended to send their sons to Germany for schooling, though the war had prevented that from happening; and had made no attempt to obtain American citizenship. ("Entire Family Sided With Germany," *Cincinnati Enquirer* 14 June 1947)

Excepting the final point mentioned, both Eberhard and Gerhard have maintained vigorously the innocence of their parents of the charges made.

358. Krause "Dangerous Enemy Aliens."

359. Eberhard Fuhr, personal interview, 27 March 1993. Former internee Arthur Jacobs also has found that other members of the German-American community were primary informants, in an effort to prevent their own internment and to prove themselves above suspicion during the war. Jacobs states that many other internees he has spoken with also support this theory (Arthur Jacobs, personal interview, 8 April 1995).

360. Krause "Dangerous Enemy Alien." Also of note is a five page, unpublished manuscript Eberhard Fuhr wrote, containing some of his memories of the arrest, detention, and internment of his family. Entitled "An Internment Story," pages 1-3 discuss their Cincinnati experiences.

Another side of the Fuhr brothers' story was presented March 24-25, 1943, when two news reports discussed their arrest. According to the former report, the brothers had been quoted as saying that they wanted "to go back to Germany and fight for Hitler" ("Brothers Want To Help Hitler," *Cincinnati Enquirer* 24 March 1943), a quote which Eberhard vigorously insists was never spoken by either brother. The latter report reiterated the comments of the day before, including the quote, and indicated that the brothers "reportedly" already were in an internment center. ("Nazi Activities Investigated by FBI," *Cincinnati Enquirer* 25 March 1943)

361. quoted in Krause "Dangerous Enemy Alien."

362. Eberhard Fuhr, personal interview, 27 March 1993.

363. quoted in Krause "Dangerous Enemy Alien."

364. Eberhard Fuhr, personal interview, 27 March 1993.

365. Gerhard Fuhr, personal interview, 27 March 1993.

366. Krause "Dangerous Enemy Alien."

367. Eberhard Fuhr, personal interview, 27 March 1993.

368. Barbara Fuhr, personal interview, 27 March 1993.

369. Krause "Dangerous Enemy Alien."

370. Eberhard Fuhr, personal interview, 27 March 1993.

371. quoted in Krause "Dangerous Enemy Alien."

372. Eberhard Fuhr, personal interview, 27 March 1993.

373. Eberhard Fuhr, personal interview, 27 March 1993.

374. Eberhard Fuhr, personal interview, 27 March 1993. According to Department of Justice documentation, there were 118 ethnic Germans still confined in the Crystal City Internment Camp as of December 31, 1946, over a year and a half after the end of World War II in Europe. Of the 118 internees, fourteen were native-born Americans, children of German internees obliged to follow their parents into internment. Five others were internees from Latin American countries. A number of rosters of enemy aliens detained at Crystal City, Ellis Island, and other internment locations, showing names; ages; occupations; registration and serial numbers; and nationalities, have been reprinted in Tolzmann, ed., *German-Americans in the World Wars*, vol. 4: 2089-2253.

Chapter VI: German-American Internees in the Post-World War II Era

375. Eberhard Fuhr, "An Internment Story," unpublished manuscript, 1992.

376. Krause "Dangerous Enemy Alien."

377. In the case of the Fuhr family, they were sent from Crystal City back to Cincinnati suddenly in April 1947, with instructions to make final preparations for deportation, as well as to report weekly to local police authorities until being summoned to Ellis Island. According to Eberhard Fuhr, who had checked in the first day after returning to Cincinnati, "The next week I called at the same hour, and the guy said, '*Don't* bother us. Don't call anymore. Forget about it.' So I did." The family moved in with old friends for some two months, with Eberhard having procured work unloading boxcars for Kroger's, until local INS officials contacted them. Local INS officials provided the family with train tickets to Ellis

Island for the next day, with deportation scheduled to take place the day after their arrival in New York. See Krause "Dangerous Enemy Alien."

378. Krause "Dangerous Enemy Alien."

379. Krause "Dangerous Enemy Alien."

380. Krause "Dangerous Enemy Alien."

381. Mike Blair, "Cruel Odyssey of Family in FDR's Concentration Camps," *Spotlight* 20 May 1991: 13. According to a contemporary report in the *Cincinnati Enquirer*, the Fuhr house, at 1907 Baymiller Street, was sold at a sheriff's sale on October 19, 1946, pursuant to a foreclosure suit brought by the Cheviot Building and Loan Company. Money realized in the sale, amounting to $1333.33 for equity in the property, was to be turned over to Carl Fuhr in New York immediately preceding the scheduled deportation of the family to Germany. ("Alien Family Being Deported," *Cincinnati Enquirer* 11 June 1947)

382. Krause "Dangerous Enemy Alien."

383. In accepting work with Kroger's in Cincinnati before going to Ellis Island, Eberhard Fuhr handled the situation as did many other of the youngest internees. He chose not to tell his potential employers that he had been interned, saying instead that it was his first job. See Krause "Dangerous Enemy Alien."

384. Krause "Dangerous Enemy Alien."

385. Eberhard Fuhr, personal interview, 27 March 1993.

386. *Personal Justice Denied* 3.

387. Gerhard Fuhr, personal interview, 27 March 1993.

388. Krause "Dangerous Enemy Alien."

389. Krause "Dangerous Enemy Alien."

390. Martin Korte, "Internierte Deutsche fordern Gerechtigkeit," *Nordamerikanische Wochen-Post* 14 April 1990.

391. Eberhard Fuhr, personal interview, 27 March 1993.

392. Gerhard and Eberhard Fuhr, personal interview, 27 March 1993.

393. Gerhard Fuhr, personal interview, 27 March 1993.

394. John, like many other of the relatively few German legal alien residents and German-Americans willing to speak for the record, is reluctant to use his last name, out of shame for the experience he endured and out of fear of a return of persecution, even after the passage of fifty years. Many others willing to speak openly have chosen to use a false name, or discuss their experiences anonymously, in an effort to guard their privacy on what remains a highly sensitive issue.

395. Alan Gathright, "Memories of Injustice," *San Jose Mercury News* 2 January 1991.

396. Gathright "Memories of Injustice" 2 January 1991.

397. Gathright "Memories of Injustice" 2 January 1991.

398. cited in *Personal Justice Denied* 18.

399. *Personal Justice Denied* 101.

400. cited in Roger Daniels, *Coming to America: A History of Immigration and Ethnicity in American Life* (New York: HarperCollins, 1990) 303.

401. "Apology, $1.25 billion go to internees," *Cincinnati Enquirer* 5 August 1988.

402. "Apology," *Cincinnati Enquirer* 5 August 1988.

403. Congressional Record, *Public Law 100-383: Wartime Relocation of Civilians* (Washington: U.S. Government Printing Office, 1988) n.p.

404. "Apology," *Cincinnati Enquirer* 5 August 1988.

405. *Personal Justice Denied* 7.

406. Joseph E. Fallon, "Hostages of Hate: German-Americans and the Home Front in the Two World Wars," paper presented at the Society for German-American Studies Nineteenth Annual Symposium, 7 April 1995: 8; see also Arthur D. Jacobs, "The Facts About Internment," *Newsletter of the Institute for German American Relations* 3.7 (1993): 2-3.

407. Fallon "Hostages of Hate" 9.

408. Cincinnati Historical Society, "New Exhibit Presents A Different Perspective of WWII," *History Express: News From the Cincinnati Historical Society* January-March 1994: 2.

409. American Library Association, "ALA plans exhibition on WWII internment of Japanese Americans," press release, June 1992.

410. Fallon "Hostages of Hate" 10-11.

411. One notable example of this is the case of Arthur Jacobs, the former internee who has taken a leading role in making known the facts of internment. Jacobs, born in Brooklyn, was forcibly interned at age 12 at Ellis Island, and later Crystal City, before being deported to Germany with family members after the war. A more detailed discussion of the Jacobs case, and his efforts to obtain redress for the internment of German legal resident aliens and German-Americans, can be found in the concluding chapter of the present study.

Chapter VII: Conclusion

412. Arthur Jacobs, "Fifty Years of Silence: All Quiet on the Arrest and Internment of German Americans in the United States during World War II," *Society for German-American Studies Newsletter* 12.2 (1991): 11.

413. Joseph E. Fallon, "The Facts About Internment," unpublished manuscript, n.d. Many of the points listed are also presented, by Fallon in another unpublished manuscript, "Summary of the Fate of German-Americans in the Two World Wars," (n.d.); and by Arthur Jacobs in "Synopsis of *Factual* Events/Actions on the 'Internment Affair'," unpublished manuscript, n.d.

414. Fallon "Summary of the Fate of German-Americans" 2.

415. Stephen C. Fox, "General John DeWitt and the Proposed Internment of German and Italian Aliens during World War II," *Pacific Historical Review* 57.4 (1988): 436.

416. Susan Canedy, *America's Nazis: A Democratic Dilemma* (Menlo Park, CA: Markgraf Publications Group, 1990) xiv-xv.

417. Canedy *America's Nazis* 225-226.

418. Jacobs "Synopsis of *Factual* Events/Actions" 1.

419. "Johnson v. Eisentrager," *Cases Argued and Decided in the Supreme Court of the United States, October Term, 1949*, Book 94, Lawyers' Edition (Rochester: Lawyers Co-Operative, 1950) 1259.

420. Commission on Wartime Relocation and Internment of Civilians, *Personal Justice Denied* (Washington: U.S. Government Printing Office, 1982) 3.

421. *Personal Justice Denied* 18.

422. *Personal Justice Denied* 66.

423. cited in *Personal Justice Denied* 112.

424. *Personal Justice Denied* 17-18.

425. In late 1994, Jacobs was featured on the NBC news magazine *Dateline*, discussing internment in the context of Latin-American detainees interned in the United States during World War II. According to Jacobs, another segment has been prepared by *Dateline*, largely concerning the internment of German legal resident aliens and German-Americans, but has yet to be broadcast (personal interview, 8 April 1995). See endnote 313 for more details on Jacobs' experience with internment.

426. "Jacobs v. Barr," case summary (n.p.: Westlaw, 1992) 5.

427. "Jacobs v. Barr" 8. Regarding the role of presumed disloyalty of American ethnic groups based on race, an article by a former attorney of the Department of Justice, Nanette Dembitz, "Racial Discrimination and the Military Judgment: The Supreme Court's Korematsu and Endo Decisions" (45 *Columbia Law Review* 175 [June 1945]), stands out as an early yet decisive critique of the factuality of racial disloyalty claims, as accepted by the U.S. Supreme Court in its decisions.

428. Stressing the lack of objectivity in the report, Jacobs pointed out that in addition to the lack of attention to the German-American case, no chapter was devoted to the Italian-American internment.

429. Arthur D. Jacobs, "Circuit Court of Appeals (D.C. Circuit) Decision Dated March 27, 1992, in the Case of Arthur D. Jacobs,"

unpublished manuscript, 30 March 1992: 1-4.

430. Eberhard Fuhr, "To President George Bush," 6 November 1992, *Amerika Woche* 21 November 1992. In recent years, Fuhr's position, like that of Arthur Jacobs, has been supported in an official capacity by several German-American organizations. In one case, the Steuben Society passed a resolution "with much fervor" at its national convention in August 1994, calling on Congress to amend Public Law 100-383, to afford German- and Italian-Americans equal treatment under the law for injustices perpetrated during the World War II era. (*The Steuben News* 68.1 [September 1994])

431. Krause "Dangerous Enemy Alien."

432. Krause "Dangerous Enemy Alien."

433. Mike Blair, "Cruel Odyssey of Family in FDR's Concentration Camps," *Spotlight* 20 May 1991.

434. Eberhard Fuhr, "An Internment Story," unpublished manuscript, n.d.

435. M.U. Eninger, "The Way I See It," *German American Journal* January 1994: 5.

Name Index

A

"ABC List," 91, 97
Adams, Glenn, 41
Akron, Ohio, 94
Alberta Province, Canada, 115
Alien and Sedition Acts (1798), 130, 134, 146, 175
Alien Enemy Control Unit, 144, 167
Alien Registration Act of 1940, 91, 133, 148
All Through the Night, 84-85
Alms Hotel (Cincinnati), 66
Amendment to Claims Act of 1948 (1951), 165
Amendment to Claims Act of 1948 (1956), 165
Amendment to Civil Liberties Act of 1988 (1992), 165, 168, 178
American Committee for the German Relief Fund, 65
American Federation of Labor, 21
"American Fuehrer Organizes an Army, An," 83
American-German Review, The, 203
American Israelite, 39-42, 62-63
American-Japanese Evacuation Claims Act, 165
American Jewish Archives, 205
American Jewish Congress, 21
American Library Association, 168
American Olympic Committee, 30
American Legion, 10, 16, 50
    opposition to German-American Bund, 48-49
American Legion National Committee on Americanization, 49
American Magazine, 83

B

American Political Movies, 76
American Red Cross, 71
American Society, 204
America's Concentration Camps, 2
America's Nazis, 174
Amthor, Gustav, 111
Andover Township, New Jersey, 28
Arch Street (Cincinnati), 124
Arndt, Karl J.R., 203
Avondale (Cincinnati), 124

B

Banater Societies of Cincinnati, 41
Barth, Rheinhold, 114-115
Bates, Mr., 177
Baumgartner, August, 108
Bavarian Club, 66
Bavarian Mutual Support Organization, 66
Baymiller Street (Cincinnati), 227
Beecher Street (Cincinnati), 124
Bell, Leland V., 36
Benefits for Certain Federal Employees of Japanese-American Ancestry (1952), 165
Berlin, Germany, 18, 22, 27, 29, 30, 57, 58, 63, 65, 80, 81, 89, 125
Berlin Street (Cincinnati), 13
Bernstein, Sam, 31
"B.G.," 69
Biddle, Francis, 69, 95, 97, 98, 100, 103, 108, 114, 121, 164
Bill of Rights, 79, 80, 82
Bishop Street (Cincinnati), 107
Black Legion, 28
Bogart, Humphrey, 85
Bohemia, 6
Bond Hill (Cincinnati), 124

D

New German-American Studies
Neue Deutsch-Amerikanische Studien

This series features scholarly monographs, published in German or English, that deal with topics in the humanities or social sciences pertaining to the German-American experience.

Original monographs in the following areas are welcome: history, literature, language, politics, philosophy, religion, education, geography, art and architecture, music and musical life, the theater, and contemporary issues of general interest.

All inquiries should be directed to the Editor of the series. Manuscripts should be between two and four hundred pages in length and prepared in accordance with the Chicago Manual of Style.

For additional information, contact the editor:

Dr. Don Heinrich Tolzmann
Langsam Library M.L. 33
University of Cincinnati
Cincinnati, OH 45221